Date Due

The Child's World:
HIS SOCIAL PERCEPTION

The Putnam Series in Education

**A Publishing Program Dedicated to
Education as a Profession: Assessment and Planning**

Consulting Editors

OLE SAND and ELAINE COOK
Wayne State University

GETTING DOWN TO CASES: *A Problems Approach to Educational Philosophizing*, Robert L. Brackenbury, *University of Southern California*

THE CHILD'S WORLD: *His Social Perception*, Frank J. Estvan, *University of Wisconsin*, and Elizabeth Estvan

FIVES AT SCHOOL: *Teaching in the Kindergarten*, Elenora Moore, *Wayne State University*

FATHER TO THE CHILD: *Case Studies of the Experiences of a Male Teacher with Young Children*, Everett Ostrovsky, *Queens College*

INDIVIDUALIZING YOUR READING PROGRAM, Jeannette Veatch, *University of Illinois*

SPURS TO CREATIVE TEACHING, Laura Zirbes, *Ohio State University* (*Emeritus*)

The Child's World:

HIS SOCIAL PERCEPTION

FRANK J. ESTVAN
University of Wisconsin
and
ELIZABETH W. ESTVAN

G. P. PUTNAM'S SONS   New York

To Our Parents

FOREWORD

WHAT children do and say and believe is a consequence of the way *they* perceive their world and the events that make it live. This truth is one of the hardest for parents and teachers to comprehend and act upon. We are almost perverse in our insistence that boys and girls see as we see, and believe as we do, and act as we would. This perversity is nowhere more evident than in the recommendations adults make about the content of the school curriculum.

This book by the Estvans should help anyone who values research and who has his resources sufficiently available to comprehend reality when it is called to his attention. The *Child's World* concentrates upon one broad aspect of his world, its social aspect and the authors use an ingeneous projective technique to learn more about the way children perceive situations in which people are central. What I shall remember longest from their findings is the inexorable need for children to read into what they see the meanings they bring with them. And these of course are learned meanings. They are rooted in the child's experience.

I will remember, too, the strong tendency for children to react to the human element in any complex situation. It is, I believe, in connection with these human elements that it is of crucial importance for us to understand and influence what the child sees and hence believes and thinks and does. Our world will end, if it does, in catastrophe not because today's boys and girls and tomorrow's citizens perceive unrealistically the physical world—be it the universe or the inside of an atom. Catastrophe will come because these children growing up in the midst of the tragic biases of us adults have had insufficient opportunity to perceive realistically the strivings and interrelationships of their fellow men.

STEPHEN M. COREY
Teachers College, Columbia University

PREFACE

THIS BOOK is about the way children view their social world: what they "see" when looking at a farm or factory, rich people or poor, a church or capitol building. It is meant for all those who are concerned with children of elementary school age.

The aim of this book is to describe what children had to say about certain life situations presenting contrasts in rural and urban environment, upper and lower socioeconomic background, and in child and adult activities. Comparisons were made of the reactions of farm and city children, boys and girls, pupils in first grade and sixth, as well as between bright and below-average children in order to arrive at an understanding of social perception. It is hoped that the findings will be helpful to students and practitioners in the field of child development and related areas.

The ideas in this book are the outcome of three separate investigations. The first was centered on the social-problem awareness of upper- and lower-status children living in an Illinois city of approximately 85,000. Under a series of grants from the University of Wisconsin Graduate School Research Committee this work was expanded. Further techniques and materials were developed in studying the middle-class children of a Madison suburb. The study on which this volume is based involved children attending one-room schools in a rural Wisconsin county and children in the public schools of a city of approximately 50,000 located in the same state.

The authors are most appreciative of the whole-hearted cooperation which they received from the children and personnel of the participating school systems. Many others have contributed to these projects in various ways. Special mention should be made of Dr. Dorothy M. Sawin and Dr. Irvin J. Lehmann, whose contributions are reflected in their doctoral dissertations, and to Wilma Youngert, who drew the pictures used in the interviews. In the writing of this book, we wish to acknowledge our indebtedness to Dr. Elaine Cook and Dr. Ole Sand of Wayne State University, consulting editors of this series, who stimulated our efforts, read manuscript, and offered helpful suggestions. We are especially grateful, also, to Dr. Stephen M. Corey, Teachers College, Columbia University, for writing the Foreword.

FRANK J. ESTVAN
ELIZABETH W. ESTVAN

CONTENTS

Part III

How Do Children Perceive Social Status
Life Situations?

Part IV

How Do Children Perceive Child and
Adult Life Situations?

Part V

What Have We Learned About Children's Social Perception?

Part I

WHY IS IT IMPORTANT TO KNOW ABOUT CHILDREN'S SOCIAL PERCEPTION?

The Blind Man's Idea of the Sun [1]

There was a man born blind. He had never seen the sun and asked about it of people who could see. Someone told him, "The sun's shape is like a brass tray." The blind man struck the brass tray and heard its sound. Later when he heard the sound of a bell, he thought it was the sun. Again someone told him, "The sunlight is like that of a candle," and the blind man felt the candle, and thought that was the sun's shape. Later he felt a (big) key and thought it was a sun. The sun is quite different from a bell or a key, but the blind man cannot tell their difference because he has never seen the sun. The truth (Tao) is harder to see than the sun, and when people do not know it they are exactly like the blind man. Even if you do your best to explain by analogies and examples, it still appears like the analogy of the brass tray and the candle.

[1] From *The Wisdom of China and India,* p. 1067, Lin Yutang (Editor). Copyright 1942 by Random House, Inc. Reprinted by permission.

NATURE AND IMPORTANCE
OF SOCIAL PERCEPTION

THE Chinese parable of the Blind Man is one of many imbedded in folklore stressing man's age-old quest to understand the world in which he lives. It underscores the problems created by limited or imperfect senses in coming to know this world. The difficulty of communicating meanings to those who have not as yet "seen" is not glossed over lightly. As one reads on, there is even the suggestion that those who try to develop understanding in others are themselves not infallible in their viewpoints. Understanding the world is not merely an adult concern. It is central in the rearing of each new generation.

How does the child "see" the world? Is the sun to him something other than a sounding brass tray or burning candle? What about the mountains, the rivers, and all the wonders of Nature—and the hurricane which has just been reported off the coast? (Is that near or far away? Are *we* in any danger?) What does the child really "see" during a period of televiewing in which troop movements in a far off part of the globe and the latest exploits of men in submarines or jet planes are squeezed between his two favorite programs, "Days of the Old West" and "Spaceship Patrol"? Like the Blind Man's, the impressions he gains are not likely to be the same as those of an adult.

Whatever the meaning of the countless stimuli which make their impact upon the child, they constitute his world. Adults who are trying to help children grow up in our culture need to know what each child's world is if they are to be effective. Somehow they must sense his point of view in order to know where to begin and what kinds of assistance the child needs to further his understanding of the physical and social environment in which he must learn to live.

Nature of Perception

The way in which things or events are viewed or apprehended is the beginning point in the development of knowledge and understanding. For instance, as long as the sun is regarded as something akin to a sounding brass tray or burning candle there is no point in thinking about its relationship to other heavenly bodies. Such a question would simply be irrelevant. Perception of the sun as a heavenly body, on the other hand, did raise this question of relationships. In finding out, man's accumulated knowledges and understandings led to broader perceptions including, among others, the sun as the center of our solar system and a source of energy. Although it is true that these ideas were the end points or products of much reflection, they *function* as beginning points in further astronomical thinking.

The way in which an individual perceives or regards a situation is directly related to his behavior. Interpretation actually constitutes one of the first steps and is a continuing phase of his adaptation to a situation. Beginning with sensory impressions, perceptions are formed which become the basis for action. When driving an automobile, for example, most people realize the importance of checking their gasoline supply from time to time. This furnishes the motive for seeking clues furnished by one of several instruments found on the dashboard of modern cars. The needle of the gasoline gauge pointing to one-half is thus singled out as being relevant sensory data. In and of itself this would have little meaning except for those who react habitually to "halfness": which might mean for the optimist half full, for the pessimist half empty. On the other hand, certain ideas might be recalled or associated with this visual stimulus of halfness. The driver's perception of the gasoline situation would be reassuring were he to recall that there is only a short distance to be covered and/or he is in familiar territory where many gasoline stations are located. The opposite would be true were the distance to be covered much greater, the territory unfamiliar with respect to service facilities, or if it chanced to be a day when many service stations might be closed. In the former case, the resulting behavior on the part of the driver would most likely be characterized as relaxed in comparison to a certain degree of tension and alertness for service signs occasioned by the latter perception of the gasoline situation.

Perception also is involved in understanding other people's behavior which, in turn, modifies our reaction to whatever they do. This interpretation of behavior is extremely important when adults try to help young children for often the things we do "for" children are interpreted by them as being "against" their best interests. This may be illustrated in such a simple thing as requiring pupils to write each word ten times which they misspelled on a weekly test. If this is regarded as punishment for failing to have a perfect paper in spelling very little learning will result from such written exercises—as many teachers can testify. Yet, every method for teaching spelling relies heavily upon writing the word as one step in the process of learning to spell.

This then, is what is meant by perception. It is an awareness or interpretation of a situation (stimuli) in terms of which the individual responds, and which he maintains or modifies in light of his experience. It involves a *selective* element for not all aspects of the situation come under the perceiver's scrutiny. It calls for an association of *meanings* with sensory stimuli which in many cases have an *emotive* or affective quality. This getting ready to respond or selection of things to respond to applies to all situations confronting human beings be they matters of the physical environment, social relationships, school subjects—even in reacting or adjusting to one's self.

Importance of Social Perception

We live at a time when the development of keener social perception is the sine qua non for effective individual and group living. Never before have there been so many changes, affecting so many people, within such a short time, as within the past quarter century—and their pace and magnitude seem destined to increase. In one generation, our homes have been filled with "invisible workers" who do our bidding at the flick of a switch. This same technology has made it possible to span continents or oceans in a matter of hours, and now we are shooting at the moon. A source of energy has been developed which has the potential for lifting mankind to undreamed heights of living or destroying the fruits of human progress including man himself. Lagging behind these changes in the material aspects of our culture have come social inventions and adaptations. In the economic sphere, automation and labor unions are developing side by side and from all quarters come pressures for varying kinds and degrees of governmental regulation. Social legislation has increased to the point where guarantees are made to the individual from the time he is born until he dies, yet battle lines have been drawn over certain problems involving minority groups. The city, suburb, and farm are being welded into regional organisms by broad stretches of concrete whose monotony is relieved by cloverleaf approaches and tri-level bridges. Equally as impressive as changes in the domestic scene are those taking place in our international outlook. Leadership in the United Nations and increasing participation on many fronts present rather striking contrasts with the isolationism of past generations.

These changes make their impact on boys and girls. For many of them, to be sure, television is not new and war—either hot or cold —may appear to be the normal state of affairs. Most children, however, cannot escape the bombardment of mass media of communication, and as a consequence their "here and now" is vastly extended beyond that of yesterday's child. Neither can they escape the increasing mobility which characterizes the present way of life. (A principal of a downtown school in a large metropolis described her pupil population in these terms: one-third had been enrolled in her school the previous year, one-third had attended schools in the same city the previous year, and one-third of the children were new to the city most of whom were also new to the state.) It would be strange, to say the least, if these increasing complexities and scope of experiencing did not present children with problems of social perception, and hence social "adjustments."

Philosophers Explain Perception [2]

How human beings go about this matter of perceiving the world has been contemplated by philosophers through the ages. For every conception of the "good life" or system of thought ultimately revolves around two pivotal questions: What is truth, reality, knowledge? How does the mind grasp (perceive) these things?

[2] For a more detailed but readable account of these various philosophers, *see* Bertrand Russell, *A History of Western Philosophy*. New York: Simon and Schuster, 1945.

That perception has no simple explanation was apparent to the ancient philosophers. In a world where everything is in a state of flux as envisioned by Heraclitus, nothing would remain constant from one moment to next. Also complicating the problem was the belief expressed by Protagoras that there is no such thing as an objective truth, but that each man has his own percepts from which he infers the percepts held by others.

Distrusting the reliability of man's senses, many early philosophers formulated dualistic interpretations to account for perception and knowledge. Democritus regarded the former as being of two kinds: one involving the senses and the other understanding. The latter is dependent only upon the things perceived which possess certain inherent properties such as weight, density, and hardness. Perception involving the senses may be subject to certain distortions, however, for qualities such as color, taste, and tone are found in the perceiver rather than in the thing perceived. Plato created a different kind of dualism, that between reality and its appearance. The limitations of man's sense perception would always result in confused versions of reality. Hence, perception was not the same as knowledge. To gain knowledge it was necessary to evaluate and judge perceptions; in a sense, to reject the sensory world in favor of the world of pure thought. For the Skeptics this meant turning away from the world as experienced by men and looking inward to engage in subjective thinking. To the Stoics, however, this unreliability of the senses was regarded as errors in judgment which could be avoided. This separation of knowledge and perception meant that for the Scholastics and other philosophers of the early Renaissance great reliance was placed on the theory of innate ideas or principles—all sorts of things which the mind was suppose to know *a priori.*

Perception came into its own again with the rise of empiricism which claimed that all knowledge is rooted in experience. Ideas were no longer imbued with mystical or subjective origins, but were regarded as outcomes of a functioning intellect. As Locke pointed out, this meant that perception was the first step or inlet of all the materials leading to knowledge. Berkeley went so far as to maintain that material things exist only through virtue of being perceived. All reality is mental, and what we perceive are qualities such as color and sound, and not the thing or substance itself. For

Hume every impression had a corresponding idea and these were the constituents of more complex ideas. To perception he allied such things as identity, time, and space which he claimed were immediately observable, but causal relationships were reserved for the realm of reasoning for they are not readily apparent. Kant, however, did not disclaim the world of objects or "things-in-themselves." Perception to him is partly due to external things resulting in sensations, and partly to the perceptive apparatus which is subjective and not dependent upon experience. It is this which creates order and relationships among the sensations received. It is *a priori* and a constant sensibility or "intuition," two such forms being space and time.

The interaction between the perceiver and object in the act of sensation or perception was singled out for closer examination by later philosophers. In his emphasis upon action, Marx tended to replace "sensation" with "noticing," his point being that we notice those things which are parts of the process or situation in terms of which we are acting. Bergson made no distinction between the subject and object, and actually considered matter and the perception of matter as being one and the same thing. For him, perception had its origin in purpose in the pursuit of which the brain served as a selective agent limiting what was being perceived to that which was practically useful or of interest to the perceiver.

Thus, we acknowledge our debt to the philosophers for making clear the central position held by perception in the affairs of mankind. In their centuries of thinking about perceptual processes, they have traced many ramifications in human thought and action, and thereby identified the major points which must be considered in any attempt to understand how perceiving takes place. Many issues are not "settled" for not all philosophers have swung away from the dualism between reality and its perception to regarding perception as the test of reality. There is even less agreement as to whether perception is one of the *givens* and, therefore, *a priori* and intuitive or whether it results from effort on the part of the perceiver in the form of "pure" reasoning or mental activity based on past experience. In the main, however, philosophic inquiries have inevitably given recognition to the existence of some kind of interaction between the object and the subject, the more recent emphasis being on the part played by the subject's purposes, interests, and activities.

Psychologists Study Perception [3]

After more than two thousand years of theorizing about the nature of perception in the course of which major reliance was placed on logical thinking, came the need for more exact data regarding the processes involved. By the nineteenth century conditions were ready for the physiological study of human behavior. Out of this was born experimental psychology which fathered several different systems of psychology. Without exception, each gave a prominent place to perception, but its role or functioning was regarded differently.

In keeping with its physiological origins, emphasis was first placed on sensation. Once it was discovered that sensory and motor nerves are different (Bell and Magendie) the way was open for Weber, Fechner, and Helmholtz to make detailed studies of about a dozen senses (touch, optics, tone, etc.) and thus demonstrate that sensation and perception are susceptible to experimental study. Emphasis upon sensation reached its peak in Wundt whose first psychological laboratory in America ruled supreme between 1880 and 1890. Through methods of introspection he arrived at the conclusion that sensations were the simple and sensory elements of consciousness and that perceptions were complexes of these sensations. His followers, Titchener, and Külpe, broke down sensations into many attributes which they regarded as the abstracted dimensions of consciousness, and in so doing they left little distinction between sensation and peception.

Contemporaneous with Wundtian concentration on the elements of mental life was the psychology of experience being expounded by Peirce, the founder of pragmatism, and William James. For Peirce, reasoning began with percepts and not sensory impressions, and meaning was not something inherent in a thing but was derived

[3] A more extended treatment of psychological developments may be found in:

Floyd H. Allport, *Theories of Perception and the Concept of Structure.* New York: John Wiley and Sons, 1955.

Edwin G. Boring, *Sensation and Perception in the History of Experimental Psychology.* New York: D. Appleton-Century Company, 1942.

from the action that it involved. James, too, emphasized that the starting point in psychology is experience as it is perceived and not simply sensation, that sensations and perceptions are abstractions of experience which are gained through analysis. This functional, organismic, and operational psychology was developed to its highest point in the writings of John Dewey. In the central position given to problem solving and critical thinking, he underscored the role of purpose as the selective agency in observation (perception).

Concentrating on the relationship of parts and wholes but rejecting introspective methods, the Connectionists (Thorndike) and the Behaviorists (Watson) studied with great exactitude stimulus-response and conditioned-reflex behavior. In so doing, discriminatory action was substituted for sensation, such selectivity being guided by certain states or conditioning of the subject. Reacting against this "piece-meal" and "mechanical" interpretation of behavior, the Gestalt psychologists (Wertheimer, Köhler, Koffka, Lewin) came forth with a psychology based on "insight" and the primacy of the whole. This was essentially a psychology of perception rather than sensation in which configuration or the whole-part relations in a "field" held the key. All this was considered to be functions of contemporary arrangements independent of past experience in which no distinction was made between elements and complexes, and in which perception absorbed sensation.

Meanwhile, other groups were concentrating more on the subjective meaning in perception than external or objective reality. Personality psychologists including the psychoanalysts (Freud, Adler, Jung, Rank) were becoming increasingly conscious of the idiosyncratic meaning which the world held for normal as well as disturbed people. To a large extent their therapy was centered on helping their patients "see things differently." The subjective aspect of perception was also used as a means of diagnosing and understanding the perceiver. The notion that perception is influenced by something other than the stimulus pattern was also recognized by social psychologists (Sherif, Cantril). They regarded individuals as adapting or conforming to "social norms," the latter constituting a frame-of-reference which was brought into play in the perceptive act. In this sense, perception merges with cognition and is regarded as the apprehension or understanding of the complex interplay of social forces constituting the social situation in which the perceiver finds himself.

Thus, we see that psychological interest in perception began with a consideration of the minutia of the perceiver's sensory equipment, and was extended to include the totality of the social milieu in which he was born. In this process, sensation, perception, and cognition have played various roles but always the attention has been upon the interaction between the stimulus-world and the perceiver's world. From the relatively simple act of combining sensations, perception has become a highly individualized complex involving motivational states, body responses, and experiential background.

STUDYING CHILDREN'S SOCIAL PERCEPTION

MAN's persistent problem, as the preceding chapter has shown, is his attempt to grasp reality, and to act "appropriately." The crux of the problem lies within man himself; in the way he perceives the life situations which make up his world. Perception has many facets, and its development—or lack—is not a matter of all or none, but a question of which aspects are attended to and in what ways. Certainly, this is a very complex form of behavior. Rather than single out any one of its constituent parts, therefore, there is a need to examine the way various components go together. While the perceptive act may be fractionalized for purposes of analysis, the pieces cannot be left lying around loose; they must be integrated in some form of content-process relationship in order that social perception be understood as *behavior*. It is quite clear, moreover, that perception is a highly individual matter, and that whatever technique is employed to secure data must leave wide latitude for the individual to respond in his own fashion. Only by giving the perceiver comparatively free rein can it be determined what elements in the total complex of stimuli he has *selected* to respond to, the *meaning* he ascribes to these stimuli, and his feeling tone or *attitudes* toward what is perceived.

An Overview [4]

The major problem, quite obviously, is to determine the nature of social perception and the factors associated with its development. This may be studied to advantage in the earlier stages of children's

[4] Only the major outlines are presented here. A more extended treatment, including a verbatim report of a social-perception interview, is available in:

Frank J. Estvan, "Studies in Social Perception: Methodology," *Journal of Genetic Psychology*, XCII (June, 1958), 215-246.

development, comparing the perceptiveness of distinctive groups to various types of social situations. From the relationships discovered in this procedure, certain inferences can be made regarding the factors which are associated with perceptual behavior. The specific questions guiding the phase of work which represents the bulk of this volume deal with the relationship between elementary-school children's social perception and differences in types of community lived in (rural-urban), sex, grade (first-sixth), and intelligence.

To secure evidence about children's social perception, a projective-type approach was used for reasons stated above. It was based on a Life-Situation Picture Series consisting of 14 scenes. These were devised in terms of three social background patterns: (a) a Community Block including rural and urban life situations, (b) a Social Status Block contrasting upper- and lower-class situations, and (c) a Child-Adult Block presenting situations commonly associated with such age differentials. (These will be described more fully in the introduction to the respective sections dealing with each Block.) The picture series was also devised to account for basic social functions: conservation of human and natural resources; production, distribution, and consumption of goods and services; transportation, government, etc. They included numerous clues regarding the placement of scenes in terms of space (community, Wisconsin, the U.S., etc.) and time ("modern days," "old times"). There was also a balance of sexes in the children depicted in the series as a whole.

This instrument was administered to children individually following a group orientation period. The social perception interview was planned so as to bring about a gradual increase in the personal involvement of children. This was accomplished in three stages each of which presented the child with a different task: (a) 2″ x 2″ black-and-white slides were projected on a 30″ x 40″ screen and the pupil was asked "What story does this picture tell?" (b) the same pictures were presented as 8½″ x 11″ photographs, and the child selected from among 8 cardboard figures of happy, sad, angry, or neutral boys and girls the one that "belongs in the picture" indicating why he made his selection, and (c) the child chose the three pictures he liked best (copies of which he was given) and pointed out the one least preferred, again telling why. All responses were tape recorded and typewritten verbatim. (*See* Figs. 1 and 2.)

	Part I	Part II	Part III
Task	To tell a story about each picture.	To select children's figures for each picture.	To designate the 3 preferred and 1 nonpreferred pictures.
Stimulus	Projection of 2″ x 2″ black-and-white slides of Life-Situation Picture Series on 30″ x 40″ screen.	1. 8½″ x 11″ photostatic copies of Life-Situation Picture Series. 2. 6″ cardboard cutout figures of 4 boys and 4 girls (happy, sad, angry, and neutral).	1. 8½″ x 11″ composite picture of Life-Situation Picture Series.
Directive	"What story does this picture tell?" (Repeat for each picture.)	1. "Which boy or girl belongs in this picture?" 2. "Why?" (Repeat for each picture.)	1. "Which picture would you like to keep for yourself?" 2. "Why?" (Repeat in modified form twice more and then in negative sense.)
Behavior	Producing a story spontaneously.	Making and supporting decisions.	Making and supporting decisions affecting the subject.

(Between each Part column runs a vertical band labeled "Instruction Period.")

Fig. 1. Design of Social Perception Interview

A total of 88 children were interviewed. They were selected at random [5] and in equal proportions from *all* the first grade and sixth grade children attending one-room schools in a rural Wisconsin county, and from *all* the first and sixth grade pupils attending the public elementary schools of a Wisconsin community of approxi-

[5] Fisher's random numbers technique was used. For more details of the considerations involved in sampling and the technique employed see Irvin J. Lehmann, *Rural-Urban Differences in Intelligence,* unpublished Ph.D. dissertation, Department of Education. Madison: University of Wisconsin, 1957.

Fig. 2. Children's Figures

mately 55,000 population located in the second most highly ur-
banized region of the United States. Sex was equated within each
grade level for both rural and urban samples thus providing eight
subgroups of 11 children each. All were white, American, free
from serious speech defects, and had birthdates between June 1
and December 21. For purposes of comparison, intelligence groups
were formed by selecting the two pupils having the highest intelligence quotient in each of the eight subgroups to constitute the
high-ability sample, and by using similar procedures at the opposite
extreme to form the low-ability group. (The comparability of all
groups in terms of chronological age and intelligence quotient is
given in Table 1 in the Appendix.)

Interviews were held over a four month period, February
through May, an attempt being made to sample the eight subgroups proportionately. All the social perception interviews were
conducted by one person. Approximately one week to one month
after this interview the Stanford-Binet Intelligence Test was administered. Typescripts were exactly as given on the tape recorder
with no attempt being made to delineate thought units by means of
punctuation or to produce "smooth" versions of children's responses. These typescripts were checked against the tape recordings
a second time to insure the highest degree of accuracy possible.

Children's responses to each life situation picture were evaluated from a number of standpoints. One was *recognition* or what
the scene represented to a child. Another was *perceptual field,* the
where and when orientation ascribed to the scene by the perceiver.
Third, was *perceptual attitude* or how the child responded to the
situation. Which of these life situations represented the greatest
values for him were indicated through his picture preferences. The
question of who, from the standpoint of the child's perception of
the appropriateness of the situation for his life space, was inferred
from the figure identified by him as "belonging" in the picture. In
addition, the length of the child's response to the picture stimulus
in Part I when he told his "story" (Attention Time in seconds and
Word Productivity or count) was regarded as evidence of the
stimulus value of the scene, and ease of interpretation.

Analyses of the data were made in terms of the total group in
order to determine the perceptiveness of elementary school children, in general, to various types of life situations. To shed light

on the factors associated with social perception and its development, four kinds of group comparisons were made: rural vs. urban, boys vs. girls, first grade vs. sixth grade, and high I.Q. vs. low I.Q. Some of the findings are presented in percentages in order to give the reader some notion of the proportion of children involved. The bulk of the analyses, however, are comparative, and in each case the null hypothesis was tested using appropriate statistical techniques. In the interest of readability, these figures are not given in the text. They may be found in summary tables in the Appendix. Differences which have not been found statistically significant are not discussed in this volume.

Evaluating Perceptual Recognition [6]

The child's recognition of a life situation is the resultant of two factors. One is the *level* of perception which he achieves. Does he: (a) merely identify certain clues or objects in the situation, (b) describe these parts in terms of form, color, movement, location, or (c) bring these clues together and interpret them as a whole? Accompanying this "process" of perceiving is *content* which consists of the ideas or meanings associated with what was attended to in the life situation. Regardless of which level is achieved (clues, part, or whole) recognition or nonrecognition is determined by the relatedness or appropriateness of ideas. Hence, the standard is "literal" perception, and misapprehensions of an unusual or bizarre nature are classified as nonrecognition. (*See* Fig. 3.)

Recognition of a life situation may center upon its objective features which is referred to as *structural,* its dynamic aspects including activities and processes which is known as *functional,* or may represent a *synthesis* of both. The latter, therefore, represents the highest level of awareness possible in reacting to a life situation.

Structure and function may be analyzed from the standpoint of their specificity or generality. An *immediate* recognition of structure would be limited to the objective elements in the scene; to the recognition of "a poor house," for example. A more extended interpretation of structure for this same situation would be represented by a broader classification involving greater abstraction or extension of the scene; in this case "a slum section." With

[6] All scoring keys evolved from an examination of children's protocols, and were checked against adult responses for verification.

Perceptual Level	Recognition	Nonrecognition
Interpretation (Whole)	Appropriate: 1. Synthesis 2. Structure only 3. Function only	Inappropriate: 1. Synthesis 2. Structure only 3. Function only
Description (Parts)	Related: 1. Human 2. Natural 3. Cultural	General: 1. Human 2. Natural 3. Cultural
Enumeration (Clues)	1. Related referents listed	1. Miscellaneous referents listed
Indefinite		1. Mixed 2. Garbled 3. No response

Fig. 3. Perceptual Recognition

reference to function, an *immediate* recognition would be limited to the description of activities or processes depicted as, for example, "people are downtown shopping." A more extended awareness of this same situation would include qualitative or judgmental reactions characterizing events such as, "it's crowded downtown with lots of cars and people busy shopping." (*See* Fig. 4.)

Type	Structural Recognition	Functional Recognition
Immediate	Limited to objective features of the immediate scene. ("a factory")	Description of events, activities, processes being depicted. ("manufacturing steel")
Extended	Extension to a broader classification or higher level of abstraction. ("an industrial area")	Abstraction of characteristics or qualitative aspects of events, activities, processes. ("mass production")

Fig. 4. Types of Structural and Functional Recognition

In dealing with *parts* of a life situation the child's attention may be centered on human, natural, or cultural elements. The first includes statements regarding persons: their appearance, what they are doing, how they feel. The second refers to the world of Nature both physical and biological. The last is reserved for all the things which are man made including objects as well as institutions.

Recognition of a life situation is regarded as *indefinite* when a child's responses are mixed or garbled, and when he fails to respond. The first is usually a reflection of the child's uncertainty, and takes the form of vascillation from one interpretation to another at various points in the interview. For example, he may call a scene "an old beach" and later refer to is as "a lumber camp." Garbled responses are those which are so confused that two or more judges cannot agree as to the essential meanings which the child is trying to communicate.

In analyzing children's responses from the standpoint of recognition, therefore, it was necessary to determine first of all the highest level reached: identification, description, or interpretation. Next, whether the meanings attached to this highest perceptual level were appropriate (recognition) or whether the ideas were inappropriate or irrelevant to the particular situation (nonrecognition). To make this determination, the responses elicited in all three parts of the interview were considered.

Evaluating Perceptual Field

The perception of a life situation may involve its placement in a larger context. This field, background, or orientation for a life situation is defined in terms of space and time. Either of these settings can be indicated through the use of associational or systematic referents. The former are places and events which have gained general familiarity in our culture whereas the latter are based upon systematic units of measurement.

The classification of *spatial* settings, therefore, includes associational referents based on Nature when the emphasis is placed upon the physical or biological world ("out in the country"), the home when reference is made to a house or dwelling place ("in a mansion"), and institutions when a connection is made with public or private agencies ("at the Capitol building"). More specific spatial designations can be expressed in political terms (community, United States) and geographically (the West, Europe). These geopolitical area definitions are classified in terms of their *distance from the observer* which, in this case, are as follows: community (in which the child lives or communities in general), state (Wisconsin), region (Midwest), nation (United States), and the world. Also worth noting is the tendency for some children to specify location in general terms ("overseas") whereas others use specific place names ("China").

Temporal settings of an associational character are classified as natural when based upon periodic changes occurring in the physical or biological world. Depending upon the length of the cycle of these events, they are diurnal when limited to parts of the day such as morning or night or annual when applied to divisions of the year including the seasons. Associational time referents can also be based upon human activities or events. These are personal when the activity is experienced by individuals as part of the daily routines of living such as "breakfast time." They are social when the event involves large numbers of people who are experiencing distinctive social conditions such as in time of war or depressions. Temporal settings of a more exact nature are based upon systems of measuring time and are, therefore, mathematical in essence although they may be expressed in general terms. Chronometric referents focus upon time measurements including clock units covering a twenty-four hour period and calendarial units covering a yearly period. Historical time, indicating chronological or sequential order of events, may also be stated in general or numerical terms to indicate the *past, present,* or the *future.*

As will be shown later, children do not use spatial and temporal settings in a consistent fashion. For this reason, each was scored separately, all of the data elicited for each life situation being taken into consideration. Except that settings were incompatible, in which case they were regarded as mixed, the subject was given credit for each type of designation.

Evaluating Perceptual Attitudes

The perceiver's general feeling tone or emotional reactions to a life situation is referred to as *perceptual attitude*. This affective set or state is described as *positive* when the observer expresses satisfaction or approval of what he sees, exhibits a high regard for the values depicted in the situation, or is generally attracted to the life situation. At the opposite end of the scale are *negative* attitudes characterized by dissatisfaction, condemnation, and aversion toward the life situation. The observer shows little regard for the values represented in the life situation, and seems repelled rather than attracted to it. Where no tendency in either a positive or negative direction is readily discernible, the attitude is described as *neutral*. It is recognized that the perceiver may not be entirely indifferent or unmoved by the life situation, and that in many cases this is probably a measure of intensity rather than an indication of a neutral attitude. Opposed to this is the individual who displays *mixed* attitudes vascillating between positive and negative feelings, because he cannot "make up his mind" or because he views the life situation from more than one point of view. Besides noting the direction of attitudinal set, it is also important to observe the consistency with which the attitude is expressed for this is a measure of the crystallization which has taken place with reference to a particular life situation.

As was true for scoring other aspects of social perception, all responses to a life situation were taken into account in making a determination about attitudes. Each was scored independently, the results being summarized in terms of attitudinal direction and consistency for each life situation.

Summary

This section has pointed out the key role of perception in human thinking and behavior, special reference being made to the importance of social perception in the modern world. That perception is no simple matter, and that its many components must be regarded in some form of interrelatedness has been made clear. How many of these variables have been accounted for in the present effort to understand children's social perception has been outlined.

Children's responses to the Life-Situation Picture Series follow. Each scene will be dealt with separately, and as part of a pattern of pictures in which similarities and contrasts are presented. Part II is devoted to the Rural-Urban Block, Part III to the Social Status group, and Part IV to Child-Adult life situations.

Part II

HOW DO CHILDREN PERCEIVE RURAL AND URBAN LIFE SITUATIONS?

Village

City

Farm

Factory

INTRODUCTION

ONE of the broad classifications of people the world over is in terms of where they live. Whether one is an inhabitant of a congested urban community or a sparcely settled region is generally associated with differences so fundamental that there is a tendency to think of such people as constituting separate populations. This feeling is still prevalent in this country in spite of the rapid urbanization taking place, and the mechanization and mass influences touching rural life.

At an early age children are introduced to these "different" ways of living. When this takes place, a number of questions present themselves having significance for the guidance of their learning experiences. Is the so-called simple way of life generally associated with rural areas easier to understand than the complexities of urban communities? How are rural situations perceived by city children, and conversely, how is an urban environment regarded by rural children? Do boys and girls respond differently to rural and urban living?

To elicit data bearing on these questions, the Community Block of pictures depicts some of the major differentials found in rural-urban living. The scene of a Village and its counterpart, the City, were intended to secure reactions to a wide variety of facilities and services offered by such communities. The Farm and the Factory were included because they represent one of the sharpest contrasts in the performance of a basic function of living—the production and the distribution of goods.

Children's perception of each of these four life situations will be described in succeeding chapters, after which an analysis will be made of the pictures as a group.

THE VILLAGE

It Looks So Peaceful and So Nice

In the country is the little village with a big street winding through it, perhaps named Cheery Street. It has a bunch of houses, a grocery and meat market, the school house with the flag standing, and next to it the church where people meet together. Children are playing along the roadside or in front of their houses for there's hardly any traffic. People mow the lawn, dig their gardens or just sit out in the front yard relaxing. And in the back are the farms and the hills. The townspeople are quiet and there's nothing to disturb them.

THE above verbal montage is representative of the concepts brought to the Village scene by elementary school children. They had somewhat more than the usual amount to say about this life situation and said it quickly. Although pupils were quite voluble, they did not exhibit a corresponding degree of productivity. Ideas about the Village were rather limited in extent, and barely average in appropriateness. In comparison with other pictures, there was a greater tendency to view this scene in a larger context with reference to time, but space was quite average in this respect. Interestingly enough, boys were associated with village life much more often than girls. Generally speaking, the Village elicited a considerable proportion of favorable as well as negative attitudes. Whatever their attitude, however, children apparently did not feel strongly. Very few either selected the Village as their favorite picture or rejected it outright.

Children's Recognition of the Village

Despite the simplicity attributed to village life by adults, this was not the easiest scene for children to interpret. In fact, only 75 per cent managed to achieve some degree of recognition, a rank of 8.5 in the series. About as many children synthesized the various elements in the situation to arrive at a fairly complete perception as those who failed to recognize it—one-fourth in each case. The same proportions generally held true regarding the recognition of either structure or function as compared to an awareness of relevant clues or parts.

The *structural* aspect of this life situation was recognized by 42 per cent of the boys and girls. With few exceptions, responses were centered on the immediate situation rather than generalized to include a farming section or region. The terms, "village" and "town," were equally popular in referring to this scene, although in several instances "little city" or "small city" were substituted. A sixth grade rural girl managed to get all three into her "story" about the picture:

> Well, about a little city with . . . a little town or village, with a church, and stores, and people going from place to place.

Functions portrayed in this rural community were recognized by 26 per cent of the pupils. Their responses were about equally divided between social processes and certain characteristics of village living. A good example is that of a sixth grade urban girl whose "story" follows:

> Well, that looks like um . . . a little town . . . a little quiet town. And it has a church in it . . . and children are playing. And then it has a . . . a store where you can buy your groceries, a grocery store. And um . . . it doesn't look like it . . . maybe, only has about five hundred people there. And a . . . you can see the road . . . and . . . and the way the trees are drawn, and the way everything looks, looks like a nice little quiet town, and you can see the hills in the background.

As indicated in the above, children saw taking place in this rural community the distribution of goods (stores, shopping), certain religious observances (going to church or Sunday school), and to a lesser extent its educational functions (going to or coming home from school). Half the children who described qualities of village living spoke approvingly of it as being quiet. There was some dissension, however, for a sixth grade urban girl complained, ". . . it looks like the boys and girls aren't having too much fun, they're just playing around by themself and walking through the streets all alone ... you don't have very many friends there." However, some characterized village life as being friendly, and others noted that it was healthful and presented few traffic hazards: "... looks like a friendly little village," "... he should like the outdoors—lots of clean air ... ," "... there's hardly any traffic."

A meaning for this life situation which involved a *synthesis* of both structural and functional elements was achieved in 24 per cent of the cases. The wide range of physical features which could be integrated to form the concept of "town" is illustrated in the reactions of a sixth grade urban girl:

> (Part I—What story does this picture tell?)
> Well, that looks like an old country road or something, a little town, and there's a church and it looks like there's a school, and some stores, and it looks like a flag standing, and a couple of boys and girls playing in front of their houses. It looks like a man's coming out of the store carrying some bundles. And people are walking down the street; they're probably going to the church. And there's a man; it looks like he's fixing ... planting his flower garden and his grass.
>
> (Part II—Which boy or girl belongs in this picture?)
> The happy girl.
> (Why?)
> Well, it's probably fun to live out in the country. And she's happy because she gets to go and play alone if she wants to, and she can play with the other kids across the street, and have a lot of fun and that.

Not only was this girl showing awareness of the external or objective appearance of this situation, she was also able to read into these symbols certain social processes such as recreation, distribution of goods, and religious expression.

There was evidence of *partial* recognition in 26 per cent of the replies. These children described one or more clues having significance for village life, but made no reference to the community as such. Three-fourths of these responses were directed toward people. The remainder were equally centered on the physical environment or natural setting of the scene, and man-made or cultural features. A typical reaction is that of a first grade rural girl:

> (Part I—What story does this picture tell?)
> A, children going to school, I think. And some buildings, and a store, and children playing out, lotsa houses, and a school house, and a barn. Boys and girls, and their father going to school.
>
> (Part II—Which boy or girl belongs in this picture?)
> The happy boy.
> (Why?)
> 'Cause he's happy ... he don't have to work.

Those whose attention was focused on people described them as going or coming from church or Sunday school in half the cases. Next in order of mention, were going to school or shopping. Children who were more conscious of Nature were well aware of the fact that this was "in the country." As for cultural references, a first grade urban boy was surprised by the lack of traffic: "... there's some people going across the street there, and there's no car coming." On the other hand, a first grade rural boy reported matter-of-factly, "There's a tavern there."

Only 5 per cent of the children went no further than to *identify* various objects or clues in the picture which are related to village life. It is significant to note that all of them were first graders, a typical response being that of a young urban boy:

> There's a church, and there's stars up in the sky, and there's a sky, and there's trees, and houses, and people, and signs, and a restaurant, and trees, and a steeple, and a church, and windows, and porches, and roofs, and fence, and grass, and a road.

Nonrecognition. A surprisingly large number of boys and girls did not recognize the Village in whole or in part. Twenty-two per cent failed because they *described* such *general* elements that no differentiation was made between this village scene and scenes in general. With few exceptions their responses dealt with human activities. Half the people were described as playing; baseball and other games of ball being most frequently mentioned. The remainder of the responses centered on various kinds of work, such as mowing the lawn, and the simple act of walking or just "going places." A number of children were conscious of certain disciplinary situations remarking that "he minds his mother," and "his mother won't let him in the house." Only two per cent of the children, however, were *incorrect* in their perception of this life situation. A first grade urban girl remarked: "It's in the city, and the people are out there . . ." An older urban girl noted: "The city is usually peaceful, but except for maybe a few people that are walking along, and have some business to do." Unlike several of their classmates who used the diminutive forms, "little city" or "small city," these pupils had failed to discriminate among communities in terms of size.

It is not entirely clear why less than half the children (44%) were community minded in their perception of this village scene. In fact, the word "community" was seldom used. This does raise the question of just what concept children have regarding a community. Does it consist primarily of massed industries, housing, and service facilities with everything else regarded simply as clusters of buildings along a highway? Do children realize that when they go to church or to school they are participating as members of *some* community dispersed as it may be or do they regard these institutions as having a separate identity—like the gasoline stations and motels which are springing up alongside traffic arteries? It may well be that the automobile has made it increasingly difficult to tell what is and what is not a rural community.

Children's Setting for the Village

Children's orientation for the Village was no better than for the picture series as a whole. They located it with average frequency (Rank = 7) in some geographical or political setting. Although fewer children were sensitive to the element of time than to space, the village scene drew forth considerably more temporal settings (Rank = 4) than most of the other life situations.

A *spatial setting* was given to the village scene by 68 per cent of the pupils. Out of ten such responses, six referred to some geopolitical unit, one was an associational referent, and three were combinations of both types. As might be expected, all the pupils who gave a specific place designation referred to its community setting. In this sense, recognition of the scene as a "village" was also an indicator of the location of what was happening; that is to say, in a village. Interestingly enough, not a single child placed the village itself in a larger area such as state, region, nation or world. The following are typical of children's spatial designations:

> He lives in such a fine village . . .
> A little quiet town, and it has a church in it . . .
> This could tell about the person who lives in the town . . .
> Just a little village with a road through it . . .
> This looks like a little farming community . . .

Of the relatively few children who used associational referents to designate location, practically all mentioned Nature. As the following excerpts indicate, "the country" was the most useful indicator of spatial setting for the Village.

> This is a country scene . . .
> That looks like it's in the country . . .
> Just a few houses running through the country . . .

Of the total number of pupils interviewed, 19 per cent placed the village scene in some kind of *temporal setting*. Those who showed an awareness of time found associational and systematic referents equally useful, one-tenth of the pupils using both. With reference to the former, children apparently found it easier to indicate time by referring to the passage of natural events for none of them used human activities as bench marks for telling time. These included such daily occurrences as:

> There's some stars up in the air . . . it's getting dark . . .
> It look's like a summer morning . .
> It's night so not so many people would be out . . .
> There's stars out . . . it looks like night . . .
> It's early in the morning and not too many people are up.
> It's getting pretty late . . . it's sorta getting dark . . .

and the following annual events:

> About a tree and it's spring . . .
> It look's like a summer morning . . .
> It look's like a summer night . . .

Systematic referents used by children included both chronometric and historical time systems. In the former instance, reference was made not to the clock, but to the calendar to indicate time of year:

Some people are going to bring their children to Sunday school ...
I think it's Memorial Day 'cause there's a flag out ...
It was close to Hallowe'en ...
They're going to church again and it's on a Sunday ...

The few children who used an historical time scale in connection
with this scene referred to the past ("It's a town in the olden
days ...") as well to the present ("In the new days ...").

It seems as though children regarded this life situation as a kind
of universal. It was not associated with any specific section of "the
country" or the world at large. With a few exceptions, neither was
it fixed in time as "old fashioned" or "modern." Regardless of
whether they recognized the village as such or were responding to
general aspects of the scene, to boys and girls these were not peculiar to any one place or to one period in history. Villages, or the
kind of living characteristics of small places, exist everywhere and
are timeless.

Children's Attitudes toward the Village

A positive attitude toward the village scene was exhibited by 60
per cent of these children. Twenty per cent were negatively disposed toward village life, 14 per cent were neutral, and only 7 per
cent expressed both favorable and unfavorable feelings. The same
attitude, regardless of its nature, was held throughout the interview
by 25 per cent of the children. None of these figures are very different from the other three pictures in this Community Block.

Analysis of children's expressions reveals their propensity to
view favorably certain characteristics of village life including play
opportunities, and to be less than enthusiastic about working or doing chores. In each case, the reverse was expressed by a smaller
number of boys and girls. Going to church and the general problem
of conduct were brought into focus less frequently, but were also
regarded in this dual light by different members of the group.

Many boys and girls were impressed by the peace and quiet of
village life. Others appreciated the various services provided by a
village, and the fact that there are many things which can be done
"around the country." Opportunities to play outdoors with other
children, with ponies and pets were highly attractive. Some even
liked the idea of helping their parents with certain chores. Opposed
to this were children who felt that very little ever takes place in a

small community, and that there are too few people to share in whatever does happen. Quite a number were very unhappy about the implications for "work" contained in this scene.

Positive	*Negative*

Village life

Positive	Negative
It's a quiet village. (6RB)	It wouldn't be very exciting there. (6UB)
There's a lot to do around the country. (6UB)	You don't have many friends around there. (6UG)
They've got a church, a school, and farmland. They got the house, the barn, and their friends, that they can play with there. (6RG)	
They can all work together, and have lots of fun. (6RG)	
There's a lot of other boys here to play with, and it looks like a nice little town to live in. (6UG)	
Maybe he lives close by the store, and he gets to buy candy a'cause his mother gives him money. (1UG)	

About playing

Positive	Negative
He can do what he wants, and he has fun, too. (1RB)	The boys and girls aren't having too much fun. (6UG)
He's going to play with some other children. (6RG)	They're playing around by themselves, and walking through the streets alone. (6UG)
His mother gave him the ball to play outside. (1RG)	He's not playing with nobody and having fun. (6RG)
She wants to ride a pony, and she minds her mother. (1RB)	He's not happy about what he's doing. He's not happy about where his party is (in school). (1RG)
He likes to bounce his ball. He likes to play outside with no sweater on. (1UB)	
She's playing with a little puppy that her daddy brought her home. (1UG)	
They're going to the festival, and they played ball and they had a real good game. (6RB)	

About working

He's helping his mother. (1RB)	He (the happy boy) don't have to work. (1RG)
Maybe he's helping his mother or father with the work. (6UB)	His father's doing the work, and all he can do is play. (6RB)
	Most boys don't like to go to the grocery store. (6UB)
	He had to mow the lawn, and his older brother didn't have to. (6RG)
	It looks like they're all doing work. (6UB)

In a number of instances, children's feelings toward the Village hinged on religion and some of the broader aspects of human relationships. For the most part, going to town to attend church or Sunday school is something which boys and girls like to do, but this is not true in every case. Also of interest is the positive approach which children assumed with respect to human relations in the Village. Any disturbance in peace and quiet was more likely to occur in the home than in community living.

Positive	*Negative*

Going to church

They can go to town, and go to church and help God. (1RG)	Because he wants to stay home, and his parents make him go to church. (1RG)
Him like to go to Sunday school, and get a lot of lessons. (1RB)	

Human relations

That guy is doing something nice, and that other guy likes him to do. (1RB)	He had a lickin' maybe. (1RB)
	His mother won't let him in the house. (1UB)

Neutral attitudes were indicated by those pupils who simply described certain features of the Village or some of the activities pictured there. A first grade rural boy said, "it looks like he's mowing the lawn," and an observation made by his city counterpart was to the effect that "he might be going to Sunday school by himself," or as stated by an older rural girl, "he has to carry things out to some other person." Noncommittal acceptance of the routines of living was expressed by a sixth grade urban boy who noted, "They're working and they wouldn't be especially happy." That even such an activity as play does not necessarily have an aura of excitement about it may be what another sixth grade boy was getting at when he said, "He's not surprised about playing baseball, and he's probably been playing for a long time."

There were comparatively few pupils who showed *mixed* attitudes toward this life situation because they were able to see both sides of the question. Although not overly surprised, a sixth grade rural boy did note that, "they've got a nice home even though it is a little village." A more personal observation was made by an older city boy who went on at some length to explain, "This boy is carrying the groceries home, and let's see, he wouldn't be too happy about goin'. But, of course, he should be kinda happy goin' for his mother; after all he's doin' somethin'."

Children, it seems, are more aware of the "nice things" about village life than the reverse. Except for contacts with Nature, however, each of the features singled out by them is the focus of pro and con feelings. To many, village life has interesting possibilities; for others it lacks "excitement." The contributions to good living made by certain basic institutions are appreciated by boys and girls, but the so-called "cultural advantages" of larger population centers are of little or no concern. Thoughts of future vocational opportunities are left to the future by elementary school children.

Children's Preferences for the Village

The Village scene was selected 3 per cent of the time as being one of the three best in the series; only 1 per cent of the children rejected it. No other picture met with less acceptance, and only one with less rejection. In short, children were not overly enthusiastic or markedly adverse to village life.

Examination of the reasons pupils gave to support their choices indicates that they placed a high value on opportunities to experience Nature, and appreciated the peaceful atmosphere of village life. Just what the objection was of the first grade rural boy who rejected this picture is something which the reader may judge for himself.

Acceptance	*Rejection*
It shows the open country, and the little boy likes that. (6RB) The father said that he could pick an apple from the tree. (1UG) Well, because it looks so peaceful and so nice there. (6RG) I've always wanted to live in a little village. (6UG)	Because my dad doesn't like so many trees, and houses, and buildings, and he likes lotsa people. (1RB)

The Village is nothing to get too excited about, quite obviously. Children who display favorable attitudes toward small-community living place greater value on other types of life situations. Those who regard the Village with disfavor attach no great cruciality to their objections. Though not exactly a nonentity, neither does the Village have outspoken champions on one side or bitter critics on the other. For boys and girls it is simply "all right" or "not too bad."

Group Comparisons

All but one of the differences revealed in comparing various groups of elementary children were associated with differences in maturity. The one exception was a minor variation in the perception of the Village by boys and girls. All these were matters of cognition rather than emotion. Not one attitudinal difference was discovered between children differing in locale, sex, grade or intelligence, this being the only instance of such uniformity among the pictures in the Community Block. There is good reason to believe, accordingly, that a village is pretty much the same sort of thing to children, except for the difference in ideas characterizing age primarily, and sex in only a small way.

Age Differences. Sixth grade pupils almost consistently outstripped younger children in the ideas or concepts they brought to bear on the interpretation of this life situation. Not only were they superior in the number of structural recognitions made, it is interesting to note that not a single first grade pupil used the term, "village." Older children also excelled in their awareness of both community services and characteristics of village life. Only rarely was a first grader sensitive to this aspect of the life situation. As a consequence, older pupils were far ahead in the ability to view both the objective and dynamic aspects of this scene as a totality. Younger children, on the other hand, exhibited a much greater proportion of partial recognitions most of which were centered on people. This same tendency to deal with parts instead of wholes led to their greater use of general descriptive statements about people indicating nonrecognition of the village as such.

Older children also had a better notion of the background for this scene. More of them gave some designation of spatial setting, and this was especially marked regarding the placement of the community in a geographical or political unit.

The great increase in ideas or concepts about the Village which accompanies age is apparent. That this gain is not uniform is reflected in the relative lack of consciousness of time by both young and older pupils. Furthermore, there seemed to be little change in attitudes with development of the cognitive aspects of perception.

Sex Differences. Boys and girls were quite evenly matched in all the various components of perception as applied to the Village. Although there was no difference in the total number of their descriptive responses (partial recognition), girls were more responsive to, or aware of the people in the situation than were the boys.

This, then, is not an indication of superiority in recognition, but evidence of greater interest in human beings and their activities on the part of girls. It may be that this is a reflection of greater socialization on their part or simply a difference in the interests of boys and girls.

THE CITY

It's a Good Thing to Go Downtown

A city is a busy place with many buildings—about one thousand buildings—with advertisements, TV antennas, and firescapes. It has theaters, playgrounds, and apartments. And there are places to buy things: supermarkets, dimestores with toys, and shops having big sales and cute clothes. At the crowded corner a newsboy is selling his papers, a policeman is directing and watching over people, and the sheriff's car patrols. Buses are getting people to work. Some people are rushing; others are walking and chatting, and going from place to place. And cars and taxis are making a noisy sound.

WITH so much going on, it is little wonder that children associated more meanings with this scene of the City than any other in the series. They did this with only a moderate expenditure of time and energy as expressed in words. Their reactions were much to the point as evidenced by the high proportion which had significance for urbanism. Children, furthermore, tended to locate this scene in space to a relatively high degree, although this was less true with reference to orientation in time. Unlike the Village, these children did not associate urban living with either boys or girls but regarded it as the province of both sexes. Children, nevertheless, were not attracted to this picture of "downtown." In terms of positive attitudes and preferences it failed to rank above the average for the series. In the same vein—it ranked above average in the number of children who disliked what they saw in the City.

Children's Recognition of the City

Pupils had little difficulty in recognizing this urban scene. Ninety-one per cent managed to do so in whole or in part (Rank = 5). The highest level of interpretation, a synthesis of structure and function, was reached by five-eighths of the group, whereas less than one-tenth failed to recognize signs of urban culture in this life situation.

A total of 70 per cent of the children gave recognition of its *structure*. Their responses were about equally centered on this scene as representing a section of a city or regarding it in more inclusive terms for the community as a whole. A sixth grade urban girl's attempt to identify this city by name: "This looks like a street in Chicago . . ." was a rare exception.

Of the more specific terms used by boys and girls, "downtown" was decidedly more popular than "street corner." "Street inter-section" was mentioned by an older rural boy, and an interesting reversal in flow of movement was provided by a sixth grade urban boy who referred to people going "up town." No child referred to Main Street, the business section, or shopping area, and in spite of the supermarket no one confused this scene with a modern shopping center. Community designations were almost equally divided between "city" and "town." That the much talked-about exodus from the city to its outlying fringes has not influenced these children to any appreciable extent may be inferred from the fact that only one child referred to "a suburb of a big town"— and this was a sixth grade city boy.

Almost as many children (64%) recognized the *functional* aspects of this life situation as did the number responding to its structural elements. Three-fifths of their responses dealt with various social processes or activities, and the remainder pertained to certain characteristics of urban living.

To these children, "shopping" was by far the most frequently thought of activity taking place in the city, and the term "super-market" was common parlance. Much farther down the list of awareness was transportation as it related to cars, trucks, and buses. Equally significant to boys and girls were the measures taken by the community for the protection of its citizens—the policeman, the squad car, and to some extent the fire escapes.

One child in ten also associated the city with employment or "going to work." Only a few referred to education, recreation, and the function of communication as represented in the news-paper stand. A typical "story" is that of a sixth grade rural girl who, in the context of a city structure, showed awareness of such functions as protection of human resources, distribution of goods, and transportation:

> Well, this tells of a busy city ... why, there's a supermarket, and a grocery store, lots of buildings, a bus even. People are busy; they're walking and chatting. And here it is spring. People have their cars. Why, there's a police car. A policeman is standing on the corner directing the cars. Some of the people are going into the grocery store, and some into the supermarket. Some people are going across the street. Some are on the bus enjoying the ride.

The aspect of urban living which was most prominent in the thinking of these children was its "busy-ness." They envisioned "many people," who are "rushing around" and where, as a con-sequence, "it's crowded." Only a scattering of responses centered on the many opportunities existing in an urban community, and the possibilities for making friends. One pupil, a first grade urban girl, was critical in her judgment that this was not "a decent town."

Sixty-three per cent of the children were able to *synthesize* the various elements pictured in the situation, and to arrive at an interpretation which included both structure and function. The degree of insight is well illustrated in the remarks of a sixth grade rural boy:

> (Part I—What story does this picture tell?)
> Well, here is a very busy street where there's a bus, cars, every-thing of vehicles, and there are people along busily trying to hurry to buy food before they can come down to their houses. And upstairs is an apartment where many people are watching out of a window, and they like to watch the busy street and its cars go by; they try to count them. And there's a squad car, maybe, even going along the street or checking meters or had stopped, and made the traffic go slower so people can go some-place across the street. And the bus down there is one that's a ... taking people to, maybe, a ... to the country where they might even see a lot of sightseeing that they might like.

(Part II—Which boy or girl belongs in this picture?)
The sad girl.
(Why?)

> Because she's going to the grocery store for her mother, and she doesn't like it too well 'cause she has to go so long, and she lives kinda far away from the town. She had to ride her bike so she was sad she hadda come that long way, and go to the grocery store and git this, just a bag of groceries.

A *partial recognition* of this urban scene was attained by 15 per cent of the children. In every case, they went beyond the mere listing or identification of objects having significance for city life to include a description of or associations with the clues selected in the situation. As a first grade rural boy said in his "story":

> There's a police car down there. I think there's about one thousand buildings down there. A...all the cars are going this way and trucks. And people are getting into the bus.

Two-thirds of the responses showing partial awareness of the City referred to the human element in the situation. Children were most likely to notice people who were riding on the bus, doing their shopping, or engaging in various kinds of work. The other third of the responses in this category involved such culturally determined things as cars, buildings, or the street in general.

Nonrecognition. Only 9 per cent of the boys and girls failed to indicate some form of recognition of the City. All were first grade children. Seven per cent *described general clues* or discussed unrelated elements so that their responses can not be considered as having demonstrated a recognition of the City or its downtown section. All responses in this category dealt with people. No one activity stood out above the others, the remarks including a miscellany such as driving, riding, crossing the street, and playing. The remaining two per cent of the reactions were *indefinite* in that they did not provide clear-cut evidence regarding just what the individual was perceiving in this urban scene.

That the majority of elementary children are in familiar territory when they enter the realm of city life is evident in the richness of meanings brought to this scene. Not only are their ideas comprehensive, they represent a fair balance between attention to the

externals as well as the dynamic elements of the City. It is interesting to speculate why shopping has made such a strong impression on so many children—more than cars, buses, policemen, and
firemen combined! All in all, children equate the city with "busy"
living.

Children's Setting for the City

Boys and girls perceived this life situation in a spatial context
much more often than with respect to time. In comparison to
other scenes, the City ranked fourth and seventh respectively.

The picture was placed in a *spatial setting* by 75 per cent of
the pupils. A significantly greater number of these responses were
geopolitical in nature, and in one-tenth of the cases their use was
combined with associational referents. The former were almost
entirely confined to references to a generalized notion of urban
communities. There was only a small scattering of responses specifically indicating where the scene might be located.

> It's on a street corner . . .
> This is in the suburb of a big town . . .
> It looks like people shopping downtown . . .
> That looks like a big town district . . .
> That's a city . . . a pretty big city . . .
>
> A busy city like Chicago . . .
> This looks like a street in Chicago . . .

The few associational referents which indicated placement, were
institutional in character. These responses, quite obviously, did
not encompass the entire situation, but were concerned with one
of its many segments. In naming the part, the stage was set for
whatever activity was described by the child. Illustrating this use
of institutional associations are the following:

> There's a lot of stores there . . . and people are going into the stores
> and out . . .
> There's a playground, he can play, too . . .
> Somethin' about a person who works in a supermarket . . .

The City was given a *temporal setting* by 14 per cent of the
children. To tell time, boys and girls made associations with hu-

man and natural events as often as they used systematic measures. Illustrating the former are the remarks of a first grade rural girl, whose pivotal point in the day seems to be dinnertime:

> ... then they go home, and then they eat their dinner, and then after dinner they always watch TV ...

In addition to using human events of a personal nature to indicate when things happen, boys and girls also referred to certain periods of the day and seasons of the year as in the following:

> One morning in the big town there was a lot of people ...
> It's a very busy day and in the city ...
> The bus is getting people to go to work in the morning ...
>
> Here it is spring ...

As for systematic measures, the calendar was resorted to in attempts to determine the day of the week or to specify certain holiday periods. Those who showed a sense of historical perspective, however, were few in number.

> Everybody's doing their Christmas shopping ...
> It's probably, maybe on a Tuesday, or a week day, because there aren't very many people ...
> That is probably on a Friday when it's busy downtown ...
> That's maybe a Friday where most of the people are out ... they're maybe going shopping as usual every week ...
>
> In the new days, this is 1955 ...
> Looks like a very modern city and it's busy ...

One of the most interesting things to note about the "field" in which children perceived the City is their use of specific referents to indicate location. To begin with, not many were used. More significant, perhaps, is the fact that although these pupils live nearer Milwaukee than Chicago, the latter appears to be psychologically closer in the sense of being more readily available for the interpretation of new situations. Do these boys and girls actually have more contacts with Chicago through travel, radio, TV? Whatever the explanation, the implication is clear: influence is not necessarily a matter of distance.

Children's Attitudes toward the City

Twice as many children (53%) regarded this urban scene in a favorable light as those who were negatively disposed toward it (25%). When compared with other life situations, these figures are less favorable to urbanism, the rankings being seven and four respectively. About one child in ten was apparently unimpressed by what he saw, and an equal number fluctuated from one extreme to another. One-fourth of the pupils never varied in the attitude expressed in all phases of the interview. The focus of all these feelings were the City in general, transportation, shopping, and the newsboy.

Generally speaking, boys and girls regarded the City in a favorable light for the many opportunities it has to offer. This was not universally felt, however, as is indicated by the negative statements quoted in the list below. Transportation and traffic or the general problem of crowding also were some of the unfavorable aspects picked out by pupils, and in this connection there was a note of appreciation of the policeman's role.

Positive	*Negative*

Urban environment

It would be a nice city to live in. And they have a policeman at the corner to stop cars so you could cross the streets, and it would be safe. And they have nice stores. (6UG)	He isn't happy about his town. His daddy and momma won't move, and he's so used to that house that he doesn't like it any more. (1RG)
He lives in town. He's got many friends. He can go most of the places he wants to—to the movies or anything, and he's got a bus that can take him and bring him home from school. And his father's probably got a good job in the city; he can be glad he's probably got enough to live on. (6RG)	

Transportation and traffic

He (the happy policeman) can direct the street. (1UB) The policeman is blowing the traffic, and he's happy as can be. He might not have been a policeman for a long time. (1RB)

The (sad boy) don't wanna go on bus. (1RB) Maybe she didn't have any money, and she was going to get on the bus, and the bus man pushed her right out. (1UG) He doesn't pay any attention to what he's doing there. He's walking in front of the bus when it can be starting up. (6UB)

The activity which drew forth the most enthusiastic response from children was shopping, but here, again, there were those who didn't like going to the store—especially when it interfered with play activities. As is indicated by the excerpts below, children were also definitely aware of the two sides to being a newsboy.

Positive   *Negative*

Shopping

She gets to go to town, and she likes to go in the stores like her mother does. (1RG) They can go to town, and there are dimestores where they can buy toys and stuff. (1RG) Most everybody looks forward to going to town, and git things like toys and stuff. (6RG) It's a busy city, and there's lotsa cute clothes—pretty clothes—for her, and a lotta big stores to look around in. (6UG) When they go to buy something they're always happy to git something. (6UB) She might like to go downtown; it's a very good thing to go downtown shopping. (6UG)

Some of them don't like to go shopping. They like to play outside instead of going shopping and they're still mad. (1UB) She's going to the grocery store for her mother, and she doesn't like it. She hadda come that long way, and git just a bag of groceries. (6RG)

Selling newspapers

He likes to go and sell the papers. (1UG)

He'd be happy in this things—selling papers or anything. (6UB)

He don't like his job. (1RG)

He's not happy; the people are not buying newspapers. (6UG)

Playing

She can't have no fun. (1RB)

She wants to play with some friends. (1UB)

They might have wanted to stay to home and play, but their mothers had to take them along because no one else is home. (6RG)

Children showed no great concern for the anonymity and lack of friendliness often charged to large-scale urbanism. Attitudes expressed in the general realm of human relations were largely centered on children's behavior or child-adult relationships. These were of both kinds, usually on the part of the younger children who had failed to recognize urban conditions depicted in the life situation.

Positive	*Negative*

Human relations

He likes everybody and he likes to go to church; he likes his mother and father. (1RB)

He minds his mother, too. (1RB)

She didn't get no licking or anything. (1RB)

'Cause he doesn't wanna do what his mother says. (1RG)

Neutral expressions included matter of fact descriptions of what was going on in the scene. "Inbetween" figures were associated with the situation by a first grade urban boy, "because he might be walking across the street, and he might be walking with his daddy," by a sixth grade rural girl who simply stated, "she's going shopping with her mother," and by a sixth grade rural boy who explained, "they're walking along probably coming from school or going shopping for their mother or something like that." Acceptance of normal living routines was indicated by a sixth grade urban boy who thought that, "maybe they're going shopping as usual every week." Another member of his group found the whole situation rather commonplace and maintained, "he's not excited about selling papers and that."

Most of the children exhibiting *mixed* feelings about the City were those who were able to perceive the advantages offered by an urban community as well as some if its disadvantages. The latter included such things as crowding, traffic, and other health hazards. An unusual instance of empathy is given by a sixth grade urban boy who felt that both a happy and sad figure "belonged" in the picture for the following reason:

> It's because of the policeman, and it isn't fun to stand on a corner; it might be cold weather. And it wouldn't be unhappy because he knows he's helping the people.

Elementary children do not seem to be unduly appreciative of the City. For those who do not regard shopping as fascinating, it has few inducements. Going to town interferes with play; besides, it is crowded and altogether too busy. It may be important for adults, but what the child wants—outside of dimestores and such— is not to be found "downtown."

Children's Preferences for the City

The City was selected by children as often as it was rejected, five per cent of the total being involved in each case. This represents low valuation in the series (Rank = 11) and a moderate degree of rejection (Rank = 6).

Reasons given by children for their choices indicate that whereas some liked the hustle and bustle of urbanization, there were those who do not feel comfortable in such surroundings. The many things which make up a city as well as opportunities to shop, and to ride on buses were highly regarded by some pupils. Others found city activities generally uninteresting. Typical of these comments are the following:

Acceptance   *Rejection*

Urban environment

It's in a city, and there's all kinds | It's too crowded.   (6RB)
of people around, and big build-
ings, and lotta stuff in there.   'Cause it's a hard one.   (1UB)
                            (6RB)
Because there's all different—
there's all sorts of things in it.
                            (1UB)
Well, it looks like it's a good important thing I could draw some-
time. I like to draw pretty good,
too.   (6UB)

Urban activities

That's a town, and you can go | It's just so normal.   (6RB)
there and buy toys.   (1RG)
I like to go downtown shopping.   Because it's not very interesting
                            (6UG)   to me, and that's what I don't
'Cause I like to buy certain things   like to do—go around and just
and, well, I like to ride on buses,   walking.   (1UB)
too.   (6UB)

Unlike the Village, children's feelings toward the City do make
a difference. When boys and girls are forced to pick and choose
their situations, it fares quite poorly. Nothing cities have to offer
gains unqualified approval—not even shopping. Is it because cities
—at least "downtown" sections—have been designed with grown-
ups in mind which fact is only too apparent to children? Or is it
that they are simply overwhelmed by the complexities of urbanization? Whatever the explanation, it may be a source of comfort to
city planners to know that for elementary pupils a city has as
many appealing features as unattractive aspects.

Group Comparisons

All but one of the differences in perception of the City by various groups of children belonged in the category of concepts or
associated ideas. Most of these were related to maturity. Only a
minor difference in conceptualization was noted in the community
groups as well as in sex groupings. Despite the many facets pre-

sented by the City, there was only one emotionally toned difference among the groups of pupils being compared.

Age Differences. From the standpoint of ideas about urban situations, age proved its superiority in almost every respect. Sixth grade pupils outstripped younger children in the number of times they regarded this scene as part of an urban community; hence, in their over-all consciousness of the structural aspects of this life situation. They were on more familiar terms with the concepts, "street corner" and "city" than first graders. Older children were also much more aware of both the services and characteristics of urban communities. Regarding the former, they showed greater consciousness of shopping activities. They also gave more attention to transportation, efforts made to protect people against various hazards associated with urban living, and to work or employment. As for urban characteristics, sixth grade pupils were more conscious of the presence of many people combined with generally congested conditions. Their discernment of the busy tempo of urban living was as pronounced as their superiority regarding shopping.

As might be anticipated, the proportion of sixth graders who viewed this situation in its totality exceeded by far the number of younger children who synthesized both structural and functional aspects of the City, the percentages for the two groups being 93 and 32 respectively. In view of this fact, it is not surprising to note that first graders exceeded older pupils in the number of partial descriptions made of this urban scene. This was especially true with respect to the number of times that their attention was centered upon people.

The gain in cognition which comes with age was also exhibited in the kind of background in which the City was viewed. Sixth grade pupils were far more inclined to indicate spatial settings than were younger children, and this was especially true regarding geographic or political designations. There was no difference, however, in their use of time concepts as was the case for all the groups.

Feelings toward the City were not as markedly discrepant as the above differences in ideas might seem to indicate. Although sixth grade pupils were much like first graders in the number of positive attitudes expressed, they did show a tendency to be more neutral or mixed whereas younger children were decidedly more negative in their emotional reactions to this urban scene.

There certainly can be no question but that older children are more perceptive of the facts of urbanism. Such increased knowledge on their part has not led to an enthusiastic acceptance of the City and what it stands for, but a softening of resistance to where it is more neutral or undecided. The relative lack of success on the part of younger children to interpret this complex situation may account for their greater degree of negativism. Does this mean that people must *learn* to like the City?

Community Differences. One would expect that children living on farms and those in the city would react quite differently to a scene of urbanism. This was not the case. There was only one slight variation in the responses of rural and urban children. The latter tended to regard the scene as being a part or section of an urban community whereas rural children reacted more generally in broad community terms. In so doing much greater use was made of the word "downtown" by the city child and of "town" by the rural boy or girl. This difference could be a reflection of the kinds of experiences which children have with the City. The urban dweller must make distinctions among the various sectors of his environment in order that he may deal with these parts in an intelligent fashion. Going "downtown" is different from going to the park. To rural people, the downtown section may be the only reason for going "to town," hence, the two are psychologically the same. All in all, however, there is remarkable similarity in their perception of this urban scene.

Sex Differences. There is no reason for anticipating marked variations in the perception of urbanism by boys and girls. No great differences were found. Their reactions were quite similar except for the tendency of girls to think of this situation as "downtown," and for boys to show a preference for "street corner." As was suggested for rural and urban children, these differences in terminology might be a reflection of experience or interest—in this case—shopping. Do girls go shopping with their parents or by themselves more often than boys? Is it possible that girls in elementary school are already aware of the fact that women do the major share of buying in this country? If so, "downtown" would have certain connotations which are absent in the matter-of-fact identification of a "street corner."

THE FARM

There's Lots to Do on a Farm

This is a nice farm near a village. It is in a farming region where one sees hills and fields. Airplanes fly overhead and big semitrucks haul things to the city to sell them on the market. There are houses, barns, and a pasture with all sorts of animals; there's even a baby pony and a mother one and a father! The boy has chores to do; now, he is going to get the family mail. He watches the animals, and he can ride on a pony. His father is working in the fields. He is plowing and planting his seeds to raise crops for the harvest. He knows it will pay him in the future.

THE above composite of children's responses is indicative of the wide range of reactions to this scene of rural production. That they were on familiar ground is evident. Pupils were highly productive in their ideas about the Farm, and everyone achieved some measure of recognition. Accompanying this was a keen sense of orientation for the situation in terms of both spatial and temporal settings. To do this required no more than a moderate expenditure of effort as revealed in the time spent examining the picture, and the amount of talking done by pupils. Practically all of them linked this farm scene with the masculine world. Generally speaking, they were favorably disposed toward it. In fact, the Farm was selected as "the one I want to keep for my very own" by more children than any other in the series.

Children's Recognition of the Farm

Only one other picture (Bedroom) was recognized by all children to some degree. Responses to the Farm, however, represented a higher perceptual level in that three out of four pupils actually synthesized both structural and functional aspects. A mere seven per cent responded only to parts or clues in this life situation.

The farm as *structure* was recognized by a total of 86 per cent of the children. This kind of recognition was almost always expressed as "a field" or "a farm," both terms being used by one-fourth of the pupils. Going beyond the scene as portrayed, and classifying it more broadly as "a farming region" was a notable exception.

Boys and girls attended to the *functional* or activities aspect of the Farm to almost the same extent as they did its structure (82 per cent as compared to 86 per cent). Nine-tenths of their responses dealt with various phases of production, the remainder referring to the distribution and exchange of goods.

Children talked about production in a general way in one-third of the cases, the great majority of their ideas being limited to the concept of work as: "he's working in the fields," "he's working on his grain." Other common expressions centered around "farming" or "growing crops." Specific activities, which accounted for two-thirds of the production responses, dealt primarily with the preparation of the soil—practically always with plowing, including the idea of "contour plowing." One child commented technically that, "a man is plowing and dragging," whereas another simply noted that, "it's a man on a tractor fixing the fields . . ." One-fourth of children's specific responses took in planting activities such as "getting ready to plant crops" and "planting (or seeding) a garden." Of the remainder, harvesting was most frequently mentioned, but seemed to be less understood judging from the nature of the comments made especially by younger children:

> he's cutting off oats . . .
> getting some hay . . .
> he's grabbing up some wheat . . .
> mowing stuff off . . .
> some hay he's raked . . .
> cutting up the grass . . .

Distribution processes were more often regarded in terms of delivering products to urban communities than the reverse. A sixth grade urban boy for example, explained that, "It tells about agri-

culture, too, and maybe how they ship all their goods to the city."
Even for those who saw the truck going down the road it was
more likely a case of, "he's going to go to town and sell his milk."
Very few children were aware of the reciprocal nature or interdependence of rural and urban production although one sixth grade
urban girl did point out, "He likes to have crops on his fields to
sell, and so he'll get enough money for the seeds and everything
to get new crops."

Both *structural and functional* aspects of this farm situation
were recognized by 75 per cent of the children. A sixth grade
urban boy, for example, brought together such external or physical
signs as "tractor," "fields," and "truck" to arrive at a recognition
of the over-all structure known as "farm." He also showed an
awareness of plowing and planting, activities related to the function of farm production. In viewing the truck as collecting the
farmer's dairy products, he also singled out one phase of the allied
process of distribution.

> (Part I—What story does this picture tell?)
> Well, this is a ... the farmer got up in the morning, and he's
> getting on his tractor, and he's plowing down the fields to get
> ready to plant. And a ... the truck's going up the road bringing
> a ... going to his farm to get the dairy products that he made.
>
> (Part II—Which boy or girl belongs in this picture?)
> The boy. Happy.
> (Why?)
> Because he lives on a farm, and I'd like to live on a farm.
>
> (Part III—Which picture would you like for your very own?)
> (Second choice) The one with the tractor.
> (Why?)
> A ... because it's a farm.

Partial recognition of this scene was achieved by six per cent
of the boys and girls. These children singled out one or more
clues in the situation bearing on farm life, but in talking about
them, they failed to indicate this relationship. These partial recognitions included such ideas as: "they're working," "his father's on
a tractor," and "he's traveling down the hill in a tractor."

Only one child simply *identified* various objects in this life situation. It is interesting to note how this young urban girl could

recognize symbols bearing on a means of production, a crop, and transportation of this crop, and yet fail to interpret them in connection with farming.

> (Part I—What story does this picture tell?)
> I see a tractor, and a fence, and some corn, I guess . . . I see some trees, two hills a . . . and a truck . . . and another fence.
>
> (Part II—Which boy or girl belongs in the picture?)
> The angry boy.
> (Why?)
> 'Cause he, it looks like he's angry. 'Cause it looks like he's running, and because he looks like he's sort of angry.

The Farm is a familiar sight to boys and girls. This is to be expected from rural children, but how can we account for such familiarity on the part of those living in the city? The school, of course, is one answer for the Farm is the focus of many learning experiences at all levels of elementary education. That even first grade children are so well versed in farm life suggests that much happens through home influences including trips to the country, TV programs, toys, etc. There is no doubt about the importance of the Farm in our culture—as in all societies—and children are given much help in becoming acquainted with it early in life.

The Setting in Which Children Place the Farm

Elementary pupils have a better notion of where this life situation belongs in space and time than is the case for most of the other pictures in the series. A spatial orientation was given by 80 per cent of the boys and girls, and temporal specifications were made by 23 per cent, each of these ranking third in the picture series.

Nine-tenths of the *spatial settings* were associational in character, the remainder being about equally divided between systematic designations or combinations of both. Most of the associational place referents were institutional being directly related to farming. For this life situation, recognition of structure was also an indication of placement. For example, a first grade urban girl stated, "A man at a farm, and some horses, and a plane, and a truck, and a man, and a tractor." Other associational indictors of location involved Nature as in the following:

He's traveling down the hill in a tractor . . .
That man was plowing in the field . . .
Around the country he's got plenty of space . . .

The few children who used geopolitical terms to indicate placement invariably referred to communities. As the following excerpts show, however, there was no specification in which state or part of the nation these communities were located.

That's a nice farm near a village . . .
It's quite a ways, but it looks like a town . . .
In the background, it looks like a city . . . looks like a big semi going down to the city . . .

When designating a *temporal setting* for this picture, pupils showed no real preference for either associational or mathematical referents, one-fourth of their time responses including both types. None of the children associated farming with the occurrence of human events either personal or social. All associations were related to natural events. In using Nature as the basis for indicating time, pupils relied more on daily activities than those which occur annually.

One morning that man was plowing in the field . . .
Well, he woke up real early . . . so he went out to get the chores done . . .
At night it gets a little cool, and then in the morning it gets nice and warm . . .
There is a man on his tractor plowing all day . . .
The farmer got up in the morning, and he's getting on his tractor . . .
He seems happy, because it must be a nice day . . .

In the fall probably . . .
It's on a spring day . . .

Of the mathematical or systematic bases for indicating time, only the historical was used. No child referred to the clock or calendar in connection with farming. As would be anticipated because of the nature of the picture, these boys and girls showed greater sensitivity to the present than to the past.

This is in the new days . . .
That's a new tractor just put out . . .

It looks kinda modern 'cause they have tractors . . .
There's a milk truck and a tractor; this ain't like years ago it used to be . . .

It looks like a kind of old-fashioned picture . . .

Clearly, there was no question in children's minds that this is a scene "on the farm." The nature of the terrain and farming equipment, however, did not suggest to them any specific locality such as their own state or this country in general. Add to this the fact that relatively few pupils linked the tractor to modern times. (One child actually placed it in the past!) One is left with the impression that, for children, this farm scene could exist anywhere at anytime. On one point there was greater discernment. No one gave the slightest indication that farms are run by "clockwork."

Children's Attitudes toward the Farm

Children's attitudes toward this life situation are comparable to those for the other scenes in this Rural-Urban Block. Fifty-five per cent of the boys and girls expressed positive attitudes toward the Farm (Rank = 5). Neutral feelings were exhibited by 14 per cent, 16 per cent were negative (Rank = 10), and another 16 per cent reacted with mixed emotions. In 18 per cent of the cases the same attitude was expressed toward this life situation each time the pupil was asked to deal with it.

Analysis of the positive and negative statements about the Farm reveals that children were quite realistic in their awareness of its advantages and limitations. A number accepted farm life without reservation, but no one was violently opposed. In keeping with the generally high number of positive reactions to the Farm were the pupils who perceived the fun element as well as the general desirability of rural living. Negative responses tended to center on the work aspect, particularly that of adults. Typifying the "halo" effect indicating the unqualified approval of the Farm are the following responses:

They have a nice place to live in the country. It looks like everybody's at work.   (6RG)
He's always been on a farm.   (6UG)
He lives on a farm, and I'd like to live on a farm.   (6UB)
He's on a farm, and you know how you feel—real happy. (1UB)

Many children felt that the Farm was fun because of the many things they could do. For example, they could ride a horse or, if "big" enough, on a "real" tractor—or just watch all the interesting things going on. For others, however, hardly anything ever happens on a farm, and not everyone gets a ride. In fact, it's more fun to "look at a book!"

Positive	Negative
	Fun for children	

Positive	Negative
He can have lots of fun out on a farm, and there's lots of things to do. (6RG)	There's hardly anything to do on a farm, and he just has to go get the mail. (6RB)
He's probably going out to get a horse and ride, and he's going to have a nice time riding. I like the farm. (6UB)	He wants to go and get a ride with his father, and he can't. (1RB)
'Cause he gets to ride on a real tractor, because he's real big. (1UG)	He wants to look at a book. (1UB)
He's probably just happy to sit and watch the farmer, and the horses, and the airplane going over. (6UG)	
He could do anything (!) (6UB)	

Work and its rewards, for both adults and children, proved to be controversial. For the man who had a good field and a good tractor, and who was doing a good job, there was pride and happiness. Yet, it's hard work sitting on a tractor all day—especially when it's muddy. For children, likewise, there is the satisfaction that comes from contributing to the household, but some "don't wanna do nothing" and would rather play.

Positive	Negative
	Work for adults	

Positive	Negative
It's spring now, and he can start planting his crops. (6RB)	The father looks kinda angry, because he's got to work. (6RG)
He's happy in his work. (6RB)	He doesn't look happy, because he has to sit on the tractor all day. (1RG)
He had his new tractor, and he's proud to have it, and glad to use it. (6RB)	It looks sort of muddy, and he

Positive   *Negative*

Work for adults

He'd have a field of his own, and he'd have a tractor, and he'd have good farming land.　(6UG)	might be having a little bit of trouble—the man on the tractor.　(6RG)
He knows he's doing a good job doing the garden—so he's pleasant about it and everything.　(1RB)	It looks like hard work, you know, keeping the land okay.　(6UB)
	It's too hard for him.　(1RG)
	It looks like his crops aren't so good.　(1UB)

Work for children

He's happy going to the mailbox or carrying something out to his father.　(6RG)	He don't wanna do nothing. He don't wanna do none of his work, and his daddy made him do it.　(1RG)
He's happy he can get mail and help his mother. Maybe his mother's sick, and she can't move out of bed.　(1RG)	His father told him to plow, and he didn't want to.　(1RB)
	He doesn't like to drive the tractor. He always wants to play with all the little happy girls, and make him happy.　(1RG)

Neutral remarks, by and large, were simple descriptions of the Farm or activities taking place without any attempt to make judgments. The "inbetween" figure was inserted in the picture by a young rural boy because "he's just gonna git the mail" and by a young urban girl who said, "Well, he's plowing the field." Acceptance of the situation for what it was without any show of emotion was voiced by an older city girl when she remarked, "He's away from the city and he lives on a farm, and he has to help his father with some of the plowing and work." In a like vein, an older rural girl stated, "He's doing his work what he's suppose to, and now, no worries." That farm life has few ups-and-downs was put very bluntly by an older rural girl who said, "He hasn't got nothin' to be happy about or nothin' to be angry about."

Children who *vascillated* from positive to negative attitudes about farm life did so because they recognized its various aspects. As a sixth grade urban boy indicated, "He wouldn't be too happy mowing or plowing his garden, and I don't think he'd be too sad about it either, because sometimes it's fun." Similarly, a sixth grade urban girl showed sensitivity to the influences that conditions might have in the performance of certain farm tasks when she explained, "He might be happy if he's doing his work, and he might not be, because he has to have it done before the winter."

The quite personal outlook which many children displayed toward the Farm is evident in the above attitudinal expressions. Whatever they liked or disliked in this situation had a direct bearing on their immediate wants and interests. Their ability to go outside themselves, and show empathy with the farmer was also demonstrated. They did not, however, deal with this life situation as an abstraction. No child, for example, regarded farming as the basis for our economy. No one got excited about "The Farm" and its contribution to the American way of life. For children, this was a scene of what people do on a farm.

Children's Preferences for the Farm

The Farm is the most wanted picture in the entire series, representing twelve per cent of the choices made by pupils. It is not without limitations, however, for three per cent of the children, all of them girls, regarded it as being the least desirable of the series (Rank = 8.5). This is conclusive evidence of the high esteem in which farm life is generally held, and of a moderate degree of rejection by some children.

Pupils selected the Farm picture for a variety of reasons. Many expressed a general liking for farm life which was the outgrowth of personal experience—either from having lived there or through visitation. Others placed great value on experiences with the physical world, machinery, and those of a recreational nature which are offered by a rural environment. Not completely overlooked was the importance of farm work, but in this connection there was some dissension.

Farm living

Well, because I live on a farm. (6RG)

Because I like the farm. I go down to the farm in the summer. My grandmother and grandfather have a farm. (6UB)

Farm experiences

I like to go in the fields.   (1RG)

I like farming; that . . . I like to grow things at home in summer time.   (6UB)

'Cause I can start up a tractor, and I can drive it, and everything.   (1RG)

'Cause there's a tractor and . . . a . . . got one of, and I like to run tractors, and my dad likes it, too.   (1RB)

Acceptance	*Rejection*
Farm work	
Because when I grow up I can probably be a tractor man myself. (1RB)	I'm not much interested in farming, and I wouldn't like to stand there watching trucks. (6UG)
He's happy 'cause he's doing a job, and he will be able to plant. (1UG)	
Because I have to farm. I need all the farming. (1RB)	

The child's need for activity and broad experiencing may account for the great interest shown in the Farm. For one thing, there seem to be fewer restrictions on what children are permitted to do in such a situation. Even a girl of six-to-seven may drive a tractor! It is interesting to note, too, that some children have caught the vocational significance of farm life by the time they enter first grade. What are the implications for education and other aspects of child rearing when a six-year-old casts the die to become a "tractor man?" Does this mean that his horizon has become restricted to one view of the world, and that it is necessary to "expand" his interests? Or will his presently conceived role in life serve as the vehicle for bringing him into increasingly meaningful relationships with other parts of "the world" and other ways of living?

Group Comparisons

Various groups of elementary children differed in some interesting ways in their perception of the Farm. Most of these were associated with grade level involving both ideas and feelings. Next were those between boys and girls—not with respect to cognition but, rather, in their emotional reactions toward farm living. Contrary to expectations, rural and urban children perceived the Farm in remarkably similar fashion, and this was also the case for bright and below average I.Q. children.

Age Differences. The margin of superiority enjoyed by older pupils in the recognition of the Farm, unlike the great majority of scenes, was not a matter of the number of pupils who did or did not achieve recognition. The difference was limited to the concepts brought to bear on this life situation. Whereas young children were content to describe the scene either as a "field" or a "farm," sixth graders often used both. The latter also recognized a greater number of functions associated with farming, and this was particularly noticeable with respect to the distributive aspects. Differences in recognition were more than quantitative, however. For young children, the man was simply "working," but older pupils were aware of his "farming" and "growing crops." This greater preciseness was also evident in their awareness of certain steps in production, especially that having to do with the preparation of the soil, including contour plowing. In keeping with their more extensive conceptualization, was the greater tendency of older pupils to indicate the spatial setting of this life situation, particularly in their use of associational referents. From the standpoint of attitudes, a considerable number of first grade children displayed indecision or mixed emotions toward the Farm whereas older pupils tended to be more positive.

All children, rural or urban, seem to have some means of access to farms and farming experience in our culture. When they are still quite young, boys and girls appear to comprehend its basic characteristics. With age comes a refinement in the perception of the Farm based on number of concepts and their discriminating power. The shift in feelings from mixed to positive does suggest a crystallization which could come about through the exercise of habit patterns. The question is: does this shift always proceed in the direction of more favorable attitudes?

Sex Differences. Boys and girls had equally appropriate ideas about the Farm, but they differed significantly and strongly in their feelings about it. The latter were decidedly negative whereas boys tended to be more favorably disposed. The strength of their convictions is noted in the fact that many more boys than girls selected the Farm as one of their favorite scenes.

One thing is unmistakable: for children the Farm is a man's world. No other picture was as closely identified with either sex. Although girls can understand it, the Farm is not for them.

THE FACTORY

There's Towers with Smoke Coming Out

In the city is a big industrial area with manufacturing plants. It's real smokey, with smokestacks and chimneys. There are telephone posts with wires hanging, gas tanks, and piles of dirt on the side of the road. People are going to work; some are poor, some are rich; some walk and some ride. The car is driving the manager. Others who have jobs are businessmen, officemen, secretaries, and workmen. They all work and make things to sell. The newsboy works, too, trying to sell his papers. Here, it is very busy and everybody has to watch their step.

As THE above indicates, elementary school children are not without ideas about urban forms of production. Yet, the Factory appears to be one of the more difficult life situations for them to interpret. Boys and girls spent more than an average amount of time in reacting to this scene (Rank = 4), but in the long run had little to say about it (Rank = 10). Their efforts were moderately successful in the production of ideas and in the appropriateness of these ideas. With respect to space and time orientations, however, the scene ranked in the low end of the series. This undistinguished performance in apprehending factory work was accompanied by stronger feelings against it than was the case for most. Only one picture elicited fewer favorable attitudes, and two more negativism; it was tied for last place in children's preferences, and ranked at least average in their rejections. On one thing pupils generally agreed: the Factory is meant for the male population.

Children's Recognition of the Factory

Although 78 per cent of the pupils gained some recognition of this life situation, their perception was not of a particularly high order (Rank = 7). About the same proportion achieved a complete synthesis, recognized either structural or functional elements, or paid attention only to parts.

Forty-five per cent of the children recognized *structural* elements in this life situation. Except for the sixth grade boy who referred to it as an "industrial section," all of their responses were centered on the factory site as depicted. Illustrating this tendency are the following reactions:

> There's a canning factory with some milk . . .
> There's a car going in . . . to the coal factory . . .
> And a factory, smoke comin' outta the chimney . . .

Boys and girls used general and specific concepts to name this scene in about equal proportions. Among the former, "factory" appeared most often followed by such terms as "mill," "plant," and "shops." An interesting variation is that of a first grade urban girl who remarked, ". . . I think there's some smoke coming from the company . . ." Specific types of factories mentioned by pupils were representative of a wide variety of industries, the first column listed below being mentioned somewhat more frequently:

coal yard, coal factory, coal field	grain mill, elevator
oil refinery, oil factory	milk factory
steel mill, smelting works	auotmobile plant
power plant	cement works
canning factory	sand yard
	junk yard
	quarry

Children recognized the *functional* aspects of this situation in 30 per cent of the cases being much more conscious of productive functions than the distributive processes associated with factory work. To pupils, a factory is first and foremost where people go to work. A few, such as the first grade rural girl whose responses follow, made clear what happens when people work in such places:

There's a car, and there's a lots of people taking pitchers of it, I guess. And I think that's where they work and make things. And you know how I know? Because there's smoke coming up and there's wires there; that means, that that's where you work.

Those who were aware of the fact that something is done with factory products did not extend their thinking to the large scale distribution of manufactured goods. Theirs was the more personal concern of "people getting" or "people buying" things to satisfy their needs. The comments of a sixth grade urban girl illustrate this point:

Well, that looks like a coal field where people buy coal . . . it looks like some people are going to buy coal or something . . .

The highest level of recognition, which includes a *synthesis* of structural and functional elements, was achieved by 26 per cent of the children. One of the older city girls, for example, began with the notion of "factory", and then proceeded to differentiate such relevant symbols as: smoking chimneys, piles of dirt (raw materials or waste?), power lines, and big tanks. In addition, she was aware of what goes on in a factory even though the kind of work or type of production was not specified:

(Part I—What story does this picture tell?)
It looks like a . . . well . . . a factory, sorta like, and a . . . people are going to work there, and a . . . smoke's comin' outta the chimney. And there's a lotta dirt laying around there in piles, and there's a car standing right in front of the factory. Looks like there's some power lines going into the factory, and, um, and there's some big um . . . tanks there.

(Part II—Which boy or girl belongs in this picture?)
The happy boy.
(Why?)
'Cause he's selling papers and making money, and people are always happy when they get money.

Partial recognition of this scene was attained by 28 per cent of the pupils who attended to one or more aspects of urban work or other activities involved in the production and distribution of goods. These responses were about equally divided between descriptions of what people were doing and those pertaining to things; none was exclusively concerned with the world of Nature. About equal attention was given to people who were going to the city and to the newsboy. The first was usually for the purpose of shopping. As a sixth grade urban boy explained, "Many people go on Saturday to the city to shop, and to see their friends, and lots of other things like that." In connection with the newsboy and his selling of papers, note the concern of a first grade urban girl:

> (Part I—What story does this picture tell?)
> A . . . this guy is crossing the street and then these people are gonna walk by . . . to go downtown and buy something . . . and some people are gonna go in the car.
>
> (Part II—Which boy or girl belongs in this picture?)
> The sad boy.
> (Why?)
> Because nobody would buy the paper.

Those who were conscious of the cultural aspects of this life situation were most inclined to note that this was an urban scene: a city, town, or downtown. The chimneys ("there's towers with smoke coming out") and the piles of dirt or waste were also given some notice. A sixth grade urban girl's remarks are typical of this kind of reaction:

> Well, it looks like a busy city and um . . . looks like Pennsylvania, all smoke stacks and real smokey . . . and it looks sorta like a modern city . . .

As for the first grade city boy who simply *listed* various symbols having some bearing on urban work, it is interesting to note that despite the variety and extent of his identifications, none was seen in the context of the production or distribution of goods.

> There's a town, and there's a lady, and a man, and more ladies, and men, and a boy, and a smoke, and chimneys, and a machines, and a car, and a building, and more buildings . . . more machines, and dirt—and some dirt.

Nonrecognition. Fifteen per cent of the children failed to recognize this factory scene because they centered their attention on *general elements* which are more or less common to many life situations. About three-fourths of these responses dealt with human activities, and the remainder with things. The majority of pupils in the first group described people who were "walking," "going down the street," or "crossing the street." The remainder were equally concerned with the "boy holding something" and "someone driving a car." Without exception, those who included a description of things gave their attention to "the car driving past" or stated that the "car is going . . ." *Incorrect* interpretations of this life situation were made by five per cent of the pupils. A first grade rural girl stated quite flatly, "They are all getting ready for a picnic." An older urban boy began with a glimmer of recognition, but arrived at the conclusion that this was a "railroad sta-ion." Of an opposite nature was an early fixation upon a "carnival" by a young city boy which was not altered even after he had correctly identified a number of clues associated with industry.

> A, there's a car driving and there's a . . . that's a carnival. And I think . . . and a little boy is selling popcorn . . . and a man . . .a boy's walking. And there's a pile of coal there, and there's some smoke going up . . . and there's a big smokestack, and there's a house there, sorta like matches the smokestack . . . and a ladder across is going from one to one—when they're walking from one thing to another.

The Factory, as children see it, is mostly a place where people work, and sometimes where they get things. It is not one segment of a highly complicated and interrelated system for producing and distributing goods. Some boys and girls revealed a sensitivity to the conditions attending industrialization such as smoke, waste products, and danger. Others made a distinction between workers and managers, but no one hinted at the possibility of labor problems or strikes. For children, there was no such thing as a Depression. Least of all did they mention capitalism or the merits of free enterprise. It appears as though elementary children are just beginning to develop an awareness of this many-sided institution, the Factory.

Children's Setting for the Factory

Boys and girls perceived this industrial scene in a spatial background more than in a time perspective. In comparison with other pictures their sense of orientation was not very strong for the Factory ranked 9.5 in space, and only one picture ranked lower with respect to time.

A *spatial setting* was provided for the Factory more often than not, 65 per cent of the children giving some indication as to where events were taking place. Their responses were equally divided between associations with familiar places, and geographical or political designations of location; one-tenth using both to indicate the spatial background for what was happening.

All of the associations made by pupils involved some type of industrial institution. As was the case for the City, naming the structure was also a way of defining the setting of the events taking place: ". . . people are coming there most likely to buy coal . . . around the coal yard . . .." Hence, all the general terms for "factory" and the more specific industries mentioned in the previous section on structural recognition served to set the scene. Except for an occasional identification by state ("Looks like a busy city and um, looks like um, Pennsylvania. . ."), geopolitical referents were community centered. Pupils tended to place the scene in an urban environment without feeling the necessity for naming specific cities or locating them by state, region, or nation. Typical of these responses are the following:

A lot of stuff in town . . .
His mother told him to go downtown . . .
A family leaving their neighborhood . . .
That shows a big industrial area . . .
People are going to town . . .
They're in a city . . .
People downtown . . .
People going to work in a city . . .

Kinda looks like sort of in a city (names city in which he lives).

The number of children who did not place this life situation in a *temporal setting* was significantly greater than those who did, the latter representing only 8 per cent of the total group. In about half the cases time sense was indicated through association with common events, and the other half was based on mathematical or systematic means of time measurement. Of the children who were conscious of time, about one-tenth used both types of referents.

Associational referents used by children included Nature ("in the morning," "it's daytime") as well as personal-human events which may serve as a rough indication of time ("The last minute when everybody is getting out of school . . ."). Systematic referents included both chronometric and historical time. Of the former there were no direct references to the clock, all the responses being based on the calendar:

> It was Sunday morning . . . Easter Sunday . . .
> Many people go on Saturday to the city . . .

The historical references were all in the present tense as indicated by the following remarks:

> This looks like in (1959) . . .
> It looks sorta like a modern city . . .

The failure on the part of so many boys and girls to place the Factory in some kind of larger context would appear to be a sign of their lack of familiarity with industrialization. They are moderately successful in their recognition of factories, but that is as far as their perception goes. Concepts about the Industrial Revolution, and manufacturing centers or industrial regions are only in their incipient stage of development in the elementary school period.

Children's Attitude toward the Factory

Children are not attracted to this life situation. Less than half (47%) revealed a positive attitude toward the Factory (Rank = 12). Neutral attitudes were expressed by 18 per cent, and 26 per cent showed negative tendencies (Rank = 3). The remaining 9 per cent of the pupils were mixed in their reactions varying all the way from positive to negative feelings. Regardless of attitude, 24 per cent of the boys and girls responded consistently to this life situation in the various phases of the interview.

Boys and girls felt that factory work is all right for adults. On the subject of newsboy activities, however, there was quite an even distribution of pupils favoring such work and those who regarded it with certain reservations. With few exceptions, going downtown and having certain related experiences appealed very much to these pupils. For quite a number, this life situation had many implications for human relations.

Children's attitudes about work were based on the notion that this is what grown-ups do; that they are happy to do their work, but also glad to rest. Attitudes expressed toward selling newspapers reveal a rather broad set of values associated with work opportunities for children. Money was only one. Some thought of it as being fun, and having many interesting possibilities—even for learning! There was also the hint of depending upon oneself. Although disappointment was shown in a lack of success (sales), no one regarded the newsboy's work as drudgery or a hardship.

Positive	*Negative*
Factory work	
Some people (happy) are going to work. (6RB)	Might be gettin' out of work, and they'd be happy that their day is over—to rest. (6UG)
Selling newspapers	
He (the happy boy) can have that job. (1RG)	Because no one would take his papers. (1RG)
If he's selling papers he's usually having a fine time, because he can meet all kinds of people, and he can learn different things. (6UB)	It doesn't seem like many people are buying the paper. (6UG)
He's selling papers. He gets money for selling them. (6RB)	He's got to sell all the papers, and he can't sell most of them. (6UB)
He hasn't got many worries. He's going to the factory delivering papers to the businessmen. (6RG)	'Cause he's always got to sell papers, and do much stuff, and gives him his money. (1UG)
He's earning his own money, and he can sorta depend on himself. (6UG)	

Surprisingly few children expressed a great desire to become better acquainted with the Factory through visitation or otherwise.

A number did voice their enthusiasm for riding in cars or trains apart from the manufacturing emphasis of this life situation. So fascinated by the prospect of "going downtown" were a number of children that they, too, overlooked the industrial significance of this scene. As was true for the City, however, there were the dissenters:

Positive	Negative
Other experiences	

He's happy 'cause he likes to see all the things in the sand (sand yard). (1UB)
He wants to go in the car. (1UB)
Maybe he's going on a train ride. He could be happy he's going on a train ride; maybe, it's his first train ride. (6UB)

Going downtown

Positive	Negative
Because it's a nice day, and they're walking downtown. (1RG)	His mother told him to go downtown, and him didn't want to. (1RB)
The ladies are just together, and they look happy going down the street (to town). (6RG)	He can't walk on the sidewalk—it's too crowded. (1UB)
'Cause he gets to go to town, and he has lots of fun, I think. (6RG)	
I don't think that anybody who lives in a city like that would have anything to cry about or to be unhappy about. (6UG)	

For a considerable number of pupils, especially those who were younger, this was not so much a scene of industrialization as it was of human relationships. The range in types of behavior which they considered both from the standpoint of what is good and what is undesirable may be gathered from the following excerpts:

Positive	*Negative*

Human relations

Positive	*Negative*
He's nice, the boy sending out newspapers. (1RB) He wants to help everybody else. (1RB) He's a good little boy. (1RB) He's glad he can be in the middle of the road, and he can stop people and tell 'em they can go through. (6RB)	She might not be feeling good, and then her mother's mad at her. (1RB) He didn't wanna get out of the way of the car. (1RG)

Neutral attitudes were expressed by children who simply described what they saw without further comment. A first grade rural boy, for example, mentioned, "she's walking along," and one of his fellow group members added, "he's just selling newspapers." Acceptance of the activities depicted was indicated by an older rural girl who stated, "he's just selling papers like a normal boy would," and her city counterpart who selected a neutral figure to add to the situation, "because people are going to the factories to work." That a factory is nothing to get excited about, was stated quite explicitly by a young city girl who noted, "nobody's smiling, and nobody's crying, and nobody's mad."

Elementary school pupils did not show any great tendency to *pro and con* regarding the virtues or drawbacks of factory work. Whatever they saw in this situation was not examined from two or more points of view. An attempt to be flexible in this sense was demonstrated, however, by a little rural girl who explained:

> He's happy that he can work, and get money, and get food together. And, maybe, they don't got any money for food, and they can starve, too, and they can die.

Apart from the wide variety of attitudes expressed toward this scene, the most striking aspect of children's emotional reactions was their apparent lack of feeling for adult work. Few even took this into account, and when they did, there was little empathy. What work means to adults in terms of training, routines, security, recognition, and job satisfaction belongs to a world behind closed doors as far as children are concerned. This is especially true regarding women in industry. Factories are for men and, of course, they like going to work there.

Children's Preference for the Factory

The Factory is the only picture which no one selected as his most preferred. It placed second or third in three per cent of the choices—the lowest valuation placed on any scene in the Life-Situation Picture Series. That children were not simply indifferent to this scene of production is indicated by the moderate degree of rejection it received: five per cent or a ranking of sixth in the series. Reasons given by pupils for their choices represent an unusual balancing of values regarding work, the unfamiliar, and the element of interest:

Acceptance	*Rejection*
Because he works, and other little kids don't work, and father and mother work. (1RG)	Well, the people are just walking around, and they aren't doing any work. (6RG)
It's some place I've never been very often. (6RB)	It wouldn't make a very good picture to color, and it's just kinda common. I like something extra in it. (6UG)
I like to see what's inside of a cement factory, and how they work it. (6UB)	It doesn't look like a very interesting place to go. (6RG)

Obviously, children do not appreciate the benefits of mass production. Whether this is because they are not especially interested in material things or because modern industrial forms are too complex for them to come to grips with is not known. Unlike the Farm picture, this scene did not stimulate future ambitions. As far as could be determined, no elementary school child has a great desire to become a "factory man." It would be interesting to know when and through what process so many eventually do come to this decision.

Group Comparisons

Differences in perception of the Factory were related to age, sex, and community background in the order named. First and sixth grade pupils varied in practically all the cognitive aspects as well as in their attitudes. Boys and girls were not as far apart with respect to both ideas and feelings, but these differences have extremely significant implications. Although factories are usually associated with urban conditions, farm and city children differed in only one minor aspect.

Age Differences. As might be anticipated, older pupils excelled in the ideational side of perception. More of them recognized this scene in structural terms, and in so doing they made greater use of both general and specific concepts to describe what they saw. Sixth graders also displayed greater sensitivity to the functional aspects of factory work as a whole, and to production in particular. A synthesis of both these components was so seldom achieved by first grade pupils that the superiority of older children at this highest level of recognition was quite impressive. There was little difference in the number at each grade level who evidenced partial recognition of this life situation, but for some reason, younger pupils were more conscious of things than were sixth graders. On the other hand, the former produced a decidedly greater number of general, descriptive responses (nonrecognition) especially regarding people. As for orientation to this scene, older pupils made many more attempts to prescribe a spatial background especially of an institutional character. In attitudes, the difference was not that older pupils were more favorably disposed toward this industrial situation, but that young children were decidedly more negative.

The conclusion is inescapable that the first grader has little perception of the Factory. His contacts with modern industry are superficial at best, and may be the reason behind his negativism. Considerable progress is made in children's apprehension of industrial production during the elementary school years. Yet, it appears that while factories are seen by children, they are not adequately understood even by the sixth grader.

Sex Differences. Girls, generally speaking, did not fare as well as boys in their perception of the Factory. More of them attained only partial recognition of this situation, and those who did were more concerned with people than was the case with boys. They, also, were more inclined to associate this scene in a general community setting than specifically with a factory as was the tendency for boys. More significant, perhaps, were the differences in valuation placed on this picture. The tendency was for more boys to select the Factory, and for more girls to reject it.

There seems to be little doubt in children's minds about the Factory belonging to the world of men. The slight advantage which boys have in the perception of this particular scene may well be a reflection of their awareness of sex role in connection with factory work. Girls of elementary school age, however, did not see themselves in the role of "office workers" or as having anything to do with the production of goods. One wonders just what concept of role these girls will have when they "enter industry" as many of them will.

Rural-Uban Differences. The only way in which farm and city children differed in their perception of the Factory was in connection with the spatial background in which they placed the people, things, and events they recognized in the situation. Urban pupils tended to be oriented in terms of an institutional or factory setting whereas rural children located the scene more generally in a town or city.

Despite the common association made between industrialism and urbanism, the perception of the Factory by children coming from different community backgrounds was remarkably similar. Have the farm and factory merged in the minds of children as simply two different kinds of work or aspects of production? Has industry decentralized to the point where many rural people are factory workers either on a full-time or part-time basis? The increasing mobility of people—from the farm to the city and vice versa—may also explain the commonality of viewpoints toward the Factory exhibited by rural and urban children.

Chapter	SUMMARY

VIII.

IN answer to the questions raised in the Introduction to Part II, it must be noted first that *elementary children are not consistently superior in their perception of rural or urban life situations*. In four of the ten aspects of perception being considered, variations among the four scenes were not related to locale (*See* Table 2, Appendix). This was most dramatically evident in the value placed on the two rural pictures: the Farm was most preferred in the entire series while the Village shared last place with the Factory. In addition to this index of preference, no consistency was shown in the total number of ideas produced in response to the situations, and the proportion which were appropriate as well as in the number of times that an effort was made to designate the spatial background for what was taking place.

There was consistency, however, in six of the ten perceptual characteristics being analyzed. These suggest that children are more familiar with and look more favorably upon rural scenes than those portraying urban culture. More specifically:

Children respond to rural life situations with greater facility than to urban. There was a much greater flow of words in response to the rural scenes even though far more time was spent in responding to the urban pictures. This may mean that children find rural situations more interesting or easier to interpret.

Children have a better temporal orientation for rural scenes than for urban. This was the only one of several cognitive aspects involved in perception where differences appeared. Children's superiority in knowing about rural life, therefore, is not general. As will be shown later, time sense represents maturity in development, and this may mean that rural scenes are easier for children to cope with.

Children like rural situations much more than urban. The former elicited many more favorable attitudes whereas the latter were the target of more negative attitudes and were actually rejected by more pupils. This difference in feeling tones represents the greatest contrast in children's reactions to rural and urban life situations.

A number of reasons can be advanced for this apparent bias in favor of rural situations. It may be that children come in closer contact with the rural scenes depicted than with the city situations. Their experiences with factories, for one thing, are certainly more remote than those with farm work. As a member of a farm family, the young child cannot help but be aware of, and soon becomes engaged in, the work of running a farm. In contrast factory work is not a shared family experience. The city child probably hears little about factory work in family conversations, and is legally barred from participation until he reaches a certain age. The chances are, too, that regardless of where children live, they visit a farm long before they do a factory, that they read books about farm life before reading about factory work, that the farm is studied in school long before the subject of major industries appears in the curriculum. To a lesser extent, this differential in experience would also hold true for villages and cities. Children associate the former with a variety of purposes including religious and educational for rural children, and vacation or recreational for urban children. "Downtown" was primarily associated with shopping and work—adult activities with children in tow, as it were, until the time when they are old enough to venture by themselves, and have the means to do the kind of buying which appeals to them—"toys" and "cute clothes." So pronounced was this orientation that the "downtown movie" drew little attention showing once more the businesslike if not adult nature of downtown activities experienced by children.

Accompanying differences in experiencing rural and urban situations, are the values being associated with these ways of living. For most children, "the country" is a place where they can go sight-seeing, ride ponies, roam about the fields, and come to know the many fascinations of Nature; there are many opportunities to play. In short, the outdoors represents a life space of considerable magnitude. For some, the city is a place full of excitement where one can take bus rides and go shopping for all sorts of things. Only a few, however, associated downtown or the city in general with recreational pursuits, and for some shopping was regarded as something that had to be done—a chore interfering with play activities. Only an occasional child was interested or curious about how things are made; factories are for men's work—a life apart from that of children.

Differences Associated with Age

The greatest differences in the perception of scenes in the Community Block were those between first grade and sixth grade pupils. These occurred in their responses to each of the life situations, involving both ideas and feelings as follows:

Older children are superior to younger children in the ideational aspects of perceiving both rural and urban life situations. More of them reacted to the whole situation instead of to fragments. In so doing, they employed a greater number of concepts including those having greater specificity. There was also a greater tendency for them to designate spatial settings. Although the extent and degree of superiority on the part of sixth graders varied among the four scenes in this block, there was no exception to this rule.

Neither first nor sixth grade children find rural or urban life situations consistently easier to recognize. Both groups reached the highest levels of recognition (structure and/or function) in responding to the Farm followed by the City. Less agreement occurred on the Village and Factory, but for no grade was there consistency in the rankings of scenes by locality.

Younger children are more negatively disposed toward urban situations and, to a lesser extent, rural situations than are sixth graders. Toward both the City and Factory, first graders exhibited more unfavorable attitudes, and more of them vacillated between positive and negative feelings about the Farm. No such differences characterized attitudinal responses to the Village. To put it another way, negative attitudes toward rural life situations are tempered or eliminated earlier than similar feelings toward urban situations.

That older pupils are better able to deal with the ideas associated with the scenes constituting this block is in keeping with expectations from increased mental maturity. Whether a life situation is rural or urban, however, seems to have but little bearing on ease of recognition. The pattern of attitudes exhibited by first and sixth grade pupils is in keeping with the previous discussion on differences in opportunities for experiencing rural and urban life, and the greater freedom that comes with age in connection with the latter. It also is an indication of young children's tendency to have negative or mixed feelings about situations which they don't understand. The Village is an instance where children come to school with rather firmly established attitudes. It may also be that what happens in the following six years, in school and out, has little effect in changing their feelings. Subsequent experiences with small communities are little different in kind or intensity from earlier contacts—an outcome which may be partially attributed to the restricted nature of village life itself.

Differences between Boys and Girls

Second in the amount of difference exhibited in their reactions to the community life situations were those between boys and girls. Variations occurred with respect to both ideas and attitudes involved in perception. More girls than boys achieved only partial recognition of the Village and Factory situations. Boys and girls used different concepts in responding to the urban scenes. The former were more favorably disposed toward the Farm and Factory, but girls disliked or rejected both. These are important differences, but they are not consistent for a particular type of locality. We may conclude that *boys and girls do not perceive either rural or urban life situations in a characteristically different manner.*

Sex differences in the perception of the Community Block scenes may be explained in a number of ways other than rural-urban differentiations. The greater number of partial recognitions may be interpreted as a sign of greater immaturity on the part of some girls. This may be accounted for by differences in the experiences provided for boys and girls in our culture. Girls tend to be more home oriented and boys more likely to be concerned with "outside" interests. The Village would be such an outside factor to both farm and city children. In a similar sense so would the Factory appear to girls. Interests associated with sex may account for the greater tendency for girls to view the City as "downtown" and to regard the Factory scene as a "town" or "city"—both situations having unusual possibilities for shopping. In way of contrast, boys simply saw a "street corner" in the first case, and identified various factory situations in the latter. Recognition of sex roles helps to explain differences in attitude toward the Farm and Factory. These are primarily representations of male occupations, and were so accepted by the boys. It is significant to note, however, that girls of elementary school age are not attracted by farm life or the prospect of participating in industry.

Differences between Rural and Urban Children

Children living on farms and those living in a city perceived the Community Block in much the same way. The one difference was a matter of kind rather than of degree. *In their recognition of and spatial designations given for the urban situations, city children use more precise terms than farm children.*

It appears as though the locality in which children live does not unduly influence their perception of rural and urban scenes. A rural child, for example, seems to have sufficient accessibility to urban situations—either through direct contact or vicarious experiences —for him to develop a body of concepts and attitudes resulting in perceptions similar to those of urban children who, as we have seen, have somewhat limited experiences with "Downtown" and "Factory." That there exist differences in depth of insight and understanding of an urban environment, however, is indicated in the more specific terminology employed by city children as contrasted with the rather general use of "town" and "city" by rural youngsters. The fact that a similar refinement in the use of rural terminology by farm children was not evident may be an indication of the relative simplicity of their environment or its commonality. In either case, the kinds of experiences which city children have with "the country" seem to be adequate for the development of basic concepts about rural situations.

Differences Associated with Intelligence

The greatest similarity in perception of the Community Block was that between the high and low intelligence groups. In fact, none of the differences for any one picture was great enough to be considered significant. When compared with differences between first and sixth grade pupils, it is clear that for these life situations perception is more closely associated with mental level than brightness. Within the limits of normality, *intelligence is not related to to the perception of rural or urban life situations.*

Part III

HOW DO CHILDREN PERCEIVE
SOCIAL STATUS LIFE SITUATIONS?

Mansion

Poor House

Resort

Old Beach

INTRODUCTION

THERE is a range in the levels of living or "standards" by which the people of any nation live. Exceptions to this rule have either been practiced on a small scale or, if broader in application, have been short lived. The peoples of most cultures, in the past at least, have tended to accept a station in life relatively fixed by heredity. America, on the other hand, has been regarded as a land of opportunity for achieving the "better life." However much disagreement there may be in defining this way of life, it is generally acknowledged that a good part of our population is striving for upward mobility. For these parents, it is important that children be motivated to be "successful." They look to the school for assistance in developing such a point of view, and the necessary qualities for attaining this "good" life.

The question arises as to whether children of elementary school age are even aware of status differentials and what value they place on "better" ways of living. If such were the case, a number of related questions would also be important. Is the process of acculturation equally effective for country children and those living in the city? Are girls more conscious of socioeconomic status than boys? Do bright children show more sensitivity to differences in social background than children who are below average in intelligence? What developmental pattern takes place in social status perception during the first six years of school?

To find answers to the above questions, a number of life situations were devised contrasting upper and lower socioeconomic levels. General environmental clues were presented in the interior views of the Mansion and Poor House. Since recreation or leisure time activities constitute one of the sharpest contrasts between status groups, the Resort and Old Beach were added to form the Social Status Block.

Children's reactions to each of these life situations will be described in separate chapters followed by a series of conclusions regarding their perception of social status.

Chapter	THE MANSION
X.	

Many People in the Town Have Rich Houses

This place is a mansion, an awful nice home, where a real rich family lives. The modern living room is a pretty decorated room with all the new style furniture. There's a big fireplace, pretty curtains, pictures, a big curved couch, a coffee table, a television, and a piano. They have servants, a butler, a chauffeur to drive the convertible, and a maid to take care of the child. The lady might be going to some big party for she is putting on a mink stole. The child is just sitting there reading a book. Rich people usually have all the pleasures they want.

CHILDREN had more to say about this upper-status scene than any other in the series, and devoted more time in responding to it than for all but one other picture. This high rate of productivity in terms of verbal output and attention time, however, was not matched by a corresponding number of meanings associated with the situation or the appropriateness of these meanings. In fact, the Mansion ranked at the bottom of the series in the number of ideas evoked as well as in their correctness. A high-average number of time orientations were given in response to this scene, but designation of spatial settings was low-average for the series. Surprisingly enough, the Mansion was very low in the number of positive attitudes expressed toward it, and was the object of a moderate amount of negative feelings. It was selected as a preferred picture somewhat more than the average, and rejected to almost the same degree. That these children were reacting to something more than social status is indicated by the fact that more of them associated girls with this life situation than boys.

Children's Recognition of the Mansion

Only 49 per cent of the children were correct, in whole or part, in their interpretation of this scene. Of these, half perceived the picture solely in terms of its structural qualities, and one-fourth failed to integrate their impressions and form an inclusive meaning for the life situation.

Twenty-eight per cent of the boys and girls recognized the *structural* aspects of this upper-status home scene. All of these responses were centered on the building as pictured, no child extending his awareness to include the idea of an exclusive residential area or a so-called better section of town.

Those who recognized the external features of this situation made far greater use of adjectives to indicate exceptional dwelling circumstances than they did in naming it something other than "house" or "home." Almost half the responses included the terms "nice" or "big" as a means of conveying the idea that this was no ordinary dwelling place. About one-fifth of the responses showed an awareness of the "modern" or "new" aspects of the home as represented in this scene. Some children were also impressed by its aesthetic qualities ("pretty," "fancy," "beautiful") which indicated to them that this was housing of an unusual character. Only a few children came outright with the expression "rich house." The range of responses in this category is evident in the following responses:

> And a new home with pretty furniture, and pretty windows and pretty fire-stuff. (1RB)
> Well, it looks like a kind of a nice home, and they have sorta modern furniture. The table's modern and the chairs are modern, they have a modern piano, they have a nice car, and they have nice pictures, and a nice fireplace. (6UG)

Of the cognates used other than "house," the one most frequently mentioned by children was "mansion." One child attempted to indicate his conception of size or pretentiousness by referring to it as a "plantation house." In short, there is substantial evidence that in responding to this home situation, children definitely relied upon descriptive terms or phrases to differentiate this house from average or typical homes.

Fewer children, 10 per cent of the total, responded to the *func-*

tional aspects of this situation than to its external features. Their responses centered on the consumption of goods and services characterizing wealth as well as the quality of living experienced under such circumstances. A consciousness of the services available to a "rich family" as well as other consequences which may accompany wealth are revealed in the following remarks:

> It tells of a real rich family and um ... that maid is helping the mistress get ready to go away in the car and um ... in the window you can see the butler waiting for them to come out. (6RB)
> I think these are very rich people. They ... a ... which are going to give a party or else are going to a party and leaving the maid to take care of the little boy.   (6UG)

When referring to financial means, children were much more likely to generalize under the heading of "rich" than to mention "good things," material possessions, or services in general. No one used the term "wealth" or such expressions as "being well-off" or "having everything they wanted." References to the quality of living under the circumstances pictured were relatively few in number and were concerned, as will be indicated by the excerpt next quoted, with "having pleasures," and certain undesirable parent-child relationships which some children associated with wealth. It is also significant that no boy or girl expressed an awareness of social position or financial security often associated with wealth.

Only 5 per cent of the pupils recognized this scene of wealth from the standpoint of both its *structure and function*. This is the lowest percentage for any of the pictures in the series, and is in keeping with other evidence pointing to children's taking for granted "the good things" of our culture.

An example of a pupil who synthesized both the external features as well as the processes symbolized in this scene is that of an older city boy who showed an awareness of the exceptional qualities of the house which he associated with wealth, and from which he proceeded to generalize about the pleasures of such a way of life.

(Part I—What story does this picture tell?)
> Well, there's a man standing out a ... out on a ... near a car, a convertible. And there's a ... well, it looks sorta like a ... it's taken in a rich house, and there's a picture on the wall, quite a few of 'em and there's a oh! it's sort of a place where you could

sit down, and there's a piano there, and there's two ladies and
a man there, and then there's a fireplace with um, stones all
around it, and there's a . . . looks like there's a TV set there.
And let's see, there's a little boy sittin' down there on a . . . on
a sort of a couch or somethin' like that and there's a little
curved table there like a boomerang or something like that.

(Part II—Which boy or girl belongs in this picture?)
The in-between boy.
(Why?)
Because he has all his pleasures. It looks like—and looks like
it's sorta like a rich house there and um, rich people usually
have all the pleasures that they want.

A *partial* recognition of the elements in this life situation was
evidenced by 12.5 per cent of the children. These responses were
descriptions of what they saw rather than the mere identification of
significant clues (2%). They were centered on people and things
pertaining to our culture, there being no references which were
focused exclusively on Nature. Typical of such incomplete awareness is the "story" of a first grade urban boy:

A . . . they're in a house and they're having a party. A . . . a boy's
sitting down and he's looking at some "Kool Aid" or something.
And there's a piano there, a picture of a man that's crying, a . . .
a servant, and then a girl, and a maid.

This sensitivity to entertainment and to having servants represents practically all of the concepts referring to people. To these
children, having a party or dance and the presence of maids, butlers
or chauffeurs were the attractive aspects of this life situation, but
they failed to indicate that these were conditions of wealth. This
was also true of one of the more unusual responses, that of a young
rural boy who was struck by the fact that the lady was putting on a
"mink stole." The majority of children who fastened their attention on things limited their observation to the room rather than
viewing it as part of a house. They recognized that the room was
"big," "pretty," and even "modern," but failed to see it as part of a
wealthy home.

Nonrecognition. A bare majority of these pupils (51%) failed
to recognize the Mansion as typifying high-status living or wealth,

this being the highest percentage of nonrecognition in the entire series. Those who did not connect this scene with high socioeconomic background were far more likely to single out general aspects (39%) than to arrive at an incorrect meaning for the situation (11%).

Almost all *general descriptions* were centered on people, there being a few dealing with things but none exclusively concerned with Nature. Somewhat more than half of the former were about the child, who, for the most part was reported as reading or merely sitting and watching the adults. The idea of having visitors or "having company" was expressed fairly often, and to a lesser extent the coming and going of parents or an older girl going on a "date." Miscellaneous remarks included such things as the child looking at TV, a mailman coming up the walk, and a family which "likes" music. Concepts about things were most often applied to the home in which case no attempt was made to ascribe qualities indicating high socioeconomic status ("That's a home . . .").

Inappropriate interpretations were largely errors involving time, such expressions as "olden days," "long time ago," and "old fashioned" being most common. To a lesser degree, this scene was confused with governmental buildings, "the courthouse" and "White House" being mentioned by some older boys. Among the miscellaneous errors were: "Abe Lincoln's house," "hotel," and even "boat."

To an adult, it may come as a surprise that more children did not view the Mansion in the light of high-status living. The symbols of upper-class background pictured in this scene were suggestive of wealth but not other aspects of social status. Children's emphasis was on the comforts and enjoyment associated with living in a "nice," "big" house and being "rich." Factors such as prestige and influence, often thought of in this connection, seem to be of no importance to children. More striking is the fact that fully half the children were unaware of the exceptional character of this scene. Does this mean that they regard the way of life pictured in the Mansion as the norm or standard? Have TV, the movies, and other forms of advertising succeeded in convincing even children of elementary school age that this is the way most people live—or should?

Children's Setting for the Mansion

Elementary school children placed the Mansion in a space relationship more frequently than in a time perspective. Compared with other pictures in the series, however, this scene ranked higher in temporal orientation than in placement (Rankings = 5 vs. 9.5).

In 65 per cent of the cases, pupils defined a *spatial setting* for the Mansion, thus indicating a definite trend for giving location. Children who did so, in the majority of cases, associated the scene with familiar places rather than specifying certain geographical or political units. Only a handful of children used both associational and systematic measures for indicating spatial orientation.

As would be expected, most of the associations used to designate space involved the home. Only a few pupils mentioned an institutional background, and no one located it in the wide world of Nature. Typical of their responses are the following:

> It looks like somebody lives in a awful nice home ...
> They're home again, now ...
> Well, that looks like people are living in their real fancy house ...
> People are coming to a house ...
> They are showing them around in the house ...

> They're close to a zoo ...
> It's on a big plantation ...
> It looks like sorta in a hotel ...

The few instances in which geographical or political units were referred to included communities in general and the nation as is indicated below. Boys and girls, surprisingly, did not place the Mansion in their own city, state, or region; neither did they transport it to areas outside their own country.

> About ladies downtown ...
> Many people in the town have rich homes ...
> This looks like a home down South.

Eighteen per cent of the children gave a *temporal setting* for the Mansion, a definite indication that elementary school pupils do not visualize this scene of upper-class living in a time perspective. Those who did, specified time in chronological terms more often than by associating it with common events. The measurement system used was not that involving clocks or calendar, but was solely historical with about equal emphasis on the past and the present.

> This looks like one of the old-fashioned homes ... the long dresses they used to wear ...
> It looks like a very rich family in the olden days ...

> Well, it looks like a real modern house ...
> A modern living room where the family is just about to receive guests ...
> This is a rich family and they have all the new style furniture ...

The few associational responses were directed about equally to natural and human events. In the former, the emphasis was upon daily rather than annual happenings whereas human events tended to be social rather than personal in nature.

> At night they went home ...
> She's gonna have guests in the night time ...

> This is the story of Abraham Lincoln and his room ...
> It could be the White House and all presidents, like James Monroe, it could be their house.

There is no simple explanation for the perceptual field in which the Mansion was placed by boys and girls. The fact that it was not identified with their own circumstances in life or relegated to foreign countries might be interpreted in two ways. For those who regard this life situation as nothing unusual, there was little reason for being so explicit. Children who realized that few farm families or city households lived in this style, and that it was not typical of any one section should be credited with realism. The divided opinion on whether this was an "old-fashioned" or "modern" scene points out another group of pupils who were at least aware of a certain uniqueness about this life situation. Was it the long dress which intrigued (and confused) boys and girls?

Children's Attitudes toward the Mansion

Contrary to what might be expected, elementary school children did not react to this high-status situation with overwhelming approval. Somewhat less than half (47%) of the boys and girls were attracted to the Mansion (Rank = 12), the remainder being about equally divided among neutral (19%), negative (19% or Rank of 7.5), and mixed (15%) feelings. These boys and girls, moreover, showed a high degree of consistency in their reactions at various points in the interview thus indicating that their minds were pretty well made up as far as this scene of upper-status living was concerned. Thirty-eight per cent responded with unvarying feelings toward the suitation; only one other picture in the series (Poor House) exceeded this degree of attitudinal set.

No child voiced any objections to having the material conveniences and comforts of high socioeconomic living. Boys and girls were divided, however, on the subject of whether or not wealth is associated with enjoyment. A number of children disregarded everything in the life situation except the factor of family and interpersonal relations which were also seen in a dual light.

Having *enough* money, a nice house to live in, adequate food and clothing ("a fur coat"), and "pleasures" in general were the symbols of wealth which children were conscious of in this scene. These were the "good things" (including the comics!) which boys and girls approved.

Toward wealth

The lady in the picture because she's got a fur coat.   (1UG)

He lives in a big house, and there's a lot of good things—comics and everything.   (6UB)

They have a nice home, and it looks like they have nice parents.   (6UG)

Because she's got enough money, food to eat, and she just likes it.   (6RB)

He has all his pleasures. Rich people usually have all the pleasures that they want.   (6UB)

For some children being rich meant having fun. There were many opportunities to "go out," to enjoy dancing and other forms of recreation, and one could always read at home. On the other hand, there were pupils who regarded high social status as setting up definite hindrances to play and having fun. There's hardly anything to do or anyone to do them with in a rich family. Reading, furthermore, was not always popular with boys and girls.

Positive	*Negative*

Recreation

Positive	*Negative*
She's getting ready to go out. (6RB)	Nobody'll play with him. (1RG)
	She can't play. (1RB)
She must be going to have a lot of fun. (6UG)	She's rich and she doesn't have, maybe, too much fun. She just has to do things that her mother would want her to. (6RG)
She wants to dance with them. (1RG)	
The lady—she's going to the dance, and she looks so pretty. (1UG)	She's not exactly happy, because she can't go along with her mother and father, and there's hardly anything to do in such a big house. And she's just looking at the magazines and papers. (6RB)

Reading

Positive	*Negative*
She's reading the funnies, and she's having a good time. (1RB)	She (sad girl) hadda read that book, that's probably why. (1RB)
He likes looking at pictures and stuff. (1RG)	She looks kinda sad because she's reading the paper, and she looks like she might have read something dreadful, too. (6RG)
	She has to look at pictures, and she don't wanna. (1RG)

Some of the children who were so engrossed in human relations that they paid no attention to signs of wealth were favorably impressed by the lack of tension between parents and children. Poor human relations, however, accounted for the largest single class of negative feelings expressed toward this high-status situation. Many pupils associated the scene with parental neglect of their children or a lack of family unity.

Positive	*Negative*

Human relations

Positive	*Negative*
'Cause see, her mother didn't scold her. (1RB)	He don't wanna go to bed. (1RB)
Her father's helping her, and he seems happy about it. (6UG)	Nobody pays any attention to her. (6RB)
Because, well, she might be get-	'Cause his mother gets new coats

Positive		*Negative*	
		Human relations	

ting married.   (6UG)   and stuff, and he don't.   (1UG)
                                          She's crying because her mother's
                                          going away.   (1RB)
                                          His mother is going away, and
                                          she has to leave him home or
                                          something.   (6UG)
                                          He can't go with his mother and
                                          father.   (1UB)
                                          Because she couldn't go to town
                                          or something.   (6RG)
                                          They are so rich they sort of neg-
                                          lect her, and just leave her with
                                          a maid.   (6UB)

Those who were *neutral* or unmoved by this scene of well-to-do living either saw little in it touching upon children's activity or associated it with commonplace or routine events. There was simply "nothing to do" in such a situation or it was a setting in which children "just looked" or engaged in other than exciting activities. Such neutral attitudes were expressed in the following ways:

She don't have nothing to do.   (1RG)
She's just sitting there.   (6RG)
All she can do is sit there, probably.   (1UB)
He doesn't have nuttin' to make him happy.   (6UB)

She's just looking at a book.   (1RB)
'Cause he's just reading a book.   (1UG)
Looking at the television set.   (1RB)
She's reading a paper, and I think their visitors are coming.
                                                        (6RB)

Mixed reactions to this living room scene were of two kinds. In the case of younger children, many expressed different attitudes to various parts of the situation which engaged their attention at different times during the interview. Older children, in reacting to high-status, usually responded favorably in their first contact with the situation, but the second or third meeting would find this attitude changed as they took into account other things besides the factor of wealth. The responses of a sixth grade urban boy, for example, reveal the impression made on him by a "real mansion" and "big party." The second time he viewed this situation, he became conscious of the "sad girl" who was being relegated to the charge of a "nurse maid."

Why was the Mansion looked upon with so little favor that only one picture (Poor House) ranked lower in positive attitude? As has been indicated, it is not because boys and girls are unmindful of the "good things" in life. Could it be that once a certain level of material possessions is assured, having fun is more important than having more money? More significant even, was children's concern for the human relationships implied in this life situation. It appears that boys and girls would rather be with and do things with their parents than be left in the care of such an exceptional "baby sitter" as a butler or maid. They recognize that there is no substitute for a happy home, and this means the presence of parents.

Children's Preference for the Mansion

Although more than an average number of children valued the symbols of high socioeconomic status represented in this scene, about as many failed to appreciate their significance. The Mansion accounted for 8 per cent of the total number of children's picture choices (Rank = 4.5) and 5 per cent of their rejections (Rank = 6). This is another indication of the "two-sided" nature of the situation as perceived by these children. Reasons given for selecting or rejecting this picture usually centered on certain aspects of the life situation rather than on the scene in general. These specifics included the appearance of the house and its conveniences or comforts, as well as recreational possibilities for people living in such circumstances. As the following excerpts indicate, these children approved of neatness and regarded a modern house in a more favorable light than one which was "old fashioned."

Acceptance	*Rejection*
I like modern houses. (6UG)	Because this is in the old-fashioned days. (1UB)
It looks like a modern home— like the homes we have now. (6UG)	
Because they got such a neat house. (1RG)	

Children were also attracted to such "nice things" portrayed in this situation as the piano, furniture, and maid service, but again, the matter of style was questioned.

Acceptance	*Rejection*
I like the piano. (1RG)	I don't like the style of the fur-
'Cause mama and daddy want me to get a piano, and that one reminded me that I'm gonna get a piano. (1RG)	niture. (6UG)
They have a nice pretty lounge that's real big. (6UG)	
I like the way the lady is dressing the woman. (1UG)	

Recreation, the third attraction of this high-status situation, met with not a single objection. It is interesting to note that it was the girls and not the boys who who made this observation, and that dancing was something that even little girls prized.

> 'Cause there's dancing there.   (1RG)
> The lady is going to a dance, and she looks so pretty.   (1UG)
> The girl seems happy because she's going away, and the boy seems happy because he's just looking at the comics or something. (6UG)

Miscellaneous responses took in other factors or were very general in nature. Among the former was shown a concern for human relationships. His regard for the human element was so great, apparently, that a small rural boy overlooked all evidences of comfortable living and rejected this picture, "Because they're sad. Because someone is going away and they like them." General or rather vague statements were more likely to indicate a feeling about the situation than a recognition of what it was. A young child selected the picture simply "because I like it" or because "I like to color things like that." He would reject it " 'Cause I went there before, and I didn't like it."

It is interesting to note the specificity and wide variety of reasons given by children in their valuing or rejection of the Mansion. No child wants to be rich simply for its own sake. There is something he definitely wants which money can bring him. A generalized state of affluence is either too intangible to satisfy him or beyond his powers of abstraction to understand.

Group Comparisons

The way in which the Mansion was perceived differed markedly between first and sixth grade pupils and to a lesser extent between boys and girls. Whether one lived on a farm or in the city, his perception of this upper-status situation was quite similar, and this was also true for children varying in ability. Age differentials included both the conceptual as well as attitudinal aspects of perception, but sex differences were limited to emotional reactions.

Age Differences. Sixth graders surpassed younger pupils in their ability to recognize this scene and to place it in a space-and-time field. More of them responded to the structural aspect of this situation, and this was particularly noticeable in their use of adjectives denoting the superlative qualities of the residence. Their superiority was especially marked with respect to the recognition of functional aspects. Whereas 20 per cent of the sixth graders recognized some functional element in the scene not a single first grade child showed an awareness of wealth or upper-status living. As a consequence, none reached the highest level (synthesis) in recognition, but neither did many of the older pupils. On the other hand, more first grade pupils than sixth graders responded to general aspects of the situation particularly to the people, and thus failed to recognize this as an upper-status scene. The greater consciousness of both spatial and temporal backgrounds by older pupils was revealed in the first case, by a greater use of associational references to home and certain other institutions. When indicating time, they were more inclined to refer chronologically to the past and present.

The contrast in the attitudes of these age groups toward the Mansion was not as striking as in their ideas. Sixth grade pupils had a tendency to look with favor upon this upper-status scene but younger children were decidedly more negative.

It would appear from the above, that the ability to understand and to appreciate this high socioeconomic situation is more related to development of social maturity as defined by our culture than to differences in children's social backgrounds. At six years of age relatively few children (30%) were able to discriminate between the Mansion and any other home situation, so they reacted primarily to its human relations aspects. By twelve, the proportion had more than doubled (68%), and with this increasing sensitivity came a higher regard for what the Mansion symbolizes in our society.

Sex Differences. Boys and girls did not differ in what they saw, but in how they felt about this situation. The attitudes of the former tended to be on the negative side whereas girls were far more favorably impressed. That these were strong convictions was borne out in their picture preferences: many more girls than boys wished to keep the Mansion "for their very own." The difference, then, is not a matter of more precise conceptualization, but in the values which boys and girls associate with this high-status scene.

The more favorable outlook which girls displayed for the Mansion may be a reflection of their greater concern for home and family life in general or a greater consciousness of the qualitative element in our culture. The former would, quite obviously, be in keeping with their sex role. The latter can be explained in terms of social maturity if we assume that girls are more conscious of socially accepted or culturally approved ways of living than are boys during the elementary school years.

THE POOR HOUSE

It's Sad to Be Poor

> *This is the story of some people who are very poor and live in a slum. They live in a broken house—kinda rickety-rackety—because they don't have enough money to buy a good house. They haven't got much of anything. The father has to find a job to get enough money to support them. Mother has her hands full with the baby, and the little children are sick. They are cold and hungry, and their clothes are ragged. None of them are very happy and they must be worried. Everything looks so wrong!*

THE above comments reflect the critical reactions of children to this situation of poverty. They felt more strongly about the Poor House than any other picture in the series. It ranked last in the number of positive attitudes that it elicited from pupils and first in negative responses; it was first in the number of times it was rejected, and near the bottom of the list of selected pictures. This strong reaction was evidenced also in the high rate of productivity stimulated by this scene; children had much to say and took a great deal of time in so doing. As a result, many ideas were forthcoming. Yet, boys and girls did not find this an easy situation to interpret, and only a little more than half achieved some degree of appropriateness in recognition. Their sense of orientation, in terms of space and time, was also below that of the majority of life situations. They were aware, however, that both boys and girls may be identified with situations of poverty.

Children's Recognition of the Poor House

Appropriate interpretation at various levels of insight were made by 59 per cent of the pupils (Rank = 12). Somewhat less than half of these represented a synthesis of both the structural and functional aspects of the situation; one-fourth were partial or incomplete.

Objective or *structural* characteristics were recognized by 34 per cent of the boys and girls most of whom were also conscious of function. Responses were definitely more centered on the specific building portrayed than upon the area or district which they might represent. In the few instances in which the latter occurred sixth graders used the term "slum" exclusively, there being no mention of tenement, broken-down section or other similar designations.

By far the greater number of references to the building were based on the concept of "house." Children defined the quality of the house by specifying what it was not as well as what it was. In the first instance, "not good" and "not nice" were used most frequently. A positive indictment of the house usually called for the modifier "old" or "poor." Some children, whether for lack of vocabulary or a preference for more picturesque speech, used phrases to describe the general condition of the house ("falling apart," "broken down") or seemed to have a language all their own ("rickety-rackety"). How these appeared in context is indicated by the following:

> Seems like a poor family living in a old, a kind of poor house . . .
> It looks like a rickety old house . . .
> They don't have the right . . . kind of house, and it's old . . .
> They haven't a good home . . .
> It's kind of a rickety-rackety house . . .
> She doesn't have a very nice house . . .
> There's a broken house in there . . .
> Their house is all falling apart . . .

Terms other than "house" used to indicate unsatisfactory shelter were few in number. "Cabin" (generally accompanied by "old") was used most often, and only infrequently did the term "shack" or "shed" appear. Only one pupil, a sixth grade girl, thought this was a family "living down in the basement."

Recognition of the processes or *functions* being depicted in this life situation, either singly but usually in conjunction with its objective appearance, was indicated by 36 per cent of the children. They were far more sensitive to consumption or distribution as related to the broad problem of poverty than they were to the processes of production as reflected in employment or work-type activities. Regarding the former, "poor" was the most convenient and almost universally applied concept to describe the lacks or deprivation portrayed in this scene. Those who did not actually use the word "poor," expressed the same idea in a number of ways to indicate what the people in the picture did not have. Only one pupil, a sixth grade urban girl, used the word "poverty" in talking about this scene. A sampling of these remarks follow:

> These people are very poor . . .
> It looks like a poor family that doesn't have much money . . .
> This is a family that, they haven't got much of anything . . .
> They're not very rich . . .

Children looked upon employment in the different ways it might have applied to this situation. Their interpretation included the idea that the father in the family was either unemployed or that he did not have a very good job, and the more positive approach that he was job-hunting. Typical of such reactions are the following:

> Their father hasn't got a very good job . . .
> The man is very sad . . . it looks like he lost his job . . .
> The father . . . has to find a job 'cause . . . the little children are sick . . .

The highest level of recognition, which included a sensitivity to both the *structural and functional* aspects of this life situation, was achieved by 26 per cent of the boys and girls. Most often such awareness was stimulated by certain physical characteristics of the house which led to the notion of inadequate shelter as well as the deduction that in the distribution and consumption of goods and services the family pictured had not fared too well. In the illustration given below, for example, the sixth grade rural boy showed awareness of this being a "poor house" that was likely to be "cold," and associated poverty primarily with illness and a lack of food and clothing.

> (Part I—What story does this picture tell?)
> Oh, this is a family that was very poor. They didn't have very much clothes, the father was just going out to buy some at the store—they had to live next door. And I guess, then, there's these clothes hanging up; they were all they had and washed

them. And this little girl had come down with pneumonia and was in bed; she tried to keep as warm as she could. This mother had her baby in her arms trying to protect her from the cold, too. And the house that they lived in was very poor, and they were cold most of the time.

(Part II—Which boy or girl belongs in this picture?)
Sad girl.
(Why?)
'Cause there it looks like it's very poor, and they don't have very much clothing. And I guess that this little girl in bed has penumonia so she's not very glad.

(Part III—Which picture wouldn't you want to keep for your very own?)
The poor house.
(Why?)
Well, because they were so poor, and I hate to see things like that at all. And it's just to see them suffer, and not have enough clothing and food.

Fifteen per cent of the boys and girls *partially* recognized this life situation in that they described one or more elements of the scene having to do with poverty. Their attention was given to people and to things, there being little opportunity to become engrossed with Nature in and of itself.

Children who focused on the people in the situation were more sensitive to emotional states than to activities. For them, anyone experiencing poverty would most likely be sad if not angered by the deprivations of such living. Being ill or quarreling seemed to be of lesser import. It was in conjunction with the identification of figures which "belonged in the picture" that such hinting at poverty was most likely to occur:

The angry girl. (Why?) Because she don't like her own home, because it's too mussed up . . . she'd have a home like the other people.   (1UG)
The crying girl. (Why?) Because she looks sad, 'cause a . . . she don't have nothing to eat.   (1RG)
The mad boy. (Why?) 'Cause the father is mad . . . 'cause his mother don't like him.   (1RG)

Pupils who were sensitive to the physical features in this situation seldom stopped short of bringing clues together to form the concept of a very inadequate house. Some of the younger children, however, did not synthesize in such broad terms. They were content to make the simple statement that this was an "old house" without elaborating on the idea of a really poor situation. Such was the case for a young rural boy who said:

> I think there's two, there's two girls there and a boy. There's a baby over there—there's a baby in the mother's hands. Looks like a old place, too. Milk's on the stove, too, think it's for the baby. Father's walking over to the bottle to get some milk, an' the girl, the girl's gonna go git her dolls. The boy's sleeping in his bed.

Nonrecognition. The difficulty level for the Poor House is indicated by the fact that whereas some pictures were recognized by practically all children, 41 per cent did not make a correct interpretation of this situation. This is not because of inappropriate responses or inability on the part of boys and girls to respond. The great majority of pupils who failed to recognize this life situation gave their attention to general features in the scene which were not considered to be signs or symbols of poverty.

Children who responded to *general* aspects of this poverty situation (34%) were definitely more attentive to people than to things. Regarding the former, they were most conscious of: (a) someone in bed, generally a child, who was asleep or in the process of waking up, (b) the laundering operations of washing and hanging clothes to dry, and (c) play opportunities or lack of such opportunities. Less frequently were pupils aware of parent-child relationships, the father going to work, and children who were eating or simply asking for food. Those who were more conscious of things, tended to mention the clothes hanging on the line and the picture on the wall without implying that anything was out of place or "wrong."

Inappropriate interpretations were made by only 5 per cent of the pupils, too few to warrant any sweeping conclusions. The increased possibilities for making incorrect associations which come with added years of experience and learning are demonstrated in the "story" of a sixth grade urban boy:

> Um, it's probably in the pioneer days, um, let's see ... maybe it tells about the pioneers or something.

It seems that children's conceptualization of lower-status living is fairly concrete but without social stigma. The three out of five pupils who recognized this scene used such terms as "old," "not good," "poor," and "out of work" to describe their reactions. Seldom, however, was this situation regarded as the more generalized state of poverty, and never as an instance of lower-class living. Children may not like what they see in this picture, but they do not blame or condemn people who are living under such circumstances. To be poor is not nice, but neither is it degrading.

Children's Setting for the Poor House

Children found it easier to think of where this scene belonged than when the events occurred. Yet, in comparison with other pictures in the series, the Poor House placed higher in temporal setting than spatial. The rankings, 8.5 and 13 respectively, indicate, however, that children's consciousness of the perceptual field for this poverty situation was not as well developed as for other life situations.

A *spatial setting* was designated by exactly 50 per cent of the boys and girls indicating an even chance that this scene would be thought of in connection with some place or location. In defining the orientation for this scene, pupils showed a much greater preference for associating it with familiar places than for putting it in a geographical or political unit. Except for a sixth grade rural boy, who provided an institutional setting, ("A store, and a man was in there and he's walking out now . . .") associational referents were centered about the home:

> Looks like some people in a house . . .
> They have to live in an old house . . .
> It looks like a house, an old house where poor people live in . . .
> That's a sad family living down in the basement . . .
> The father's leaving the room . . .
> The father goes to work and um, the girl and a mother is staying home . . .

When it came to a geopolitical location, children gave the Poor House a wide distribution. They were aware of the fact that poverty existed in a community setting, in the nation, and in other parts of the world. Typical of their comments are the following:

They live in the slums . . .
The man can't find a job and they live in the slums . . .
This is a story of a . . . some poor people who live in this village . . .

When people just came to America . . .

It looks like some people are in China . . .
A kinda poor house in Europe . . .

A *temporal setting* was provided for this situation by 11 per cent of the pupils, conclusive evidence that they were not conscious of time or did not choose to describe this situation in terms of time. Temporal designations were about equally divided between references to familiar events and systematic measures of time. The former, associational referents, included daily changes in the world of Nature, such as day or night, and human events of broad scope characterizing social epochs or eras.

This is when Bobby wakes up in the morning . . .
A poor family ready to eat in the morning . . .

It's probably in the pioneer days . . .
That could be in the frontier days . . .

When children attempted to use a more systematic basis for placing the Poor House in perspective, they tended to use the historical past. Only once was the calendar referred to, and it is interesting to note that the month on the calendar was "recognized" as being the same as when the interview took place ("I think it's March on the calendar there . . .") Those who sensed chronology placed great reliance on the term "old" to stand for dates and centuries, the latter term not being used in a single instance.

That looks like in the old days . . .
In the old days where some of the early settlers lived . . .
That looks like it's in the older days; it doesn't look like it would happen now . . .

Certain aspects of the perceptual field in which the Poor House was visualized have interesting implications. Children were more conscious of the world-wide existence of poverty situations than for the majority of life situations. Yet, no child made sweeping generalizations or regarded this as the stereotype for an entire race, people, or nation. Time, in a number of cases, was specified as the historical past one of the few such instances occurring in the picture series. Both orientations placed poverty at some distance from the child and may be one way in which consciously or otherwise he was expressing his rejection. It may mean that many young people have little direct contact with such extreme poverty; others may not recognize that they are poor. Consequently, "the poor" live "far away" and "long ago."

Children's Attitudes toward the Poor House

Boys and girls expressed more disfavor in connection with this poverty situation than any other and, conversely, the fewest positive or favorable reactions. In fact, the number of children who expressed negativism toward the Poor House exceeded that for the other three attitudes combined the percentages being: 69 per cent negative, 7 per cent positive, 6 per cent neutral, and a mixture of positive and negative attitudes 18 per cent. These attitudes, moreover, were expressed consistently throughout the interview by 41 per cent of the pupils, the highest for the Life-Situation Picture Series.

Both *positive* and *negative* feelings were expressed about family relationships and a state of well being in general. Some children were more impressed by family unity than by the impoverished circumstances depicted in the situation. In like manner, interpersonal tensions, rejection, and discipline were of greater importance to some children than conditions of poverty. For some of the younger children physical and mental well-being were still possible under the circumstances pictured whereas others rejected the effects that such a situation would have on physical development.

Positive	*Negative*
Family relationships

She's with her father and her mother, and they got a little baby and stuff like that. (1RB)	'Cause his mother don't like him. (1RB)
'Cause there's another girl. (1UB)	She can't go along with her daddy. (1RG)
Maybe she's got a little sister. (6RG)	She might be crying because something happened to her dad. (6UB)
	Perhaps he's sad because he had a spanking. (6RG)

Positive	*Negative*

Family relationships

The husband is angry and he's mad, too, because somebody hollered at him, or he's mad at somebody like the child or the wife ... a, he could be angry at everybody. (1RG)

General well-being

He's laying in bed. (1RB)	He just doesn't look good. (1RG)
She isn't in bed, and she must feel good. (1RB)	'Cause he doesn't feel good. (1UB)
She's thinking about something real good. (1RG)	It looks like he's kinda sick or something. (6RG)

Although one or two children accepted the fact of poverty, as will be shown later in the analysis of neutral responses, no elementary school child spoke approvingly of such circumstances. In their *negativism* toward poverty, about as many talked about being poor in a general way or included several elements commonly associated with poverty as those who singled out only one of these factors on which to shower their disapproval. Typical expressions of each are as follows:

Poverty

Don't have enough money to buy good things. (6RB)
Because I don't like to see poor people. (6RB)
She isn't very rich. She doesn't have nice clothes, and she doesn't have a very nice house. (1UB)
She lives down in the basement. The clothes are ripped and she's got a ripped dress. (6UG)
It looks like it's very poor, and they don't have very much clothing, and I guess that the little girl in bed has pneumonia. (6RB)
They're kinda poor people, and she couldn't get all the toys, and their clothes are kind of raggedy. (6UB)
Because he looks somewhat angry and he might get mad at somebody. Because it looks like they're poor and they haven't a very good house. (6RG)

They're poor, and they don't have very much to eat, and they have
to live in an old house. (6RG)

It looks like they're poor, and their father hasn't got a very good
job, and they haven't got a very nice house to live in, and a nice
yard to play in, and all the other nice things that we have. (6RG)

Food

'Cause she don't have nothing to eat. (1RG)

'Cause there's no milk. (1RG)

'Cause she doesn't have enough food. (6RG)

They don't have food. They must be worried. I don't like to hear
sad stories like that. (6UG)

Shelter

Their house there is all falling apart. (6RB)

They have no nice house. (6RB)

The house is all tattered up. (6UG)

He doesn't look very happy in a home like that, and I don't think
I'd be very happy in a home like that either. (6UG)

Recreation

Nobody wants to play with her. (1RG)

Maybe she couldn't play with her friends or somethin'. (6UB)

'Cause he ain't got nothing to do. 'Cause there ain't no trains
around the house to play with. (1UG)

They don't have very many pleasures. (6UB)

Unemployment

He's got to support his family, and he doesn't got no job to get
any money. (6UB)

Her father is probably out of a job, and she might not be able to
go to school or anything. (6UB)

Mixed reactions were exhibited toward the Poor House for a
variety of reasons. The most common cause was a failure to recognize this as a lower-status situation and to respond to something
different each time the picture was viewed. Others were based on
reasons more obscure. Among the latter was a sixth grade urban
girl who appears to have started out by rejecting the idea of poverty,
which she recognized readily enough, and who ended by selecting

this as her second choice for reasons having to do with the picture itself rather than the conditions portrayed.

(Part I—What story does this picture tell?)
Well, that looks like it's in the older days, it doesn't look like it would happen now, I mean with the clothes hanging indoors, and the pictures are crooked and everything. It looks like a poor family that doesn't have very much money.

(Part II—Which boy or girl belongs in this picture?)
The sad boy.
(Why?)
Well, maybe he's sad, because he didn't get enough money to give his family.

(Part III—Which picture would you like to keep for your very own?
(Second choice)
(Why?)
Well, a ... there's a lot of expression you could put into that picture. You could make their clothes look dirty and that'd be fun mixing colors together that way.

The relatively few children who maintained a *neutral* attitude toward the Poor House were those who failed to recognize poverty and who, instead, singled out certain common activities such as sleeping and walking. On the other hand, there were several instances where the condition of poverty apparently did not touch children or result in a show of strong emotion.

Because he's sleeping.   (1RG)
'Cause she's walking, and she's happy when she's walking.   (1UB)
Can't explain. It's sorta like a poor family and a rich family, in-between.   (6UB)
The mother and father are very poor, and she's not too happy about it and she's not too sad.   (6UG)

Children did not find this scene of low socioeconomic living attractive. They voiced disapproval of a variety of factors including material necessities of life, health, and recreation. Little or no concern was shown, however, for the effect which poverty has on more subtle aspects of child rearing including education and other "cultural" advantages as well as delinquency, and various forms of anti-social behavior. Neither did boys and girls show much awareness of the cause or cure for poverty in their attitudinal responses. For them the crux of the matter is having a good job, but the personal and social implications for employment were not made explicit. Least of all did they look for certain outside forms of "assistance" as the remedy. They didn't like poverty, but blamed no one for it.

Children's Preferences for the Poor House

This was the most rejected picture in the series (44%). On the other hand, one-eighth of the pupils included it among the three they wished to keep, thus accounting for 4 per cent of the picture choices (Rank = 12). In their reasons given to support their selections, children referred to the state of poverty in general, singled out one aspect of low-status living, or based their decision on a composite of factors. In many cases, children tended to make a simple and sweeping condemnation of the situation. An exception to this rule were the reactions of a sixth grade rural boy who recognized the wretched state of poverty, but who chose it as his first picture to keep for reasons which might indicate sympathy or empathy:

Acceptance	*Rejection*
Well, it's kinda, well a . . . it's like that house there, like the—they're kinda poor and everything. (6RB)	They're kinda poor. (6RB) Because it looks like everybody is so poor, and having a hard time. (6RG) 'Cause everything looks so wrong. (1RG) Because that wouldn't be a real good one. (1RB)

The unsatisfactory condition of the house, interpersonal conflict, and the resulting unhappy emotional states were the *specific aspects* which many children singled out for rejection. These same factors were also given as reasons for the selection of this scene. Having shown a very real awareness of the hardships associated with poverty in his previous reactions, there is reason for attributing the selection of this picture and accompanying remarks of an older rural boy as reflecting compassion for the less fortunate.

Acceptance	*Rejection*
I know some people that are poor, and it's sad. (6RB)	I think there's a broken house in there. (1UG)
	They don't keep their house clean and nice. (1RG)
	They had a fight. (1RB)
	It's a sad family. (6RB)
	It's so dreary. (6RB)
	They don't look very happy where the family's all working. (6UG)
	I'm only taking the happy ones. (1UG)

In many cases, the decision to reject the Poor House was often based on a composite of the values mentioned above. By way of contrast were the responses of several pupils who selected this scene because of the lesson it taught or the moral it held for present and future behavior. This is the only instance in the series where children selected a picture because it showed what *not* to do, and may be a reflection of the emphasis our culture places upon being "well-off."

Acceptance	*Rejection*
When I can't have anything it would remind me of that little boy. I should wait until supper-time. (1UB)	The calendar's tipped over and they look angry. (1RG)
'Cause you see what it is— when you go and spend all your money when you're little and you don't save it. Then you don't got no money to live with when you're grown up. (6UB)	They're living in the slums and they're re-real poor, and they don't look very happy. (6UG)
Because we're going to study China, and that looks like it's about China, and because they have communist leaders there. (6UG)	It looks like the people are sad, and they don't have enough money to buy a good home and clothes and that. (6UG)
	They're poor. They're probably unhealthy, and I wouldn't wanna be that way. (6RG)

In spite of the rather striking presentation of poverty as portrayed in this scene a considerable number of children either failed

to recognize it or placed greater value upon the human elements in
the situation.

Acceptance	*Rejection*
I like little girls and boys. (1UG) 'Cause they're walking out a the house, and there's a baby there. (1RG) Because everybody's happy. (1RB)	Because they all look sad. They thought their grandmother was coming but their grandmother didn't come. (1RG) Because he has a mustache. (1RB) I wouldn't know what color to color the clothes. (6RG)

That children do think about income or status levels as they
grow older, and that they are in the process of forming realistic
attitudes toward wealth and poverty which are not based on
"either-or" considerations are indicated by the responses of a sixth
grade urban boy who selected this picture as his first choice because:

> Well, a let's see—there isn't too much pleasures and there isn't too
> much sadness. Anyhow, well, poor people have a, well, they got
> things that a, rich people haven't got. Like a . . . well . . . they can
> find a way of getting things, and a, rich people—all they have to do
> is go to the store and buy something.   (6UB)

and by a sixth grade city girl who rejected this picture because:

> I wouldn't want to live in a poor house or anything like that. I'm
> glad I'm right between. I don't wanta be poor, and I don't wanta
> be rich.   (6UG)

Most children were definitely against being poor. Their objections
were more than materialistic in nature, and included some social
and emotional considerations. The culture in which they lived has
made such an issue of poverty that children are very conscious of
the lesson to be learned even to selecting the Poor House "for a
reminder." Despite this, a number of children displayed an empathy with the poor and a compassion giving evidence of something more than ignorance. They seemed to realize that there were
other values in life than wealth. They were condemning poverty
not people.

Group Comparisons

The reactions of various groups to the Poor House indicate that it takes time for children to learn to perceive poverty. Once this condition has been met, there is little difference in the perception of low socioeconomic status by community, sex, and intelligence groups.

Age Differences. During the elementary school years, development in the perception of poverty takes place with reference to ideas and emotional overtones. Sixth grade pupils were better able by far to recognize this scene, and place it in some kind of spatial setting than were first graders; their attitudes were more "conventional."

The highest level of recognition, synthesizing both structure and function, was reached by 50 per cent of the older group in comparison with 2 per cent of the younger pupils. As for structure taken separately, sixth graders excelled in: number of pupils attaining this level of awareness, total number of types of such recognitions, sensitivity to the situation as a building or home site, and use of adjectives or modifiers in evaluating the "house" as pictured. Their superiority in recognizing the functional aspects of this scene was even greater. To begin with, the older pupils accounted for all of the ideas regarding employment. Also, a total of 70 per cent grasped the situation in functional terms as compared with only 2 per cent of the first graders. This constituted one of the sharpest differentiations to be found in the picture series. In way of contrast, first grade children showed greater disposition to simply respond to the Poor House in general terms, thus failing to evidence an awareness of lower-status conditions. This was evidenced in the number of first grade pupils involved, the number of different types of such responses, and especially comments about people bearing no relationship to poverty.

In keeping with their superior recognition powers, more sixth grade pupils than younger children specified a spatial background for this life situation. In so doing, they used more associational referents, and were the only ones to think in geopolitical terms. This great development in spatial consciousness, however, was not duplicated in time settings for this scene.

Attitudinal changes were in the direction of a more definite shift away from this lower-status situation. Unable to grasp the full significance of this scene, some of the younger pupils reacted positively to its family significance. No sixth grader, however, responded favorably to the Poor House without also including certain reservations.

It is clear that the strong, consistent, and negative feelings which children have about this lower-class scene develop early and are widespread. Even the child, too immature to conceptualize in terms of poverty, may be aware of certain undesirable elements in this scene. As they grow older, pupils have a much better grasp of the ideas or concepts involved and this strengthens their prior feelings about poverty. The processes of acculturation have been so effective in this case that regardless of community background, sex, and intelligence, by the time pupils reach sixth grade they know and feel strongly that poverty is to be avoided.

THE RESORT

It's Nice to Go on a Summer Vacation

*This is a summer resort, a real nice place to stay and have
a summer vacation. It's in hilly country, and has a beautiful
stone wall with bushes and many trees. You can rest, relax
or lie in the sun and get a suntan. It has a stable, and people
are going horseback riding. Some are playing tennis on the
tennis court and some are golfing. There is diving and swimming at the swimming pool, and they even have a swimming
teacher to teach them how to swim. You can have lotta fun,
but you have to watch out what you're doing in the swimming
pool and riding horses and all that.*

THIS scene of high-status recreation was one of the
most favorably received in the series. Not a single child rejected it
—a distinction shared by no other picture. Coupled with this is
the fact that it brought out the greatest number of favorable attitudes. Further evidence of the high regard that children had for
this Resort scene was the above average number of times that it
was selected as a favorite picture and the below-average ranking in
negative attitudes. The Resort, moreover, was seen as having universal appeal for it was identified as a fitting place for both boys
and girls. In spite of such favorable reception on the part of
children, measures of productivity and the ideational aspects of
perception were just average. Attention time and words produced;
meanings attached to the scene and their appropriateness, spatial
and temporal backgrounds in which this situation was placed—
each ranged no more than one step in either direction from the
average rank for the series.

Children's Recognition of the Resort

Almost as many boys and girls (70%) made some form of correct interpretation of this life situation (Rank = 11) as for the comparison scene of the Old Beach. A little less than three-fifths of these responses were partial in character, almost two-fifths combined a sensitivity to *both* its structure and function, and the remainder were *either* structure or function. Thus, there was no significant differences in the number of children who grasped the Resort scene as a whole and those who were only partially successful.

A total of 28 per cent of the pupils viewed this scene from its *structural* aspect. These responses were equally divided between references to private and public places. Those who were aware of a home-like character to this situation made equal reference to its superior qualities and to a type of house implying something above average. "Rich," "great big," and to a lesser extent "nice" were the terms which these children associated with homes having a swimming pool and stables. As for type, they thought of it primarily as a "summer home" or "ranch type" with a scattering of "very modern" or "new." An example of an older rural boy who was conscious only of the structural aspects of the situation is the following:

> (Part I—What story does this picture tell?)
>   That's a great big a . . . house. And there's a kennels out in back of it, and there's a riding stable over at the other corner, and uh . . . a lotta people there, and big cars . . . a swimming pool.

> (Part II—Which boy or girl belongs in this picture?)
>   The happy girl.
> (Why?)
>   She's going to this swimming pool.

References to public places of recreation were more varied in nature than those pertaining to private homes. The most frequently used term, accounting for approximately one-third of the responses, was "resort" used by itself or in a phrase such as "summer resort." About an equal number of references were divided among the terms "vacation spot," "ranch for guests," and "a camp" for boys or girls. Among the miscellaneous designations were: "coun-

try club," "lodge," "hotel," "the Y.M.C.A.," and the general
specification of "recreational place." In each case the identification
of this scene as a commercial recreation center was accompanied
by a consciousness of the types of activities in which people were
engaged; to talk about a resort without mentioning what was going
on seemed incomplete even for children.

A sensitivity to the *functional* aspects of this life situation was
exhibited by 30 per cent of the pupils. This consciousness of the
dynamic elements in the scene was directed far more to recreational
opportunities and activities in general than to symbols denoting
high quality or upper-status recreation. For every six children who
went on to describe the various "pleasures" that people were en-
joying, there was only one child who mentioned that these were
"rich people" having fun or the availability of "swimming lessons."

As an illustration of this point are the remarks of a sixth grade
rural boy who displayed an awareness of recreational functions and
the possibility of organized instruction although he did not identify
the place structurally in upper-status terms.

(Part I—What story does this picture tell?)
Well, here is a place where a couple of cars came by and did
some sightseeing, and here's what they saw. They seen a couple
people by this river a ... swimming. They thought they might
even go in, too, and so they came in and enjoyed their swim,
and after awhile they dressed and watched the others. And they
seen these barns and the horse riding, and after a little while
they got acquainted with these people which were known as
very close neighbors of theirs. And after while they thought
they'd ride these ponies that they seen there, and they got on
and went around the countryside horseback riding. And they
thought very much that this was one of their ver ... very best
enjoyable nights or even days.

(Part II—Which boy or girl belongs in this picture?)
The happy boy and girl.
(Why?)
Here they'd be happy. Again, as I told you, that they had been
swimming and horseback riding, and they liked this very much
because they'd never done it. And that this summer they had
learned how to swim and ... and had the swimming teacher
with them to teach them how to swim even in here, to teach
them more swimming lessons in here. And after they got done

riding horses they liked it, and thanked their mother and father for having them come on the ride and come here to their neighbors.

In referring to recreational activities, children were much more likely to name specific kinds of activities than to refer to play in general. As might be expected from the nature of the scene, swimming and riding constituted more than half the number of recreational activities singled out. Tennis, golf, "getting a suntan," and picnicking accounted for another fourth of the responses. Children who talked about recreation in general terms tended to use such expressions as "having fun" or a "good time," noted that people were relaxing by "just sitting around" or "resting," and were aware that some were "on their vacation."

The excellent physical conditions and the various activities falling under the heading of recreation were recognized by 27 per cent of the children. This attention to both *structure and function* is more than five times greater than was the case for the companion picture of a Mansion. Illustrating this ability to take into account external features as well as social processes are the comments of a sixth grade rural boy, who made note of the various kinds of recreational activities being engaged in at a summer resort, and who was aware of the more than moderate circumstances being pictured in this scene.

> (Part I—What story does this picture tell?)
> It tells of a . . . um, summer resort and a . . . they have a . . . riding and swimming and a . . . tennis playing and a . . . golfing and a, real nice places to just enjoy themselves and a stay, a have a summer vacation.
>
> (Part II—Which boy or girl belongs in this picture?)
> The happy boy.
> (Why?)
> Because . . . because um, he can go with his mother and father to a real nice summer resort.

A *partial* recognition of the Resort scene was achieved by 39 per cent of the pupils. Many children, apparently, were satisfied to mention specific kinds of recreational activities without tying these together in larger terms as to place or failed to disclose the distinctive character of the functions being depicted. Those who exhibited partial awareness concentrated heavily on people, only one-tenth of the responses focusing on man-made things, and half as many dealing with the world of Nature. An instance of this type of response is given by a young rural girl who noticed certain kinds of play activities, the shade trees, and the swimming pool, but did not indicate that this was an exceptionally good recreation center.

(Part I—What story does this picture tell?)
Well, there's a lane to walk down, and there's houses and there's trees, too, where people can get shade out of, and that's the only place where you can get shade. And there's cars and people. And a girl sitting down with a swimming suit, and there's a swimming pool there with a . . . which I just noticed. I thought that was a lane, but that's a swimming pool. And there's horses, and buildings, and places where you can play, too.

(Part II—Which boy or girl belongs in this picture?)
The happy boy and girl.
(Why?)
Be . . . because they can go swimming, and they can play around where there's a swimming pool, and they got their swimming suits on and everything.

As was true regarding awareness of function, children were much more likely to describe what people were doing in specific rather than in general terms. One-half of the partial interpretations of this scene dealing with people were references to swimming ("jumping in the river," "going in the water," "playing in the water," "coming out from the pool"). Another fourth had to do with riding ("riding a pony," "horseback riding," "people on horses"). Of the rather limited number of general statements about people, "having fun," "people playing," and "playing sports" were most commonly used.

Children who concentrated on things portrayed in this Resort scene picked out the pool in every instance, and in some cases included an unspecified "building" or stables. The few children who became absorbed in the natural world spoke at some length on the subject of horses and, as in the example given above, "shade trees."

Nonrecognition. Thirty per cent of the pupils failed to interpret this scene of upper-status recreation. Unlike the great majority of pictures in this series, nonrecognition of the Resort was due primarily to incorrect interpretations rather than to singling out general or common elements which might apply to almost any life situation.

Inappropriate responses were made by 23 per cent of the children. The greatest source of error was in confusing this situation with a farm or, in some instances, a ranch. Children were conscious of the wide open spaces pictured in the scene as well as the horses and what to them was a barn, but failed to continue in their search for clues and ultimately differentiate such things as the tennis court, golf course, and of lesser significance, perhaps, the "modern" shape of the swimming pool. Among the remaining inappropriate responses were such miscellaneous interpretations as "a race track," "beach," and "old hotel."

Few pupils (5%) reacted in such a *general* sense that they gave no indication of recognizing the recreational signs depicted. All of these responses were centered on people rather than on things or Nature, and the majority were descriptive rather than the simple act of enumeration. A young urban boy recognized a boy talking to "his uncle," and a first grade urban girl saw "people walking." Coming closer to the idea of recreation, but far from being explicit, were the observations of a first grade urban boy:

> A . . . that's a . . . two horses, and a car, and a house, and some stage coaches, and a man leading a horse, and there's a man, and a boy, and the man next to . . . in front of a car.

Children's interpretation of this high-status scene is more notable for its variety than number of ideas. The many different types of private and public recreational facilities "recognized" by boys and girls suggests a high degree of familiarity or vicarious experiences. Their relative insensitivity to the exceptional quality or exclusive nature of the situation depicted does raise the question, however, as to whether children have much comprehension of the cost of such recreation. Have public parks and other agencies expanded both in number and quality to the point where children take the Resort scene for granted—and "for free?" Is this the stereotype for recreation which many children assume is natural and normal?

Children's Setting for the Resort

Children were more aware of the spatial background for this scene than its setting in time. The ranking for temporal referents, however, was higher than for spatial (6th vs. 8th) although both were in the average range for the series as a whole.

Orientation in *space* was demonstrated by 66 per cent of the boys and girls, thus indicating a definite consciousness on their part for the placement or location of this particular scene. Instead of using geographical or political concepts to specify a spatial field, most children made reference to familiar places without pin-pointing their location. One-tenth of their responses were a combination of both associational and geopolitical referents.

There was a wide distribution of associational responses. The majority were institutional in character, this scene being likened to a great variety of recreational agencies. One-fourth were related to home situations, and the remainder were attached to the world of Nature. This variability is well illustrated by the following excerpts:

> It looks to me like the Y.M.C.A.; that's where I'm going to go . . .
> I think this is out at a camp or lodge . . .
> People are like on their vacation or something in a hotel . . .
> It's some kind of a resort or a rich place . . .
> That's at a race track . . .
>
> Well . . . that's at their home . . .
> That's a little swimming pool by this house . . .
> This looks like a rich person's residence . . .
>
> It's in the hilly country . . . hilly country . . .
> That could be on a vacation . . . out in the country . . .
> Looks like some great big house in the country . . .

These children did not see the Resort in terms of their own state, the Midwest or the world at large. The scattering of geo-political referents which they used were divided between community areas and the nation such as:

> That's a new family moving into the neighborhood . . .
> Well, that's in the city, at their home . . .
>
> This looks like a summer home, in Kentucky . . .

A *temporal setting* was mentioned by only 16 per cent of the pupils indicating a lack of time consciousness for this Resort situation. Those who did reveal such sensitivity, were more likely to use associational referents than systematic measures of time. In the former case, associations were made with happenings in Nature far more frequently than to human events, this being the only picture in the Social Status Block for which this occurred. References to natural phenomena took into account both daily and annual happenings as the following indicate:

> They got up at midnight every night . . .
> Others are lying down reading and having a nice afternoon . . .
> They swim and play tennis every day . . .

> They . . . have a summer vacation . . .
> This summer they had learned to swim . . .
> It's nice to go on summer vacations . . .

The few mathematical observations of time were based on the clock as well as the historical past and present:

> They all go to bed after supper at 7:30 . . .

> There's a hotel of them . . . in the old times . . .
> In the new days . . .
> A modern place to live . . .

The preponderance of institutional orientation which children displayed in connection with the Resort reveals their awareness of the many different agencies serving to meet recreational needs. It is surprising that so few references were made to state or national parks although this may be due to differences in the nature of the facilities usually available in public recreation centers. Regardless of type, however, it is significant that boys and girls did not associate high-class recreation with any specific locality. The Resort, as far as children are concerned, exists anywhere or everywhere. No one place has a monopoly on recreation of this kind.

Children's Attitudes toward the Resort

Boys and girls had more favorable things to say about this scene than any other in the Life-Situation Picture Series. A highly significant proportion of the group, 74 per cent, were positively oriented toward the Resort. Of the remaining pupils, 15 per cent displayed negative attitudes (Rank = 11), 7 per cent were neutral, and only 5 per cent gave evidence of a mixture of feelings. In 28 per cent of the cases, children reacted with the same feeling tone each time they were presented with this situation. This represents about average consistency for the series.

Children were very *favorably* impressed by the Resort scene, because of the many opportunities for play provided in the situation. Some children merely approved of there being a number of possibilities while others expressed an appreciation for the opportunity to choose among them. A few of the older children showed great satisfaction with the situation because it could accommodate the interests of boys as well as girls. In keeping with this attitude toward play opportunities was the insight shown by a young rural girl who placed a crying boy in the picture " 'Cause he has to work all the time." Other positive expressions included:

> There are so many things to do around there.   (6RG)
> Because they can go swimming here, and they're riding over there; picnicking.   (6RB)
> She can either take her choice of swimming, sightseeing, or horseback riding.   (6UG)
> I think the boys would like golfing a little better and riding horses, too.   (6UG)
> One boy is going horseback riding. The girl, perhaps, is doing something else like reading and enjoying herself or else relaxing in the sun.   (6RG)

The child who was appreciative of the health aspect of recreation was the exception. While it is true that some liked to think of "relaxing in the sun," not a single child made direct reference to mental or physical health as such. The closest that anyone came to expressing this idea was the approval given by a sixth grade rural boy when he said, "They're all happy because they can have a vacation now, and rest and have fun."

Positive and *negative* attitudes were expressed toward certain recreational activities and their human relations aspect. The former were the basis for the great majority of attitudinal responses to this situation. Some children talked in general about doing something nice or having fun. Others concentrated on one activity such as swimming or riding. Many children expressed attitudes toward a number of recreational pursuits which they identified in the picture. It is not at all surprising that, with few exceptions, children liked what they saw. In spite of the rather exceptional facilities represented in this scene, however, some of the younger girls expressed a dislike for swimming.

Feelings about human relationships constituted a fairly sizable group of the attitudes. On the positive side, were those involving parental permission or facilitation of play activities as well as the desirability of having a family play together. Disapproval was shown for such things as failure to be included in the play group and competition. The degree of projection elicited by this scene may be gathered from the remarks of a young urban boy who placed the "frowning" boy in the picture because, "He's there talkin' to the man. He wants to stay with his uncle." The same explanation might apply to the remarks of a first grade rural boy who noted, "I think that lady's mad. That man's going out with a different lady."

Positive	*Negative*
Recreational activities	
He did something real nice that day. (1RB)	'Cause she doesn't wanna go swimming. (1RG)
They're having fun playing around. (6RG)	
Everybody likes to do it—swim. (1UB)	
They're happy when they're diving and swimming and such. (1UG)	
They've been swimming and horseback riding, and they like this very much. (6RB)	
They had company—a lot of friends there, and they're gonna go swimming. They got horses to ride, football court or tennis—a lotta places they can play games. (6RG)	

Positive	*Negative*
Human relationships	

She could swim in deeper water than the other kids can, and some kids—their mothers won't let them go. (1UG)	She doesn't like nothing at all. She wants to play with others and they won't play with her. (1RG)
Their mother and father done what they wanted them to do, and their ponies were their own, and they could do whatever they wanted with them. (1RG)	She looks kinda mad at these two here 'cause, maybe, they swim so good and she can't. (6UB)
She's having a fine time playing tennis with her father and mother. She had a nice fine day. (6UB)	
Because he can go with his mother and father to a real nice summer resort. (6RB)	

There were relatively few reactions to this scene of upper-status recreation which did not reveal a definite attitude one way or the other. *Neutral* responses were usually simple statements of what the observer saw in the situation devoid of any expression of emotion. In most cases garbled or inappropriate interpretations were likewise unaccompanied by emotional tone. The few *mixed* reactions to the Resort scene, usually were indicative of the absence of an attitudinal "set" which resulted in shifting between positive and negative feelings. This was more evident in the responses of younger children, and is well illustrated in the remarks of a first grade rural girl who changed from a neutral attitude to one of anger, but who finally decided that she wanted to keep this particular picture.

(Part I—What story does this picture tell?)
   About boys who are going swimming, and some cars, and going horseback riding, and a house, and a lotsa fields; trees, bushes, a swimming pool.

(Part II—Which boy or girl belongs in this picture?)
   The angry girl.
(Why?)
   'Cause she don't wanna go swimming.

(Part III—Which picture would you like to keep for your very own?)
(Third choice)
(Why?)
'Cause of the water.

Several things are worth noting about children's attitudes toward the Resort. First, was their great desire for variety in recreation. No one activity seems to meet with everyone's approval. There must be things for boys to do and things for girls to do—with freedom to choose. Second, is the importance of the social aspects of play. This involves both adults and peers. Some children may chafe under the restriction of adult supervision, but others want very much to engage in recreational pursuits with their parents. As for playing with age-mates, there is always the question of being invited to participate, and the embarrassment of not doing as well as others even when there is no formal competition. For children, play can be quite a serious matter.

Children's Preference for the Resort

Not a single child rejected this picture. Further proof of its popularity is the fact that 25 per cent of the pupils selected the Resort as one of their three favorite scenes. This accounted for 8 per cent of their choices, and gave the picture a 4.5 ranking in preference. From the standpoint of both pupil selections and rejections, this was the most preferred picture in the series.

Boys and girls placed the highest priority on the things or activities depicted in this situation which symbolized "having a good time." This valuing on their part was expressed in a general sense as follows:

Because it's so nice.   (1UG)
They're having a whole bunch of fun.   (1UG)
It looks to me as if everybody's having a good time.   (6RG)
It looks like it would be a nice place to live, and it just looks nice.   (6UG)
They seem like they're having a lot of fun, and that's the kind of vacation I like to go on in the summer.   (6UG)

Of the various activities pictured in the scene, swimming and riding were the ones that children valued most. No one was greatly excited over the possibilities of picnicking or following a nature trail. Neither were court games—tennis, badminton or basketball—nor golf mentioned by children as reasons for selecting this picture. Typical of their responses are:

'Cause of the water.   (1RG)
Because I like to go swimming in there.   (1UB)
I would like to go swimming if I lived close by it.   (1UG)
I kinda like horses.   (6RB)
Because that has a picture of children riding horses and swimming, and I like some kinds of sports, too.   (6UB)
You could have a lotta sunlight, swimming, and horseback riding.
                                                              (6UG)

Among the miscellaneous responses is that of a young city boy who seemed to place a great deal of emphasis upon learning certain recreational skills ("because I can take swimming lessons"). Another boy in the same group, apparently, was much more impressed by the human relations element than by play opportunities, his reason for selecting the picture being, "Because it has so many people in it." In view of the attitudes expressed toward the Resort scene, described previously, it is not surprising to note that no child selected this life situation for the reason that it was "good" for one's health or social position.

"Having a good time" is a key phrase for children. Almost no other reason was given by the many boys and girls who chose to keep the Resort picture. The child, quite obviously, does not play for reasons of health nor is he much interested in relaxation. The most popular activities, swimming and riding, were also among the most active and "exciting" of those mentioned. Least of all do children engage in recreation to learn for the nature trail was hardly noticed. The most important thing about recreation is: IT'S FUN!

Group Comparisons

Age differences again proved to be the greatest among various groups of elementary school children. Girls and boys, and pupils of different intellectual capacity varied but slightly in their perception of the Resort. Rural and urban children differed not at all. All group differences involved the ideational aspect of perception, but in the case of first and sixth grade pupils feelings were also included.

Age Differences. Sixth grade pupils excelled in recognizing this scene. They were able to synthesize objective and dynamic elements more effectively to reach the highest level of interpretation. Taken separately, older pupils were more conscious of structure. Whether the life situation was regarded as a private dwelling, a public recreation area, or both; whether the analysis was in terms of the number of their responses—in each case sixth graders were definitely superior to young children. Similar findings were obtained from an analysis of function. Older pupils, both in terms of their number and their responses, exceeded in an awareness of the recreational activities being pictured. Awareness of the qualitative aspects of this life situation were too few for comparison, but all were made by the older pupils. Conversely, in the number of pupils involved as well as the total number of such responses, first graders only managed a partial interpretation; usually this was a reference to people.

Older pupils were also superior in perceiving this situation in a spatial background as was apparent in the greater number of such designations given, particularly those of an associational nature. Although the total number of temporal settings was not too different from that of first graders, older pupils also used more associational referents to specify time.

There is evidence, too, that attitudes toward the kinds of recreational opportunities pictured in this scene become more favorable with age. First graders had a tendency to be neutral and mixed in their attitudes or decidedly more negative than sixth graders, who regard this situation more favorably.

Children, apparently must learn to like some types of recreational activities usually associated with high socioeconomic background. The young child is satisfied with far less. Some of his real concerns are being granted permission to play or being part of a play group. As he grows older, his concerns broaden to include competition with peers and satisfactory play relationships with adults. At the same time, he raises his sights regarding recreational possibilities.

Sex Differences. Boys and girls reacted in similar fashion to the Resort. Quantitatively speaking, there was no difference. In their partial interpretations, however, girls centered more of their attention on people. Recreation, clearly, is not enjoyed only by boys. It may be that they have a preference for the more active pursuits whereas some girls are more interested in relaxation and sunning. Boys and girls may also place different emphasis upon competition and social relationships in play. Both, however, find attractions in outdoor recreation as depicted in the Resort.

Intelligence Differences. Bright children and those with less ability perceived this recreation scene in much the same way. The only difference occurred in their recognition of recreational activities. The number of pupils aware of such functions was not materially different, but those with high intelligence noticed many more things underway. This difference may be less related to recreational situations than to characteristic forms of behavior on the part of these groups of children. Bright children simply know more about recreation as they do about everything else. Similarity in feelings about the Resort suggests, however, that participation in recreational activities is not dependent upon intelligence. All children like to play outdoors.

THE OLD BEACH

Having Fun at the Beach

There's an old beach for all sorts of children that come and want to go swimming during the summer when it's hot. It has an old pier for children to dive from, and a little shack for them to change their clothes in. It looks like it's pretty dangerous; it's not very sanitary. There could be a drowning or they might get hurt. Some boys are fighting, but others are having a lotta fun there. Children are swimming, playing ball, and even making a campfire for a wienie roast. You can have a good time when you run around on the beach.

GENERALLY speaking, children's reactions to this scene of an unsupervised, disorganized, and ramshackled swimming place were in the average range for the series. The picture ranked low-average in the time required for pupils to respond as well as in the flow of words produced. The outcome of such productive effort was a high-average number of meanings derived for the situation, and these were fairly appropriate. The spatial orientation for boys and girls, and their sense of time for the life situation was also in the average zone. This tendency was also evident in their attitudes. The number of negative feelings expressed in this case was just average for the series, and positive attitudes just a step higher. Also in keeping with this general trend, was the average rank achieved in the number of times it was selected as a preferred picture. An exception occurred in the great number of children who rejected the Old Beach for a variety of reasons. Neither was this averaging out process reflected in children's identification of sex figures with the situation. There was widespread agreement that the Old Beach was meant for boys rather than girls.

Children's Recognition of the Old Beach

This life situation was recognized to some extent by 75 per cent of the children (Rank = 8.5). Of those who were correct in their interpretation, the great majority achieved only partial recognition. The highest level of perception, including both structure and function, was reached by approximately one-fourth of this group. No one regarded structure independently and only a small percentage reacted solely to its functional aspects. In short, pupils were decidedly more inclined to seize upon parts of this life situation than to synthesize various clues and arrive at a meaning for the whole.

Eighteen per cent of the boys and girls recognized the Old Beach in terms of its *structural* appearance. As might be expected, children tended to think of this scene in terms of a "natural" environment rather than one which was institutional in character. References to the former were almost entirely focused on the concept of "beach," there being but a few children who mentioned "seashore" or "lakeshore." That this beach was not all that might be desired for recreational purposes was indicated by children in a variety of ways:

> There's a beach around there ... and there's a little shack for 'em to get in their bathing suits ... (6UG)
> They should watch out cause there could be glass in the water at shore ... (1UG)
> That beach looks sorta rackety-rickety ... (6RG)
> Sort of a beach ... looks like an old pier there ... old house of some kind or a house to change your clothes in ... (6UB)
> At a resort—an awful old resort, too ... (6UB)
> It looks like a summer camp or something but the house has got broken windows in it ... (6UG)
> It's sorta like in the slums, and it's sorta like the pier is all cracked up ... (6UG)

An interpretation of the Old Beach from the standpoint of its *functions* was made by 23 per cent of the pupils. This awareness was about equally centered upon various kinds of recreational activities in which children were engaged as well as on the unsatisfactory or hazardous aspects of such play.

Pupils who were conscious of the recreational activities taking place in such unsatisfactory surroundings were far more likely to refer to specific sports or games than to make broad generalizations about what was going on. Swimming was mentioned in the great majority of instances; playing baseball and roasting wieners headed a long list of miscellaneous activities. Those who referred to activities in general, made about equal use of the concepts, "playing," "having fun," and "having a good time."

Children who were sensitive to the undesirable forms of recreation pictured in this situation stressed the physical danger resulting from such play activities. Out of all the responses, there were only two which referred to the possibility of windows being broken or the house being set afire because of activities taking place near the building. Children's consciousness of the human aspects involved in this scene was equally centered on the relationships among the participants as well as general bodily harm which might result from such play. In the former instance, objection was expressed toward acts of aggression ("fighting," "picking on everybody") rather than being left out or ostracized. Physical hazards covered a gamut of possibilities ranging from such specifics as "drownding," "getting a nail in the foot," "falling off the boards," "getting hit in the eye," "being cut by glass," to simply "getting hurt." Illustrating a recognition of the functional elements in this situation is the "story" of an older city boy which reveals his awareness of certain recreational activities and unsatisfactory aspects portrayed in this scene.

> This shows a . . . some bathers swimming and running around on there, the boards. It looks like the boards aren't too sturdy or anything. And um . . . then there's some people a bo—fighting, and um . . . playing baseball or something, throwing balls . . .

A *synthesis* of both structure and function was achieved by 18 per cent of the children. For this life situation, the tendency for one kind of perception to be accompanied by the other was particularly noticeable. Once he put water, shoreline, and other physical features together to arrive at some notion of a dilapidated swimming place, the pupil inevitably went on to describe the activities. An example of this tendency is given by an older city girl who recognized certain inadequacies in the physical environment, identified a number of recreational activities, and was conscious of the accompanying hazards. Interestingly enough, this pupil was one of many who discounted certain shortcomings in the situation in favor of "having a lotta fun."

> (Part I—What story does this picture tell?)
> These are people going to the beach, and some of them are in the water, and there's two boys fighting, and there are pictures on the window, and the bridge isn't very good, and they might get hurt.
>
> (Part II—Which boy or girl belongs in this picture?)
> The happy boy.
> (Why?)
> This boy would prob—one of these boys would probably be angry but I think they're all happy. They look happy, because they're going swimming and they can have fun.
>
> (Part III—Which picture would you like to keep for your very own?)
> (Third choice)
> (Why?)
> Because they're having a lotta fun at the beach.

A *partial* recognition of this scene was evidenced by 52 per cent of the pupils. This is a comparatively large proportion of incomplete interpretations. Although all were descriptive in nature, none being a case of simple identification, the missing ingredient was a recognition of the inadequacies or hazards associated with this particular recreational scene. Apparently children "saw" what they enjoyed —play, and overlooked or ignored what they did not want to see— danger. Those who were only partially aware of the elements in this situation paid a great deal more attention to what people were doing than to objects and natural environment combined. How a child can select clues regarding people, things, and Nature without being conscious of any of the undesirable elements is illustrated in the remarks of a young rural boy.

> There's a lotta people and they're coming in on ... they're, they're walking on this shore. And some of them are swimming and then the cottage, there, where they can put their clothes on. And there's a lotta people and um ... there's a couple of things on the grass and the ... they got their bathing suits on, some of 'em, and some of 'em haven't, and some are little kids and some of 'em are big kids, and some of 'em are big girls. And the water, it's got waves.

And a . . . that's all, oh, there are some people that are gonna dive—in the water.

References to people dealt with specific types of activities much more frequently than to recreational activities in general. Of the former, swimming was mentioned by the majority of children, as would be expected, followed by a long list of activities in which playing with or building a raft, fishing, playing ball, and building a fire were mentioned most frequently. When speaking in general terms, pupils used such expressions as "having fun," "playing," and "having a good time."

References to things were about equally divided between that on which children were playing and the part of the building shown in the picture. The former was described in a number of ways: "a raft," "boards for diving," "pier at a river," and "broken bridge." For many children the building was simply "an old house," "a log house," or "a house with broken windows," but some recognized it as "a cottage for changing clothes."

Concepts dealing with the natural environment were about equally centered on the shore and the body of water. The former were used by children who recognized the "beach," but none of its undesirable features, as well as those who saw this as "a swimming place with sand," or simply that this was "by an ocean or lake." Children who were attracted by the water recognized that this was a lake, or a river, that "the water had run over," or that "the water, it's got waves."

Nonrecognition. Twenty-five per cent of the children failed to recognize the significant features in this scene of undesirable or unorganized recreation. Those who failed to achieve some measure of recognition did so for the most part because they arrived at an incorrect interpretation of the scene. There were some which represented a mixture of correct and incorrect perceptions. Only a few pupils responded in such general terms that their remarks could apply to almost any life situation.

Incorrect or *inappropriate* responses were produced by 16 per cent of the pupils. Half dealt with various forms of work: building a house or tearing down an old one, the work involved in piling wood, "getting ready for a storm." The remainder were divided about equally between those who identified this as a camping situation and certain miscellaneous interpretations. Failing to note signs indicating a lack of supervision, some children seized upon one or two prominent aspects of the scene and came to the conclusion that this was a scout camp, a summer camp, or a vacation center "like the Dells" (a tourist attraction in Wisconsin). A far greater error on the part of younger children is evident in such remarks as:

They're building over a deep hole.	(1UG)
That looks like a city and a store.	(1RG)
That looks like in the cowboy days . . . there's a cowboy house . . .	
	(1UB)

Seven per cent of the pupils *combined* a correct interpretation with one which was inappropriate. These responses represented a mixture of work-type activities on the part of adults and play on the part of children. The former usually involved men who were lumbering, "cutting timber" or building something. Children, on the other hand, were regarded as playing around and having fun in the same general vicinity or, more specifically, swimming near the working party.

Unlike the rest of the pictures in the series, only 2 per cent of the pupils reacted to this recreation scene in such *general* terms as to indicate a lack of awareness. Such responses included the miscellaneous listing of objects in the picture, and that of a young rural boy who noted that "She (sad girl) wants to go to bed."

For children, the Old Beach proved to be stimulating, but not too clear-cut. Half could only succeed in partially recognizing it, and quite a number failed outright in their interpretation. Those who did integrate various clues saw this as a beach in a state of disrepair rather than a dilapidated resort; they were equally conscious of the play activities going on and certain inadequacies with reference to bodily harm and fighting. There is no question but that this scene of lower-status recreation created certain perplexities in the mind of some children.

Children's Setting for the Old Beach

Children were better able to tell where this scene was located than when the activities were taking place. Of the four pictures in the Social Status Block, this life situation ranked highest in terms of space designation (5th) and was tied with the Poor House with respect to time orientation (8.5).

Spatial settings were mentioned by 73 per cent of the pupils, indicating a decided consciousness of background on their part. Responses were more likely to be expressed in associational terms than as geographical or political divisions, although in a little more than one-tenth of the cases a combination was used. As might be expected, Nature was the referent most frequently associated with this particular life situation although several pupils mentioned the home and certain other institutions. The great variety of associations brought to this scene may be gathered from the following:

> I think this is out in the country . .
> Children are going swimming in a big lake . . .
> These are people going to a beach . . .
> They're going out on the pier at the river . . .
> Some people are playing on the sand along the beach . . .
> It looks like it's at a seashore . . .
> This is down by a ocean or a lake . . .
> This is a picture up on the mountains . . .
>
> They live in that house . . .
>
> That'd be like a little camp . . .
> People are going swimming at a resort . . .
> That looks like they're at a beachhouse . . .

Only a few pupils made use of geopolitical terms in describing the locale for this situation, and in each case reference was made to a community setting ("it's sorta like in the slums," "that looks like a city").

The Old Beach was placed in a *temporal setting* by only 11 per cent of the boys and girls. When they did mention time, pupils were more likely to associate the scene with certain events than to use a chronological or historical basis for designating temporal orientation. A greater diversity of associational referents were used in responding to this picture than for any other in the Social Status Block. They touched upon daily and annual occurrences in Nature as well as human activities, personal and social.

> They woke up in the morning 'cause they saw lots and lots of water . . .

They wanted to go floating on that very afternoon . . .
It looks like it's on a Sunday morning . . .

They like to go swimming during the summer . . .
They stay for maybe two weeks in the summertime . . .
It looks like a summer camp . . .

They all go in and eat dinner and supper, and then they go back
out and start working . . .
A couple boys had come from school, the lower grades had come,
got out earlier . . .

That looks like in the cowboy days . . .

The infrequent use of mathematical measures by these children involved the calendar ("it looks like it's on a Sunday," "it's on a Saturday"). It is interesting to note that although the companion picture of lower-status living, the Poor House, was regarded as a thing of the past by a number of children, this was not the case for the Old Beach.

That boys and girls saw this scene in a natural setting is evidence of their familiarity with such forms of informal recreation. Yet, they attached relatively few specific place names to this situation. It may be that the automobile and camp sites have made this type of recreation so common that children fail to differentiate between unsupervised and "undeveloped" play areas, and lower-status or slum living. Once having made a general association with Nature, children felt no need to identify it with any particular place in Wisconsin, the nation, or the world. This might also explain why relatively few boys and girls attempted to place the Old Beach in a time perspective.

Children's Attitudes toward the Old Beach

Approximately half the children (53%) expressed favorable attitudes toward this scene (Rank = 6) as compared with 19 per cent who looked upon it with disapproval (Rank = 7.5). That many boys and girls were torn between conflicting values is evidenced by the fact that 24 per cent showed mixed reactions as they viewed this life situation, the highest for any picture in the series. In short, children were definitely not neutral in their responses. Only 3 per cent failed to show any strong emotion, this being the lowest for the picture series. Furthermore, in 38 per cent of the cases the attitude expressed by the child in his first encounter with the situation was maintained throughout the interview, representing a high degree of consistency.

The great value which children placed on "having fun" is brought out in the numerous *positive* attitudes expressed toward a variety of recreational pursuits or to play in general.

He's having a good time.	(6UB)
They're playing and having fun.	(6RB)
They're running around and so happy.	(1UB)
They're playing ball and they're just running around.	(6UG)
You'd have fun on a camping trip.	(6UB)
They're all enjoying theirselves, and it seems that all the work is done, and they don't have anything to worry about.	(6UG)

So strong was this feeling that not a single child flatly condemned the Old Beach because of the hazards presented by the physical environment. Those who were aware of its unsuitability in this respect, tempered their judgment by noting all its recreational possibilities. Some children merely recognized this feature in the situation, but apparently discounted its effects as far as having fun was concerned.

(Part I—What story does this picture tell?)
That looks like a fish seashore and there's a big wind blowing. And lots of them are swimming and that beach looks sorta rackety-rickety. And some boys playing in the sand, building sand castles, and some boys are just watching.

(Part II—Which boy or girl belongs in this picture?)
The happy boy.
(Why?)
He's happy at the seashore, 'cause he has fun in the water.
(6RG)

Attitudes toward swimming, health factors involved, and fighting were divided. Opportunities for swimming and the fun there was in water activities were highly regarded by some pupils. There were others, especially the younger children, who disliked or had a fear of swimming or recalled parental admonitions against "going in the water." By way of contrast to the extreme emphasis placed upon play, were the scattering of responses which revealed a sensitivity to health. Out of the total group of children, only one attempted to show any of the physical benefits to be derived from swimming. On the other hand, illness or physical debility were regarded more as a hindrance to recreational participation than a reason for engaging in such activities.

Positive	*Negative*

Swimming

Positive	*Negative*
He's down at the beach and he likes it there. (1UB)	She doesn't wanna go swimming. (1RG)
'Cause maybe she gets to live by the beach, and gets to go swimming, and a lot of kids don't. (1UG)	She's scairt, 'cause she doesn't wanna go swimming. (1RG)
I think they're having fun swimming. (1RB)	His mother and dad wouldn't let him swim in the water. (1RG)
Because everybody, of course, likes to go swimming. (1UB)	She can't go swimming with the others. (1UB)

Health

Positive	*Negative*
They can go swimming, and they're happy that they can get fresh stuff to put on their skins and go swimming, because that will help them. (1RG)	Some are sad because they're left out. They can't help (building a raft) because they're weak and they've been sick. (6RG)

The divided stand which children take on the matter of aggression is highlighted in their reactions to the Old Beach. Although some boys and girls overlooked environmental inadequacies in this play situation, not all of them accepted fighting or equated it with recreation. These pupils accounted for practically all the negative feelings expressed toward this scene. That some youngsters do not disapprove of fighting—like it, in fact—is also borne out by their comments:

Positive	*Negative*

Aggression

Positive	*Negative*
I can see somebody's fighting and a, well, it looks like they're having a good time. (6UB)	He's mad at somebody, and they don't let him do anything. (1RB)
Well, they're having a lotta fun there. Then they—swimming and	That boy's picking on everybody. (1RB)

Positive	*Negative*
	Aggression

they're fighting sometimes. (6RB)	They don't look happy—they're fighting and everything. (1RG) 'Cause he's mad and he's gonna get ready to fight. (1UB) He's kinda mad at somebody. He's chasing another boy that it looks like hit him. (6RG) It's in the slums and I don't think he'd be very happy here. And he'd be sort of . . . like a boy for fights and arguments. (6UG)

Mixed responses were usually the result of being able to see both sides in the situation. A sixth grade urban boy, for example, placed both a happy and a sad boy in this scene giving as his reason, "They might get a nail in their foot and that wouldn't be too happy. And you can have a lot of fun being happy in the water." In a number of instances, a change in attitude took place as pupils proceeded from one part of the interview to the next. The first time one of the older city boys looked at the scene, he was conscious of the undesirable character of this "awful old resort." On next meeting it, he tempered his judgment by adding the quality of friendship. When, at the end of the interview he was permitted to take the pictures he wanted, this was his first choice!

> (Part I—What story does this picture tell?)
> People going swimming at a resort, an awful old resort, too. It looks like a lotta people going swimming, a lotta kids by some place. It looks like it's pretty dangerous.
>
> (Part II—Which boy or girl belongs in this picture?)
> The in-between boy.
> (Why?)
> Well, a . . . maybe he's swimming with his friends.
>
> (Part III—Which picture would you like to keep for you very own?)
> (First choice)
> (Why?)
> Good picture.

The few neutral reactions to this life situation were primarily statements of fact (" 'cause there's a boy playing with a man," "they're building a raft"). To one of the older city boys, swimming had apparently lost its savor or was taken for granted, for he remarked, "She's probably been in the water, and she's not excited about going in the water."

"Playing safely" is not a controlling desire on the part of children. In spite of the care which adults give to the suitability of recreational activities, the majority of children seem to be more concerned about having fun. Neither is "playing nicely" something which is ingrained in the child's consciousness. Sometimes he relishes just the opposite. Both of these concepts are in process of development during the elementary school years as witness the pro-and-con attitudes expressed toward the Old Beach by a considerable number of pupils. Health and play are more remotely associated: if you have the first you may engage in the latter. There are few things about which children feel more strongly or about which attitudes may vary so much as play.

Children's Preferences for the Old Beach

This scene of unsupervised recreation under hazardous conditions was selected to about the same degree that it was rejected. Twenty-three per cent of the pupils included it among their first three choices. This represents 8 per cent of their selections in comparison with 7 per cent of the times that the picture was designated as the one which pupils "wouldn't want to keep." In contrast to its moderate degree of acceptability in the series (Rank = 8), is the fact that only three pictures met with as much rejection (Rank = 3.5).

Those who chose this picture placed great value on the general elements of fun, action, and interest as well as upon certain types of activities. Some children could see fun in this situation regardless of circumstances. Others placed a premium on the great amount of activity portrayed in the scene. The novelty of the experience was a source of interest to a young rural boy whereas an older rural pupil regarded the interest value of a beach more generally:

It looks like they're so happy.   (6UG)
They're having lotsa fun.   (6RB)

'Cause there's lotsa excitement.   (1RB)
It looks like there's a lot of action in it.   (6UG)

'Cause I never went to a beach before.   (1RB)
It's just interesting.   (6RB)

Among the many activities selected for specific valuing were
swimming and those involving a raft. The joy of "running around,"
however, was not overlooked by a young rural boy. Of such reasons
given for the selection of this picture are the following:

You can swim if you're close by.   (1UG)
I can swim real good and I like to swim.   (6RB)
'Cause I like that, 'cause they're building a raft.   (1UB)
Where the children have a raft, and are going on a picnic.   (6RG)
Because they're running and they look happy.   (1RB)

This life situation was *rejected* by pupils who could not accept
the conditions under which children were playing, and the fact that
fighting was going on. These two factors seemed to loom largest
in the thinking of young children and girls, but the numbers are too
small to warrant any definite conclusions. Their responses include:

The house is kinda wrecked.   (1RG)
Because it's all mixed up.   (6RG)

Because they're fighting down there.   (1UB)
It looks ... some of the kids are kinda mad there.   (6RG)
These children are fighting, and I don't think they have very much
fun.   (6RG)

The Old Beach presents boys and girls with a dilemma. It com-
bines fun and action with fighting and danger. On this issue children
are quite evenly divided. For some, play is the thing, and they are
unmindful of hazards or willing to take their chances. Others are
more demanding of recreational experiences. This division poses
two complex problems in the rearing of children. One has to do with
the concept of normal prudence as distinguished from overcaution
and foolhardy behavior. Children must learn that play like everything else, cannot be guaranteed safe, and must develop a healthy
respect for its hazards—but not a blind unreasoning fear of "getting
hurt." Related to this is the question of supervision. Since children
need to *learn* how to play properly, adult guidance is important.

Part of their learning, however, is knowing how to play by themselves; the implications for adult supervision are obvious.

Group Comparisons

All differences in the way various groups of children perceived the Old Beach were concerned with ideas rather than emotions. The sharpest distinctions were related to age, and only minor variations were revealed between community and intelligence groups. Although this situation is one which boys might be expected to enjoy more than girls, the responses of sex groups did not vary significantly in any of the cognitive or attitudinal aspects of perception.

Age Differences. The growth in recognition which accompanies age was manifested in a number of ways. More sixth grade children achieved the highest level of recognition. In fact, only 7 per cent of the first graders were aware of both structure and function as compared with 30 per cent of the older pupils. This superiority in integrating various clues was also evident when structure and function were analyzed separately. Not only did more sixth graders recognize the scene structurally, they also excelled in the number of types of recognition made; as an unorganized swimming place and a run-down vacation center. With reference to the former, older pupils used a greater number of concepts. As for the latter, it was only the sixth graders who made reference to dilapidated or deteriorating recreational institutions. These two grade groups differed even more markedly regarding the functional aspects of this scene. More sixth grade pupils succeeded in recognizing each of the categories involved: recreational activities as well as undesirable play. They were also far more prolific in the number of different sports and games which they saw depicted in the life situation. Sixth graders who were only partially successful in interpreting this scene did not differ significantly in number from lower grade children. They did reveal, however, a greater tendency to use such general terms as "having fun," "playing," and "having a good time." Surprisingly enough, these groups were quite alike in the number of inappropriate, mixed or other types of nonrecognition responses.

Sixth graders were less advanced in their awareness of the context or field for the Old Beach. More of them specified a spatial setting, particularly through associations with familiar places. A similar development did not take place, however, in the ability to visualize this life situation in time. That no differences in attitudes or preferences were brought to light may arise from the dualism represented in this scene, and because conflicting forces of pleasure and pain were not resolved in terms of group characteristics. Neither young nor older pupils decided in favor of pleasure to the utter disregard of the possibilities for pain or vice versa. The fact that neither group showed a decided preference for the Old Beach is evidence of the highly personal nature of the values perceived in this situation and the priorities given to conflicting values. Apparently, this is something which is not changed during the elementary school period—if ever.

Rural-Urban Differences. Farm and city children differed but slightly in their perception of the Old Beach despite its association with the natural world. The number of pupils showing a functional awareness of this situation was about the same in each group, but urban children were more aware of the different types of functions being depicted. This superiority was especially marked in their recognition of the hazardous, unorganized, and unsupervised nature of recreational activities both in terms of number of pupils and illustrations of such activities. In short, urban children were far more impressed by unsatisfactory play conditions. It may be that city children were more fearful, because they have less acquaintance with such informal recreational activities. In contrast, rural children have greater access to a "swimming hole" nearby. On the other hand, this awareness of danger may simply be part of the city child's greater consciousness of hazards in play and life in general as it is lived in a highly complex urban community.

Intelligence Differences. Being bright or below average in intelligence does not make a great deal of difference in reacting to this scene of lower-status recreation. In their partial recognitions, however, the less capable group used more general concepts to describe what was going on than did high-ability pupils. "Having fun," or "playing" as opposed to such specific activities such as "swimming" or "playing on a raft" might represent the difference between a general response to a situation and one which is more highly differentiated. This explanation is given some support in the fact that sixth grade pupils who merely achieved partial recognition (and, hence, were *low* achievers in dealing with this scene) used more general terms than first graders who partially recognized this situation (thus being relatively *high* achievers in their group). In any event, a child does not have a different outlook on lower-status or unsupervised, hazardous recreation merely because he has a high I.Q.

| Chapter | SUMMARY |

XIV.

THE foregoing chapters have clearly indicated that responses to the various levels of social status depicted in this block of pictures have differed. Some of these are characteristic of all the children interviewed whereas others are typical of various groups of pupils. From the standpoint of elementary school children, in general, the following statements describe their perception of social status.

Children are not more perceptive, generally speaking, of one level of social status than they are of another. Rankings of the pictures in the Social Status Block (Table 2, Appendix) reveal that neither set of status situations was consistently higher than the other. For example, children had more to say about the Mansion than any other picture in the series. Yet, the Resort ranked below the Poor House in this respect. Similar inconsistencies among the status scenes appeared in the majority of aspects of perception being analyzed. Generally speaking, therefore, no single statement can describe how children perceive different levels of socioeconomic status.

Children are more likely to recognize deviations from an "average" standard of living which are qualitatively inferior than those which are superior. A more specific analysis based on number of children rather than rank of picture discloses that children differed significantly in only one respect as far as the ideational aspect of perception was concerned. They were less aware of the qualitative nature of upper-status living than of lower-status life. For every child who was conscious of rich people and their "pleasures" depicted in the Mansion scene, there were almost four who recognized poor people and their financial needs in the Poor House. The same proportion held true for the number who were aware of the exceptional forms of recreation portrayed in the Resort as compared to those showing sensitivity to the inadequacies of play pictured in the Old Beach. In the latter picture, however, there was no real difference in the number of pupils who recognized recreational activities as such. Children were equally adept at recognizing swimming in a modern pool or swimming at a "wrecky" beach, but were less inclined to associate the former with a relatively good station in life than to identify the latter with poor living circumstances. The difference, therefore, does not apply to the broad area of functional recognition, but to that part dealing with awareness of kind or quality.

Children are attracted to upper-status living and have an aversion for lower-status conditions. Children's feelings about social status presented certain sharp contrasts as evidenced in their attitudes and picture preferences. Attitudes were remarkably consistent; both pictures in each status group varied in the same direction from both pictures of the contrasting group. Children responded more favorably to high-status pictures than to low-status scenes, and this was particularly evident of the Mansion as compared with the Poor House. The same thing was true of the relatively few neutral responses. On the other hand, children responded more negatively to lower-status situations, especially the Poor House, and displayed more mixed emotions toward such situations, the Old Beach scoring highest in the picture series.

Confirming this strong opposition to low-status circumstances were children's picture preferences. Their rejection of the Poor House was so emphatic that this scene headed the list of unwanted pictures, far above the Mansion. The Old Beach was high on this same list whereas not a single child rejected the Resort. No corresponding pattern occurred in the children's selection of pictures, for the Old Beach had certain play attractions for children, and the Poor House was chosen for a number of reasons based on some thing other than an affinity for poverty.

Children's regard for status differentials is influenced by the type of life situation being considered. The ways in which children differed in their reactions to the status situation makes quite clear that the perception of social status is not a constant. The Poor House-Mansion contrast was more critical than the Old Beach-Resort accounting for six of the seven significant differences in children's reactions. It is conceivable that the social status contrast in the latter pair of life situations is of a lesser degree than in the two contrasting home situations. Furthermore, informal types of recreation are more widely experienced, and are regarded as acceptable under certain circumstances. Nevertheless, children's responses to the Old Beach indicate that in many cases they were willing to put up with inadequate conditions for the sake of "having fun." They placed considerations of play above those of social status. That this was not always an easy decision is indicated by the great number of mixed attitudes expressed toward the Old Beach.

Differences Associated with Age

Developmental differences in the perception of social status were far greater than differences in sex, community background, and intelligence combined. They accounted for 19 of 29 such differences found in making these four types of group comparisons. The advantage was always on the side of the older pupils as far as the cognitive aspect of perception was concerned, and what might be considered the prevailing attitudes toward social status.

With age there comes an increasing awareness of both upper- and lower-status symbols and their implications for ways of living. More younger children than sixth graders merely reached the level of general description (nonrecognition) in reacting to Poor House and Mansion and that of partial recognition of the Resort. In each case, their focus was on people rather than on natural or man-made environment. On the other hand, sixth grade pupils were consistently superior in recognizing these life situations in terms of structure, function, or both with the possible exception of the Mansion scene where the numbers were small. Regarding the functional-type of recognition, older children were far more sensitive to the quality of living represented in various status scenes. In fact, no first grade pupil showed such an awareness in three of the four situations; it was only in the Old Beach that they identified certain recreational activities of dubious nature.

Errors in the recognition of high- and low-status are not fewer in number, but differ in kind by the time pupils reach sixth grade. It is important to note that for none of the social status pictures was there any appreciable difference in the number of incorrect interpretations made by first or sixth grade pupils. Errors committed by young children were due to fixation on a portion of the situation which then stood for the entire scene or were so erratic that they could not be accounted for. Older pupils usually erred in the associations they made of the scene with a variety of situations spread out in distance and time. Such was the case of the pupil who, failing to note the TV set and parked automobile, stated that the Mansion scene looked like Abraham Lincoln's home.

Negative attitudes toward lower-status living develop before children reach first grade, and remain relatively unchanged by the end of the sixth. Whereas sixth graders consistently outstripped younger pupils in their ideas about various types of social status situations, differences in attitude were related to the level of socioeconomic status being considered. Lower-class scenes evoked practically the same emotional response from young and older pupils. There was little variation between these two groups in the number who showed positive, neutral, negative, or mixed attitudes, and the number of times that the Poor House and Old Beach were selected or rejected.

Children acquire a high degree of appreciation for upper-status living during the first six years of schooling. In contrast to the uniformity of feelings about the low socioeconomic scenes was the marked difference in attitudes expressed toward upper-status pictures. Young children were more negatively disposed toward the Mansion and Resort whereas sixth grade pupils showed far more approval of both upper-status situations. In connection with both lower- and upper-status situations, it must be kept in mind that older pupils were responding more directly to the status significance of these situations whereas first grade children were reacting to those parts which were related to certain of their ego needs.

Differences between Boys and Girls

Boys and girls viewed the pictures in the Social Status Block in a similar fashion. Except for a minor difference in the Resort scene all others were confined to feelings about the Mansion situation. It is clear that *boys and girls are equally competent in recognizing both upper-status and lower-status life situations.* For each of the pictures in this block, the number of boys was not materially different from that of girls whose interpretation was classified as:

Synthesis (structure and function)
Structure only
Function only
Partial recognition
General description
Inappropriate
Indefinite

Neither was there any difference in the number of boys and girls specifying any one of approximately twelve categories of spatial setting and an equal number of temporal settings for the four status situations. This across-the-board agreement in cognition had only one small exception. Although there was no difference in the number who achieved partial recognition of the Resort scene, girls were more conscious of what people were doing than were the boys, there being little difference in attention given to things, and the world of Nature.

Boys and girls have similar attitudes and feelings about lower-status situations. The number of boys and girls exhibiting positive, neutral, negative, and mixed feelings toward both lower-status situations was about the same. This was also true of their selection and rejection of the Poor House and Old Beach pictures. These facts, combined with the findings regarding the cognitive aspect of perception, indicate that boys and girls have been equally sensitized in thought and feeling to the undesirability of lower-class living in our society.

Girls are more attracted to upper-status life situations than are boys. Whereas girls tended to display favorable attitudes toward the Mansion, more boys were negatively disposed. Furthermore, more girls than boys decided to keep it as one of their favorite pictures. Attitudes of boys and girls to the Resort scene, however, were much the same, and the number of girls who selected it was not significantly greater than for boys. Both status pictures were given a high preference rating by the girls (third and fourth), whereas they were in the middle (Resort) and below-average (Mansion) preference ranking of the boys. It would appear, therefore, that the greater premium which girls placed on upper-status living, was almost concealed in the Resort scene by the attraction which recreation held for boys. In other words, girls were favorably inclined toward both high-status situations; many boys were also attracted by high-status when it was combined with recreation, but a considerable number were less than enthusiastic about an upper-class *home* situation. This interpretation is in keeping with the notion that girls are more socially responsive; that acculturation, as far as values are concerned, takes place more rapidly in the case of girls than boys.

Differences Associated with Intelligence

There were two instances where children of high and below average ability differed in their reactions to the social status situations. About the same number of pupils in each group managed to partially recognize the Old Beach situation, but low I.Q. children made greater use of such general concepts as "playing," "having fun," and "having a good time." Similarly, the functional aspect of the Resort scene was recognized to about the same extent by the two groups, but high I.Q. children identified a greater number of recreational activities. These differences do not appear to have a bearing on social status awareness as such, and lead to the generalization that *children who are above average in intelligence do not differ from those below-average in ability in the perception of social status.*

What seems to be involved here are certain mental characteristics associated with intelligence. The generality of the lower-ability group's concepts would seem to indicate less preciseness in thinking and in the analysis of the situation. On the other hand, the ability to make finer discriminations and to be prolific in ideas are the marks of superior intelligence. That these mental processes were not observed systematically in either the upper-status or lower-status situations would seem to rule out the possibility that these levels of intelligence are related to the perception of social status.

Differences between Rural and Urban Children

Of the possible 45 categories and certain of their combinations in terms of which rural and urban children's responses were compared to each of the social status pictures, a significant difference was found in only one. More urban children than rural were conscious of the hazardous disorganization and unsupervised nature of the recreational activities portrayed in the Old Beach scene.

One interpretation of this difference could be that urban children are more concerned about "standards" or social status, because life in a city is more competitive, and that could include considerations of social position. If this were the case, the expectation would be that this greater perception would manifest itself in more than one instance. Pooling the replies of the two status scenes, and even for the total group of pictures in this block failed to reveal any other deviations in ideas or feelings between rural and urban children. The more tenable conclusion, therefore, is that *there is no difference in the perception of social status by rural and urban children.*

The exception to this generalization can be accounted for in two ways. One is that children reared in a crowded complex urban community have impressed upon them from an early age the cruciality of avoiding danger and "playing safe." Their reactions to the Old Beach, therefore, were a reflection of this general alertness to hazards in their environment. Added to this is the fact that urban children are likely to experience more organized forms of recreation. Informal, "swimming hole" types of situations are not as available to them as to rural children. This unfamiliarity resulted in a greater concern about the unsatisfactory conditions pictured in the Old Beach scene. In light of the above interpretation, the difference in sensitivity to inadequate recreational functions depicted in the Old Beach is more likely to be related to differences in community background than to differences in awareness of socioeconomic status.

Part IV

HOW DO CHILDREN PERCEIVE CHILD AND ADULT LIFE SITUATIONS?

Bedroom

Dam

Church

Capitol

Schoolroom

Dock

INTRODUCTION

For a child there are two worlds. One is close and personal. Surrounding this on all sides and extending as far as he can see is the world for adults. The former is largely centered on his "growing up"; the latter is geared to the business of running the world. These are not mutually exclusive spheres of influence or fields of activity. Adults still play the dominant role in the child's world, but whenever the child steps into the grown-up world, his role is not clearly defined or is extremely limited.

Somehow the child must learn to live in both of these worlds. Those in charge of his development, while cognizant of the importance of the child's here-and-now living, are also mindful of the many demands which will be made of him as an adult. How much advance preparation can there be?

Part of the answer lies in the meaning (as perceived) which adult activities have for children. We would expect that sixth grade pupils would have a better grasp of such things than first, and that children of higher intelligence would excel as compared with those below-average I.Q. Would girls be better acquainted with grown-up concerns than boys, and would there be any difference between children living in the city and on a farm?

The Child-Adult Block was designed to provide data bearing on these questions. It consists of three paired comparisons of child and adult experiences in the areas of conservation (Bedroom, Dam), personal-social values (Church, Capitol), and human relationships (Schoolroom, Dock). That these do not connote mutually exclusive activities on the part of children and adults is readily apparent. Yet, it can be argued that children deal with home, school, and church to a far greater degree than with the conservation of natural resources, government, and world relationships. Hence, the three areas in which contrasts are being presented, while common to children and adults, do serve to bring out some very important distinctions. This block consists of six life situations instead of four in order to increase the number of stimuli related to age differentials there being no possibility of presenting a "general" child or adult picture containing a variety of clues as in the Community and Social Status blocks.

THE BEDROOM

It's Time for Bed

In a nice home, a little girl is sleeping in her bedroom. Her mother has tucked her in her nice warm bed so that she won't get cold. The shade is pulled down, the door is open, and someone is looking through. Perhaps this little "sleeping beauty" is dreaming about candy and dolls. Or she might have a stomach ache, and they are waiting for the doctor. Sleeping is good health, and children should get plenty of rest for the next day.

THE Bedroom was one of the easiest scenes to interpret. Children required relatively little time and few words to express the meaning that this situation held for them. Representing moderate productivity as far as quantity was concerned, their ideas all gave evidence of some degree of recognition. This distinction was shared with only one other picture in the series—the Farm. Children also exhibited a very real awareness of bed time, but gave less thought as to where this scene might be located than for other pictures in the series. In spite of the ease with which it was recognized, the Bedroom was not a stimulating situation. It drew the greatest number of neutral reactions and, consequently, ranked low in the expression of both favorable and negative attitudes. Yet, there were many who valued the Bedroom situation, and only an occasional pupil was so violently opposed to what he saw as to reject it outright. Interestingly enough, the Bedroom was linked with girls much more often than with boys.

Children's Recognition of the Bedroom

The fact that everyone achieved some measure of recognition of the Bedroom does not necessarily imply superior perceptiveness on the part of children to this situation involving human conservation. A greater number of children only succeeded in partially interpreting this situation as compared with those who integrated the various elements and arrived at a structural or functional recognition, or a synthesis of both. The latter was primarily due to the fact that children did not identify this as a Bedroom scene. They were much more aware of the human conservation activities being portrayed, but for every such pupil there were two who gave only a partial interpretation of the life situation.

In only 7 per cent of the cases did children express a *structural* recognition of this life situation. It may be that pupils were so engrossed by the prominence given to the figure in the bed that they went no further to identify the room in which events were taking place. Then, again, it might be that this scene was so obviously a bedroom that children did not bother to mention it. Also, it appears that children were more inclined to react to the immediate scene that to a larger classification for practically all of the identifications were in terms of "bedroom," the extension of this scene to include type of dwelling or hospital being an exceptional response.

An illustration of the recognition of this scene in structural terms without any implication of sleep as a conservation function may be found in the remarks of a first grade city girl:

(Part I—What story does this picture tell?)
A boy's going to bed in his bedroom.

(Part II—Which boy or girl belongs in this picture?)
The in-between boy.
(Why?
'Cause he isn't sad and he's not happy. 'Cause he's in bed—he's sleeping.

(Part III—Which picture would you like to keep for your very own?)
(First choice) The boy that's in bed.
(Why?)
I like the way he sleeps.

More children were conscious of the Bedroom in terms of *functions* (38%) than of structure. These responses were about equally centered on various forms of human conservation, and the factor of supervision or the agent involved in the process. Boys and girls

were far more inclined to mention specific kinds of human maintenance or well-being than to refer generally to "good health."
They were much more alert to the physical needs being met in this
situation than to the mental or emotional. As for the former, children were equally sensitive to illness and conditions of general
fatigue ("he's tired," "he needs to rest," "maybe he's sick").
"Mother" was mentioned more than any other person as the one
who was ministering to the needs of the child or supervising this
instance of human conservation. The "doctor" came in as a poor
second, and "father" was seldom mentioned. There was an overwhelming tendency to regard mother in a helpful light rather than
disciplining or punishing the child by making him go to bed.

A recognition of the functional aspects of this situation without
involving structure is illustrated in the reactions of a young rural
girl who showed sensitivity to physical needs, and the part that
mother played in satisfying the child's needs in this respect.

> (Part I—What story does this picture tell?)
> She's now going to sleep, and the mother just went out of the
> door and shut the door, and she was going to sleep. They cov-
> ered her up, and then they went out.
>
> (Part II—Which boy or girl belongs in this picture?)
> The in-between girl.
> (Why?)
> 'Cause she's um . . . it looks like she's kinda tired.

The number of children who recognized the Bedroom as a *synthesis* of structure and function was very small (6%) due to the
fact that so few pupils specified its structure. No definite conclusions
can be drawn from such small numbers, but it is interesting to note
that more first graders than sixth reached this highest level of
recognition, a tendency which was not duplicated in any other
picture in the series.

The contrast between these two age groups in the interpretive
processes is well illustrated in the remarks of a young rural girl who
recognized the scene as taking place in a bedroom and saw the
connection between sleep and health, and a rather unusual interpretation on the part of an older rural boy who was reacting to a
hospital scene where a doctor was caring for someone who was ill.

(Part I—What story does this picture tell?)

That's a little girl. Someone is standing in the kitchen, and a tel . . . telephone there, and they got kind of a little drawer there on the cupboard, and a door, and a radio, and a television's in the bedroom where the little girl's sleeping. Well, then, it's got a big bed, and a big room, and a big door where you can . . . where you can walk in. And then they got a little drawer where they keep their stuff in, and then they got a light in the room, to put the lights on so they can see, and she is sleeping and dreaming.

(Part II—Which boy or girl belongs in this picture?)

The in-between girl.

(Why?)

Because she's got her mouth that way, too, and she's got her hair the same way, and she ain't angry or sad or happy, she's just in-between.

(Part III—Which picture would you like to keep for your very own?)

(Second choice)

(Why?)

Because you can sleep and that's good for you, too.　　(1RG)

(Part I—What story does this picture tell?)

A, ah . . . a good night's sleep. Looks like a . . . well, it could be somebody that's sick, too. Looks like there's a doctor or something outside the door; could be in a hospital.　　(6RB)

A *partial* recognition of the Bedroom scene was achieved by 61 per cent of the children. All of these were in the form of descriptive statements, none being on the lowest level of mere identification of relevant objects in the life situation. Children's concern for people was evident by the fact that their responses about the human elements in the situation greatly outnumbered their reactions to both the natural environment and man-made things depicted in the scene.

As might be expected, many more comments were directed at the figure in the bed than to the suggestion of a person outside the doorway. For these children, who were only partially sensitive to the meaning of this life situation, there was little doubt that the person in bed was sleeping although a few merely indicated that a child was "in bed" or "going to bed." In way of contrast, only one pupil saw the child as "getting up." The figure seen through the doorway was noted in a stationary sense as being "outside," "at," or "in" the door as often as it was seen in movement—either coming into or leaving the room. It was identified as father or mother to about the same degree that it was regarded vaguely as "someone."

Concepts centered on the world of Nature were almost always involved in designating the time for events taking place in the life situation. Just as children had a preference for sleeping or going to bed as opposed to getting up, the majority of children referred to "night" rather than to "morning." An exception to this referral to Nature in a time sense were those who noted the weather ("it seems like a awful day to get outta bed").

Only a few of the pupils exhibiting partial recognition gave attention to the things in the scene, and when they did it was accompanied by an awareness of people as well. The majority of references were to the bed and its equipment ("covers" or "blanket," "pillow"), certain parts of the room ("open window," "shade pulled down"), and certain furnishings ("dresser," "radio to help her sleep").

Illustrating how many clues regarding people and things may be identified without coming to an awareness of human conservation are the following remarks of a young city girl:

> (Part I—What story does this picture tell?)
> I think she's going to sleep . . . I think she's asleep already . . . and I think Father and Mother's coming in or something . . . and I think the radio's making her go to sleep . . . a . . . let's see . . . I think the lights are out . . . a . . . I think the father's going to look . . . he's coming in . . . a . . . I think the telephone's ringing . . . I think that's why he's looking . . . a . . . let's see . . . I think the covers are on so she's just sleeping . . . I think she's just falled asleep anyway . . . let's see . . . a . . . I think the cover's on close and she's getting warm.

Boys and girls were undoubtedly on familiar terms with this Bedroom scene. Familiarity should not be confused with insight, however, for many children could not "see" beyond the fact of somebody being in bed or sleeping. That this had anything to do with human conservation was not widely realized. Such awareness was largely limited to physical aspects including rest and illness, and in this connection "Mother" played the dominant role. For the majority of children, sleeping is sleeping, and they do not understand its importance to their well-being. That this can create problems many parents can testify.

Children's Setting for the Bedroom

The number of children who were conscious of bed *time* was somewhat greater than the number placing it in some spatial background. Since, for the series, children exhibited far less sensitivity to time than to space, this placed the Bedroom next to the top in temporal ranking, but at the very bottom in spatial orientation.

Only 20 per cent of the pupils identified a *spatial* background for this life situation, making this the only picture in the series where the number of children who did not place this scene in a spatial context outnumbered those who did. Responses indicating a spatial field for the Bedroom were definitely associational in character. There was nothing in this scene to prompt boys and girls to specify geopolitical placement such as the state or nation. As would be expected, children related this scene to a home situation much more frequently than to an institution, and in no case was it thought of in terms of the natural world. Characteristic of these associations with home and institution are the following:

> There's a girl sleeping in her bedroom . . .
> Her father or mother's coming into the room . . .
> It's a little girl, she came in the room and she's tired . . .
> She has a nice home . .
>
> It tells a story about a farm and a little girl . . .
> Could be in a hospital . . .

Temporal settings for the Bedroom scene were designated by 33 per cent of the pupils. Thus, in spite of the high rank in the series which this represents, it cannot be said that there was a great consciousness of time for this life situation. As was true for space, there was a decided leaning toward the use of associational referents for indicating time although in this case systematic measures were also used.

Children who designated a temporal orientation for this scene drew upon events in Nature much more often than upon human activities. The former were entirely linked with the day-and-night cycle rather than with annual or seasonal changes. The latter were just as exclusively matters of personal rather than social activities. The various ways in which these were expressed are indicated by the following:

> One morning the lady was sleeping . . .
> This is Bobby's bed where he goes to sleep at night.
> It's night time . . .
> The little girl is just going to sleep for the night . . .
> It's early in the morning . . .
> It might be night yet . . .
>
> He played with his blocks a long time until it was time to bed.
> This is a picture of a bed story.
> It's about time, her bedtime . . .
> It's the first day of school . . .

Some children referred to the clock or calendar in their attempts to be more precise in specifying time. There was nothing in the scene to suggest historical time, and no such designations were made by boys and girls. Their use of chronometric measures included the following:

> A boy sleeping in the morning—let's see, about 7:30.
> A little girl is laying down at night about 9:00 o'clock.
> The children go to bed about 8:00 o'clock.
>
> That could be a Saturday morning . . .
> It's probably on a Saturday morning . . .
> It looks like it's Christmas and a little girl is sleeping, and she's dreaming.

Sleeping seems to be a matter of time rather than place in children's responses to the Bedroom. This may actually represent their greater concern for the former. Perhaps the place for sleeping is simply assumed by children: home is where one sleeps. "Bedtime," "time to go to bed," or "time to get up" are so universally understood in our culture that they are used as reference points for ordering activities within the family and in informal social relationships. Boys and girls soon learn their significance.

Children's Attitudes toward the Bedroom

This Bedroom scene was not looked upon with particular enthusiasm by children. Only 48 per cent expressed favorable attitudes toward it, this degree of positivism ranking tenth in the series. Neither did children regard this life situation with disfavor, for only 12.5 per cent were negatively disposed toward it. No other picture in the series drew less negative feeling than this. Although positive attitudes definitely outnumbered the negative, it is equally important to note that this picture was less stimulating than any other in the series. Thirty per cent of the pupils were quite indifferent to the Bedroom. A number of pupils (10%) were able to view this scene in more than one way, and expressed mixed feelings. Attitudes were expressed consistently, however, by 37.5 per cent of the children. Greater consistency than this was shown to only one other picture (Poor House).

Without exception, the pleasant emotional state associated with the act of sleeping was highly regarded by children. No one, for example, complained of "bad dreams" or connected sleep with disturbed mental or emotional states.

Positive

She looks so peaceful and happy while she's sleeping.   (6RG)
She looks content sleeping in that bed.   (6UG)
She looks like she has a good dream.   (6UB)
He's dreaming a nice dream, and he likes the girl he's dreaming about.   (1RG)

Differences in attitudes were revealed toward such things as going to bed or getting out of bed, the health aspect of sleeping, and human relationships entering into this type of situation. Going to bed seemed to be a far greater issue than getting up. In fact, few children seriously objected to getting up in the morning or greeting the events of a new day. The reverse process, however, was regarded in a number of instances as a matter of morality. A child in bed might be "good" because he had gone to bed as he had been told or he might be in bed as a consequence of having been "bad." The beneficial effects of sleep, which so often are extoled by adults, were not lost sight of entirely, but neither could this be said to have been of great importance to children.

Positive	*Negative*

Going to bed

She's (happy girl) in bed. (1RB) 'Cause he's got to go to bed. (1UB)	(Angry boy) 'Cause he's sleep-ing. (1UB)

Human relationships

'Cause her mommy doesn't shame her. (1RB) He's a good little boy. (1RB) 'Cause that little girl went to bed like her mother told her to. (1UG)	His mother's punishing him. (1UB) Her mother put her (sad girl) to bed. (1RB)

Health

She seems to be having a nice rest, and she must be dreaming of good things. (6UG) When you take a rest, and when you get up you're feeling good. (1UG)	She might have a stomach ache, and she doesn't like to be in bed. (1RB) One of her nephews might have died or something. (6UB)

Getting up

It must be a nice morning. (6UG) It's the first day of school. (6UG)	You're so sleepy now; everyone calling to ya to get up. (6UB)

Many children were not strongly impressed by the factors men-tioned above, and were quite *neutral* in their reactions. Some re-garded sleeping as a state of unconsciousness to which they at-tributed little or no significance. Others, apparently, regarded sleeping merely as one of the routines of living—something which everyone did—and this often held true even when there was a consciousness of the element of rest.

> Because she isn't a . . . happy, she isn't mad, or she isn't crying. She's just laying down peacefully-like.   (6RG)
> She's sleepin' and can't do nuthin'.   (1UB)
> 'Cause she doesn't have any cares or anything.   (6UB)

'Cause he's going to bed.	(6UB)
She's sleeping.	(1RB)

She's kinda tired.	(1RG)
Just laying there resting and trying to go to sleep.	(6UB)

Many of the children who had *mixed* feelings about the Bedroom scene were torn between their attraction for sleep and its association with illness. An older rural girl, for example, reacted first in terms of illness. Her next exposure to the picture resulted in a rather confused explanation of why she identified a neutral figure in this scene. In the final phase of the interview, this was one of the pictures she selected to "keep for her very own."

> (Part I—What story does this picture tell?)
> Well, let's see, a little girl laying in bed and she's sick, and it looks like a man going up . . . coming in that door, which means it could be a doctor.
>
> (Part II—Which boy or girl belongs in this picture?)
> The in-between girl and boy.
> (Why?)
> Because they aren't sad and they aren't happy. Well, I don't know for sure—well, because that girl, a boy is laying in bed, and it looks like he's sick, and he can't go to school.
>
> (Part III—Which picture would you like to keep for your very own?)
> (Third choice)
> (Why?)
> Well, well, I don't know—I just like it.

Children certainly regard "sleeping" in a variety of ways—and for different reasons. One which is least directly related to the conservation of human resources involves the question of "good" or "bad" behavior. It may be that sleeping has become a matter of right-or-wrong because children cannot understand or accept hygienic explanations of its importance. Perhaps, parents are so conscious of the need for sufficient rest that they use morality as additional support or authority. This is why one goes to bed! What happens to the child's sense of "rightness" may be surmised from the fact that a number of boys and girls recognized that being sent to bed was also a form of punishment for naughtiness. Under these conditions, children might come to regard going to bed as a highly arbitrary matter, to be engaged in as a matter of course rather than one of conviction.

Children's Preferences for the Bedroom

This life situation attracted a far greater number of children than it repelled. Thirty-five per cent of the boys and girls selected it as one of their three favorite pictures thus accounting for 12 per cent of their choices. Only the Farm exceeded this degree of acceptability, but the margin was inconsequential. The degree of acceptability of the Bedroom is further indicated by the fact that only 2 per cent of the pupils definitely rejected it. Only the Resort and Village met with less disfavor.

The reasons which children gave to support their selections indicated quite clearly the premium they placed upon the pleasant state associated with sleeping, health, and the human relations aspects of going to bed and sleeping. Except for an older girl who viewed this scene as "a mystery story," pupils expressed a value for sleep because it was comfortable and peaceful—there were no worries attached to sleeping—because they enjoyed good dreams, and because it was a relatively simple and uncomplicated act. The latter, however, was objected to by an older urban boy who seemingly was far more interested in activity ("because it doesn't show much activity"). The healthfulness of sleep had evidently been firmly impressed upon the minds of a few children. They seemed to accept this on faith or, at least, felt no further explanation was necessary. Positive values toward sleeping and health were expressed as follows:

Sleeping

I like to sleep. (1RG)
Because she just looks comfortable. (6RG)
Well, she just looks peaceful and happy, and she doesn't have to worry about anything. (6RG)
When I sleep, and then I dream about something good. (6UG)
Well, mostly because it's simple and, well, it looks like . . . um, most of all I think it's simple. (6UB)

Health

'Cause it's good health. (1UG)
Because you can sleep, and that's good for you, too. (1RG)

The importance which parents attach to "good" sleeping behavior was again voiced by a number of the younger children. They reflected the value judgments made of boys and girls on the basis of their sleeping habits. Some of the problems which children have among themselves in connection with sleeping "standards" were also brought out.

Acceptance	*Rejection*
	Human relationships
I alway go to bed when my mother tells me to. (1UG) Because the girl is sleeping, and my dad likes boys and girls when they sleep. (1RB)	She's sleeping, and my sister wakes me up in the night so I'm gonna sock her one. (1UG)

The majority of boys and girls like to sleep because it "feels nice." Theirs is a somatic response seemingly devoid of considerations bearing on the conservation of human resources. Occasionally a child gives tacit recognition to its health implications, but just as often he will be "a good rester" to please his parents. In short, children do not generally value sleep as meeting a basic need. It is nice to do if it doesn't interfere with more exciting things—things which have more action.

Group Comparisons

The Bedroom is the one life situation for which differences in feeling were greater than in thinking. It is the only one, moreover, for which grade differences did not loom largest. Children interpreted this scene in very much the same way. It seemed to make little difference whether they lived in a rural area or in the city, whether they were boys or girls, first grade or sixth grade pupils, or whether they were above or below average in intelligence— there were no marked variations in their recognition of this Bedroom scene. The one ideational difference dealt with its setting, on the part of grade groups. The differences in feelings were greatest between boys and girls.

Sex Differences. Boys and girls differed in their attitudes and preferences. Many more girls expressed positive feelings whereas boys were more neutrally disposed toward the Bedroom. Accordingly, more girls than boys selected it as being one of their favorites.

Why girls should regard a sleeping scene more positively can be explained in a number of ways. They might require more rest than boys although this has not been established for the elementary school period. It might be that girls are more anxious to do the "right" thing and to please their parents. Perhaps, they are more adaptable and adjust to routine more readily than boys. The scene may suggest a needed security. The fact that this was regarded as being more appropriately a girl's situation, and that "mother" was seen as the supervisor and ministrator to children's needs would also suggest that girls of this age are already conscious of their role. They saw this life situation as one in which women played a major part—and they liked what they saw. The neutrality of boys may, likewise, have its source in the same set of reasons. Occasionally, one would express the conflict he sensed between the nice feeling accompanying sleeping, and his desire for activity and excitement. Boys, too, may place a greater value on physical prowess, and thus look with less favor upon a scene which might suggest illness and confinement to bed.

Age Differences. These were limited to an awareness of temporal setting for the Bedroom, in which case sixth grade pupils excelled in the use of both associational and systematic designations. The extent of their superiority may be gathered from the fact that not a single first grade pupil made use of a precise time measurement (clock or calendar) in referring to this scene. This was, nevertheless, the smallest change to take place in the development of meanings about any of the life situations.

Sleep, of course, is not strange to children. By the time they enter school, boys and girls have acquired the ideas and attitudes necessary for dealing with it for all "practical purposes." These appear to suffice for the elementary years. The lack of sensitivity to the physiology of sleep and more rational approaches for governing such habits await further development.

THE DAM

They Built the Dam to Harness the River

Out in the country, in this setting of beautiful scenery are some interesting things to see. This picture shows conservation. There is a lake and a water dam, with water just running down. An electric company is powering electricity, and has many poles and cables. Also they can use the water to irrigate crops when it is dry. A farmer is contour plowing so his soil won't run down the hill. On the other side of the lake is a burnt forest. A man is surveying, and others are evening land off for families to make their homes. These men seem to enjoy their work and get good pay, too. And a boy, going fishing in the lake, is whistling on his way. Usually all boys like to go fishing.

THIS scene of a Dam was designed to tap children's perception of the conservation of natural resources which was considered to involve more adult ideas than its comparison picture, the Bedroom, which focused on human conservation. It was not an easy scene for children to interpret. They took more time in responding to it than for any other picture, and used almost as many words to express their reactions. The effort brought relatively low returns in the form of meanings and their relevancy. Concepts of the spatial and temporal setting for the Dam were similarly limited. Boys and girls did find something appealing in this life situation, however, for only one other picture (Resort) drew more favorable comments, and negative responses were in the low-average range for the series. Nevertheless, the picture was not strongly valued one way or the other: it was selected an average number of times and rejected an average number of times.

Children did agree, however, that boys belonged in this situation much more than girls.

Children's Recognition of the Dam

This scene depicting natural conservation was recognized in some fashion by 73 per cent of the children (Rank = 10). More than two-fifths of the interpretations were of a partial nature, but this was not markedly greater than the number of whole responses. Most recognitions were based on the external appearance or structure of the life situation, the number of pupils showing awareness of its function or the combined aspects of structure and function being significantly less.

Twenty-four per cent of the pupils were attentive to the *structural* elements of the Dam scene. Those who were responsive to objective aspects were definitely more attentive to the specific or immediate scene as portrayed than on the Dam as a part of a large scale conservation project. Concepts describing the immediate scene were limited to "dam" and "reservoir," the former being the overwhelming favorite for these children. The few responses which implied some complex or system of structures were limited to the idea of power or electricity such as "power plant," or "electric plant." The idea of a reclamation project such as the TVA was mentioned by no one.

The range of meaningfulness of structural identifications is well illustrated in the remarks of a young rural boy who simply recognized the dam with "water flowing out of it" and an older rural boy who picked out the dam, wires, and power plant.

> Well, he's a . . . he has something and then he's a . . . and then he's watching a dam, it's a . . . there's water flow . . . flowing out of it. And then there's a . . . there's some boys at a river, and then there's some rocks, and a house, and some . . . a whole lotsa trees, and a . . . and two more houses, and then a field.   (1RB)

> It looks like a man surveying a . . . a power plant, and they have wires going, and a big dam, and he was in a field.   (6RB)

Fewer children (11%) responded to the Dam in terms of its *function* than was the case for structure. They focused almost wholly upon various forms of conservation unlike the Bedroom scene where more emphasis was placed on who was supervising or engaged in conserving human resources. Conservation activities recognized in the Dam scene were attributed to people in general through the use of such terms as "they" and "men." An older rural girl identified these individuals as farmers. Corporate management was vaguely implied by a sixth grade city girl who remarked that "it looks like . . . an electric company." No one, however, thought of the government in connection with conservation.

These boys and girls were equally sensitive to water and soil conservation. The former was seen in connection with "making electricity" or "powering electricity," and to some extent with irrigation. A sixth grade urban girl even saw the river bed being straightened out to improve the general drainage system! All of the remarks about soil conservation had to do with "contour farming." In spite of the interest that children have in plants and animals, and experiences in camping, no one reacted to the significance of a burned-out forest, or mentioned the possibilities and importance of reforestation and the conservation of wild life.

The remarks of one of the older urban girls indicate how children reacted to conservation activities without recognizing the dam site or signs of a hydroelectric plant.

(Part I—What story does this picture tell?)
Well, it looks like that man is . . . is trying to keep his soil so that it won't run down the hill by um, making those um, those things go sideways on the hill instead of up and down. And it looks like there's a bridge in the back and a river—there's . . . and a little waterfall.

(Part II—Which boy or girl belongs in this picture?)
The in-between boy.
(Why?)
Because he doesn't have anything to be sad about or happy about, and he hasn't got anything to be crying about.

(Part III—Which picture would you like to keep for your very own?)
(Second choice)
(Why?)
Because it shows conservation.

Because of the relatively few children who responded to the functional element in this life situation, only 7 per cent reached the level of *synthesis* in recognition. In the illustrations which follow, an older rural girl saw the Dam in its capacity to conserve water, and at the same time recognized the benefits to be obtained from contour plowing. With less explanation, a sixth grade rural boy recognized the same aspects and added the power plant to complete his interpretation.

> This is a dam that's holding back the water from—it looks like there's contour farming—that's for the crops. And they have to hold the water back because there's some . . . so much of it, and later on when it gets dry they can always let down the water to water all the crops. And there's a little boy goin' ta go fishin'. And the man in the field is—in the contour field—is surveying it; it looks like he's surveying it.   (6RG)

> It tells of a great big dam where they're using it to irrigate, and there's contoured land where they are surveying on, and there's a big power plant down by the dam, too . . . and someone's coming up with a fish line, from one corner.   (6RB)

Those who recognized this life situation *in part* constituted the largest single group, 44 per cent of the pupils. More of their attention was given to people than to both the natural environment and man-made things depicted in the scene. Identification of "the boy" in the picture was not noticeably greater than that of "the man." Fishing, however, was far more popular than either farming or surveying, and in one instance a boy combined it with "butterfly hunting"! The few children who were conscious of Nature were most impressed by the water or "waterfalls," and by the crops. As one older rural girl stated, "It looks like there's maybe, corn or something coming up through the ground." Those who were partially correct in their interpretation as far as things were concerned gave their attention to the farm or to "the bridge."

Illustrating how a child can select clues bearing on people, Nature, and things which have a certain implication for conservation and yet not fully sense this relationship are the remarks of a young urban boy.

> (Part I—What story does this picture tell?)
> There's a mountain, and there's a river, and this looks like it's a . . . Berry River and no . . . that's Niagara Falls, 'cause I didn't

see that falls ... a, there's a ... there's Niagara Falls. And there's a cliff there at camp, and there's lots of rocks in there. I see some cactus, and there's hills, and there's some trees way back in there, and there's some corn crops, and a farmer working, and a radio tower, and a ... and a radio house, and a boy's going fishing.

(Part II—Which boy or girl belongs in this picture?)
The happy boy.
(Why?)
'Cause he ... he looks happy 'cause he's taking pictures in there.

(Part III—Which picture would you like to keep for your very own?)
(Third choice)
(Why?)
'Cause, 'cause I've been on a farm, and it's the same thing in the two pictures of a farm.

Nonrecognition. Twenty-seven per cent of the children failed to recognize the Dam scene, all of them because they described general features of the situation that might have applied to many life situations. What they responded to most were people and their activities, the number being far greater than for references made to the natural world or things of human origin.

Of the things said about people, recreation accounted for the majority, being mentioned far more frequently than work, which was second in frequency. The most popular pastime recognized by children was that of "taking a picture" followed by "looking through a telescope" or simply "playing." The men were generally regarded as "working," "building," or "helping someone." Other general references singled out various features in the landscape, especially the "hills," and the "house" which may have applied to the power station or the farm house in the distance. The mindset which many of the younger pupils had for the picture-taking theme is illustrated by a first grade urban boy:

Um, that's a photographer taking pictures of a lake, and um ... he, um, standing on some ... on a hill. And there's grass growing and um, there's hills over, and the bridge.

The generally low perceptiveness of children in recognizing the conservation of natural resources may be a reflection of their lack of experience with these functions. Ideas about not wasting or saving resources for future use, including future generations, apparently, are too far removed from the child's thinking to have a strong sense of reality. The balance of Nature, involving the interdependence of plants, animals, soil, and water, appears to be too complex an idea for young children to apply with great facility. Even when certain basic processes such as contour plowing and irrigation were understood, children's conception of the agency involved or organization of these projects was almost totally lacking. In short, ideas about natural conservation among elementary pupils appear to be in their formative stage.

Children's Setting for the Dam

Children were more aware of a spatial setting for this scene than they were of its placement in time. In comparison with the series as a whole, however, the Dam ranked at the lower end in both types of background settings (11 and 11.5).

A *spatial setting* was indicated by 57 per cent of the pupils, this being one of several pictures where there was no appreciable difference between the number of pupils who were conscious of a space dimension for the life situation and those who were not. In spite of the fact that a number of hydroelectric projects have become so well known that their names are a part of common usage in our language, at least for adults, most of the children attempted to define location through associations with familiar places rather than by designation according to geographical or political units.

Associations were made most frequently with the physical or natural world followed by references to institutions including two "famous" dams. The variety of ways in which these were expressed may be gathered from the following:

Well, that looks like a picture out in the country . . .
Well, it's on a hillside . . .
It looks like a man was surveying . . . he was in a field . . .
Well, a man's working in a field on top of a mountain . . .
A boy, he's gonna fish down at the lake . . .
It probably tells about a . . . agriculture, and what they do on a farm . . .

It tells of a great big dam . . .
Well, that looks like the . . . we'll call it the Hoover Dam . . .
Um, that looks like that could be Grand Coulee Dam . . .

Placements of the Dam in more precise terms were relatively few in number, and no child expressed an awareness of the fact that dams or conservation existed in countries other than the United States. One older rural boy saw this scene taking place in the state in which he lived: "it looks like he's taking a picture of—it could be the Beaver Dam River . . . ," and the sixth grade urban girl who saw this as the Hoover Dam added, "it's in California." A first grade urban boy who noticed "waterfalls" identified it as Niagara Falls.

Only 8 per cent of the boys and girls remarked about *temporal setting* as they viewed this scene. Quite obviously, natural conservation was not linked with time in the minds of children. This lack of temporal orientation was further borne out in analyzing types of referents used. All those which were associational dealt with natural time divisions rather than human events, which was to be expected. Not a single child intimated, however, that conservation is "modern," that it has been given more emphasis in the past century, or that it probably would expand in "the future."

One day the farmer was going up, and making flowers . . .
He has a big rake in his hand, and he works all day . . .
I think it's a . . . a hillside on a nice day . . .

It looks like a nice summer day out . . .

Well, they woke up at 4:30 in the morning. They started eating breakfast, and they had a nice big breakfast . . .

Children's lack of familiarity with efforts to conserve natural resources was also revealed in their awareness of the setting for this scene. For many, it was simply a "nice day out in the country." Their use of place associations (Hoover and Grand Coulee dams), encouraging as it may be, is no guarantee of correct spatial orientation. These may be located almost anywhere—even "California." More striking is the lack of awareness shown by pupils to damsites in their own state some of which resemble the one portrayed in this scene. Whether near or far, dams have not made an impression on these children.

Children's Attitudes toward the Dam

This scene stimulated considerable feeling tone; only 10 per cent of the children reacted neutrally. By far the greatest number of attitudes were positive, 68 per cent of the responses being in this category (Rank = 2.5). Such high approval of what children saw in this situation was exceeded only by the Resort. Seventeen per cent of the remarks indicated an unfavorable attitude toward the Dam (Rink = 9), but only 5 per cent of the children sensed what they considered to be both positive and negative aspects. This latter figure was the lowest for any of the pictures. Nevertheless, pupils' reactions toward the Dam were not very consistent. Only 18 per cent maintained the same attitude toward the life situation throughout the interview, a figure which ranked next to the last in the series. This was due to the fact that many pupils tended to react first in a neutral manner, but upon repeated exposures to the picture they discovered something which they liked.

Positive attitudes were shown first and foremost to fishing: for the fun it provided, the element of relaxation, making a good catch, and even to its utilitarian aspect. Several of the children who recognized the Dam spoke approvingly of such projects, but in general terms rather than in appreciation of its contribution to the conservation of natural resources. Even though there was little in this scene to suggest parent-child relationships, some children managed to project such feelings. Typical expressions of positive attitudes in these three areas follow:

Fishing

He's going fishing, and I think he should be happy.   (1UG)

He's walking down to go fishing, and he's having a good time.
                                                                      (6RB)

He can go fishing. He has to help his daddy and his mother for something to eat.   (1RG)

He's going fishing and he'd be happy—just didn't have no worries.
                                                                      (6RG)

He must be thinking he's going to catch a lot of fish.   (6UG)

He just got them fish, and he looks like he's got quite a catch on there.   (6RB)

Dam

I like dams and lotsa water.   (6RB)
He's seeing the dam running, and he would get a lotta enjoyment
watching it. I would like to see a dam.   (6UB)
Looks like this man is surveying some land, and that they're gonna
have a reservoir or something, and they're happy that it's gonna
be there.   (6RG)

Human relations

'Cause hims mother didn't give him a licking nor nothing.   (1RB)
'Cause his father most likely let him go fishing.   (6RG)

As was the case for other life situations depicting work, children displayed various attitudes toward the subject. The same was
true with regard to recreational opportunities other than fishing.
In both instances, however, the dissenters were in the minority
and, with few exceptions, were first grade children.

Positive	*Negative*

Recreational activities

Because he's playing. (1RB)	He doesn't wanna do nothing,
Because he's wading. (1RG)	and he doesn't know what to do.
She's lookin' at the truck, and	(1RG)
she's real happy. She likes to see	He wants to go outside. (1UB)
that picture. (1UB)	He doesn't wanna take the pic-
He's so glad to get this pretty	ture he has ta. (1RG)
scene in his camera. (6RB)	

Work

He's happy when he works.	(Sad boy) He's got overalls on.
(6RG)	(1RG)
He's having fun surveying.	Because he don't like to work in
(6RB)	the garden. (1RG)
Looks like a nice summer day	
out, and he's out working, and he	
looks as though he's happy.	
(6RG)	
Because they seem to enjoy their	
work, and I think they get good	
pay, too. (6UG)	

Neutral attitudes were expressed toward the above factors by children who simply described what they saw in matter of fact terms. Although no one spoke against fishing, an older rural girl did not appear to be too excited about such a prospect. "Taking pictures," apparently was not enthusiastically accepted by all children. As for work, it was regarded as something that adults have to do—so why get excited about it? Children, therefore, gave the following reasons for inserting an "in-between" child in the Dam picture:

He's going fishing.   (6RG)

She's just taking a picture—medium-like.   (1RB)
He's just taking some pictures that he wants.   (6UB)

He doesn't look too happy or too sad—just resting. It looks like he's been working hard.   (6RG)
She's suppose to be helping him.   (1RB)

The occasional *mixed* attitudes expressed by children was usually due to a change in attitude which took place from one showing of the life situation to another. An older urban girl, however, was aware of the fact that disappointment might color the pleasure that one might get out of fishing, depending upon the value placed upon the catch.

(The happy boy) Because he's going fishing, and he . . . he can probably catch something, but if he doesn't he won't be happy.

Boys and girls appear to be more interested in consumership than in conservation. They seem to approve of dams, but were more enthusiastic about out-door recreation. Using Nature for recreational and other purposes is dynamic and immediately satisfying. Saving Nature, in contrast, may be viewed as being static and having delayed returns. At this age most pupils do not see the relationship between saving and using. Neither have they acquired a sense of stewardship over the bounty which is for all mankind.

Children's Preferences for the Dam

This picture was tied for sixth place in popularity, and tied for eighth in terms of rejection, thus being in the middle range of children's valuation of the picture series. Twenty-four per cent of the pupils selected the Dam as one of their three preferred pictures thus accounting for 8 per cent of the total number of choices made. The latter figure is not so greatly different from the 3 per cent of rejections accounted for by this scene to be considered statistically significant.

The arguments which children gave for supporting their choices included a consideration of the dam and conservation, the farm and farming, recreation, and the beauties of Nature. In many cases, their valuation of what they saw in this life situation was based upon actual experiences. This was not the case, presumedly, of the few pupils who rejected the scene. As one young city boy said, "I just don't like it," and an older city girl exclaimed, "I don't like to work like that." The approval which children expressed for the Dam situation took the following forms:

Conservation

It shows conservation.	(6UG)
Because I like the dam, and things like that.	(6UB)
It shows the water running, and all the contour plowing.	(6UB)

Farm

'Cause I've been on a farm.	(1UB)
'Cause we live on a farm.	(6RG)
Because he's got a lot of farming to do.	(6UB)

Because there are a lot of farmers. The way they do their farming, and their dam that they built, and shows how to do some of them things, and the way that they do it.   (6RG)

Recreation

I like to go fishing, and that boy likes to go fishing, too.   (6RB)
Because he can go out and take pictures of anything that he wants to.   (1UB)
Well, he's looking through one of these kinda round things, and I like to look through those, and play pirates and that stuff.   (6UB)

Nature

That looks like a pretty countryside.   (6UB)
Because I like to look across and see what's across the mountains.
                    (6UB)

Children who had high regard for this scene because of the dam and other symbols of conservation expressed a general appreciation of their importance. They did not appear to value conservation for its effects upon their own way of life; neither did they place a value on it for the sake of future generations. They seemed to be taking conservation on faith without making explicit the various ways in which their welfare and the common good would be affected. The conclusion is inescapable: the conservation of natural resources has low priority in children's scale of values.

Group Comparisons

The Dam is one of the few pictures which revealed differences in the reactions of all groups of children. Those associated with sex, intelligence, and community were minor compared with the markedly different responses of the age groups. These variations occurred in each of the perceptual components being examined indicating, quite conclusively, the widespread nature of differences in children's perception of natural conservation.

Age Differences. Conservation of natural resources meant so little to young children that sixth graders surpassed them in practically every aspect of perception. Older pupils excelled in each of the recognition categories. In fact, not one of the younger children managed to reach the highest level of synthesis. In their recognition of the structural aspects of this life situation, more sixth graders gave attention to the specific scene and used the word "dam," and they made all of the references to an extended project involving the dam and generation of power, thus ending with a far greater number of structural responses. In like manner, they were the only ones to recognize various types of land and water conservation, not a single functional recognition having been achieved by younger pupils. Although there was no difference in the number of pupils who partially interpreted this scene, sixth graders were the only ones to note "people surveying." Conversely, many more first grade pupils failed to recognize this picture because they were preoccupied with common or universal symbols found in this life situation. This was particularly evident in their awareness of people especially with reference to "taking pictures." Although fewer in number, they also provided all the general references to Nature and things. Older boys and girls were also more advanced in their spatial orientation for this scene. This was particularly evident in the number of times that they associated the Dam with natural or institutional settings.

Feelings about the Dam also differed quite markedly. Older pupils tended to react more positively whereas younger pupils were decidely negative in their outlook. The strength of the former is indicated by their greater selection of the Dam as a favorite picture.

All this represents one of the greatest developmental changes taking place in the perception of any of the life situations. It suggests that the conservation of natural resources is not a part of the young child's world, but that he is introduced to some of its phases during his elementary years. The relationship between familiarity and feeling is also suggested in that the nonrecognition of first grade pupils was linked with a greater number of negative attitudes; the greater degree of recognition on the part of sixth grade pupils was associated with more positive attitudes and a higher valuation placed on the conservation of natural resources.

Sex Differences. The one difference in the perceptive behavior of girls and boys toward the Dam was the higher value which the latter placed upon this life situation. More of them regarded it as being one of the three best pictures. That boys rather than girls "belonged" in this scene was further indicated by children. The difference, then, is not that boys understand this portrayal of conservation better than girls. They have different feelings about it. This, again, may be an indication that children begin to learn the sex roles played in our culture at a very early age. Through actual experience, observation, and various forms of communication they have come to know the "great-outdoors" as the male's domain. Girls, apparently, are not unduly troubled by this allocation of life space for the sexes and give it tacit approval.

Intelligence Differences. Although there was no difference in the number of bright and low-ability children who recognized this life situation structurally, the former were more prolific in their ideas. Pupils above-average in intelligence produced a greater number of responses representing a greater variety of structural types. They recognized it not only as a dam, but as a structure having to do with the generation of electricity which was not the case for low-ability pupils. The contrast is between a general observation repre-

senting the least common denominator (dam) and finer discriminations based on a more extensive stock of concepts (power station).
Development of the latter seems related to intellectual capacity.

Rural-Urban Differences. The recognition of this life situation
and feelings toward it by children coming from rural and urban
backgrounds were strikingly similar. In fact, the only divergence
occurred in their nonrecognition responses. There were approximately the same number of pupils in each group who described the
scene in general terms unrelated to conservation, but more urban
children than rural were conscious of people in the act of "taking
a picture." This could mean that photography is more of a hobby
for urban dwellers or that they usually come to the country as
"sight-seers." On the other hand, the desire to record this scene
on film might be an expression of the value that this landscape held
for children. The fact that there were no real variations in attitudes
and preferences for this scene, however, would tend to rule out
such an explanation. More significant than this consciousness of
picture taking by urban children is the fact that farm boys and girls
are not overly alert to conservation. The emphasis on conserving
natural resources is so great in the state in which they live, that it
would be difficult for rural children to avoid contact with conservation practices. Yet, such opportunities have not resulted in a
corresponding degree of insight. Conservation concepts, apparently,
are difficult for all children to grasp.

THE CHURCH

Children and Parents Go to Church on Sunday Morning

People are going to church to worship God—all the families in the town. It's a nice place to be going on Sunday. There are two different churches; big stone churches that look like big castles, with steeples and a cross on them. The people can go to whatever church they want to, and can worship God whenever they want to. Some children go to Sunday school where they learn a lot of things, and others go to church where they read, sing hymns, pray, or give thanks for what the Lord had done for them. Outside the church they are meeting their friends and talking. Most people are happy when they go to God's House.

CHILDREN'S reactions to this scene of religious activity were short and to the point. They took less time in responding to it than to any other picture in the series, and, except for the Bedroom, required fewer words to express their reactions. Almost everyone recognized this as a Church scene, and showed the highest sense of its "where" and "when" than of any of the life situations. On the whole, however, children's ideas about the religious significance of this scene were limited. Nevertheless, no picture was regarded more favorably for the Church was exceeded by only one picture (Resort) in the number of positive feelings elicited, and none produced less negativism. Children's positive orientation toward the Church, however, was not accompanied by great feelings of worth or value for the picture's popularity was only low-average even though it was associated with boys and girls.

Children's Recognition of the Church

This Church scene was recognized by 95 per cent of the pupils (Rank = 3), very conclusive evidence that they are on familiar terms with certain religious institutions. Although two life situations (Bedroom, Farm) were recognized in some degree by everyone, in no instance did children achieve a higher level of interpretation. In fact, there were no partial recognitions. This does not mean, however, that pupils were conscious of both the external features and the life-processes being depicted. They responded to this situation primarily in terms of its structure, combining this with a sensitivity to various forms of religious expression to a much lesser degree.

Hence, recognition of this Church scene almost invariably entailed an awareness of its *structural* features. Such a consciousness was voiced by 94 per cent of the pupils. The number who took into account only one of the structures was not significantly greater than those who extended their observations to include both churches or the idea of a religious center. Children who concentrated on one of the structures, with very few exceptions, used the term "church" in referring to the building. One youngster called it "God's House," and another identified the building as a "Sunday school," but no child used such terms as cathedral, temple, tabernacle, or house of worship. For most of the children, this was simply a case of people going to church, and they went no further to explain why. It is conceivable that many children were including the idea of religious services in the expression, "going to church." To put it another way, they might have assumed that church attendance could mean only one thing—some form of divine worship. Whether or not such meaning should be read into their words is not so important as the fact that these children did not choose to elaborate on their religious experiences. The comments of one of the older urban boys illustrates this point.

(Part I—What story does this picture tell?)
I think it's about a family that goes to church, and then they go on with what they do with their afternoon then.

(Part II—Which boy or girl belongs in this picture?)
The in-between boy.

(Why?)

> A 'cause he doesn't look very happy or sad. Let's see, well, a he's not surprised that he's goin' to church.

Those who saw more than one building in this scene were likewise more aware of "churches" than they were of a religious center which might include a church and Sunday school building. Regarding the first category, children often were conscious of architectural differences in the two church buildings, but did not associate these with differences in religious form or beliefs. Those who attained this level of recognition, it should be noted again, did not make explicit the spiritual and moral significance of church going.

> (Part I—What story does this picture tell?)
> One morning they went to church, and them read and sing. And them went to Sunday school, and learn a lot of things.

> (Part II—Which boy or girl belongs in this picture?)
> Happy boy.
> (Why?)
> 'Cause him is happy going to Sunday school.   (1RB)

> (Part I—What story does this picture tell?)
> Well, there's a church and everybody's come out of it . . . and I think the priest is there . . . and let's see . . . the people are waiting for their cars, I think, so they can drive them home. See, the trees, and the people in the other church. I think they're waiting out, too, for their friends.

> (Part II—Which boy or girl belongs in this picture?)
> The mad boy.
> (Why?)
> That's why—he's kind of mad . . . 'cause to go to church. (1UG)

The expression of religious sentiments in connection with this Church scene was emphasized by 26 per cent of the pupils. This sensitivity to religious *functions* was accompanied in each case but one by a recognition of the physical environment in which such activities took place. (The lone exception was a young urban girl who saw a wedding but did not mention the church!) Children's description of various religious observances was not markedly greater than their awareness of certain qualities or characteristics of these religious experiences.

Boys and girls were more inclined to refer to general religious
experiences than to specify certain types of church services. The
latter, in fact, were confined to the "wedding" referred to above,
and another child's consciousness of people attending "Mass." The
great variety of interesting expressions used by children to denote
religious experiences in general is indicated below. Of these, "worship" and the idea of "prayer" occurred most frequently, but
accounted for less than half the number of expressions used. In
short, there was a singular uniqueness in the way that children
expressed the relationship which they sensed between the individual
and God or described certain religious practices. Theirs was a very
personal approach, for they used the names "Jesus" and "God"
most frequently; only occasionally did they refer to "The Lord,"
and no one spoke about "The Creator," "He," or "Him."

'Cause it shows you for a—your faith in God . . .   (6RB)
'Cause after this dry season—a he, it had rained. And he had
thanked God that it had rained, and he prayed, and the Lord
had answered it . . .   (6RB)
Because she's gonna see God . . .   (1RG)
And these men and little children, they help God to live and stuff,
and they pray for sick people . . .   (1RG)
And Jesus said you should always go every Sunday if you have a
chance to go.   (1RG)
Some people coming home from their religion . . .   (6UB)
People are coming from all over the country to worship.   (6UG)

The two major values expressed by children regarding qualitative aspects of religious experience dealt with differences among
religions and religious freedom. In case of the former, very little
use was made of denominational names. The terms "Catholic" and
"Lutheran" appeared only a few times, but no one classified the
latter more broadly as "Protestant;" the use of "Christian" by an
older boy was synonymous with "religious" and not in way of contrast with other forms of religions. Likewise, very few children
referred to the clergy; the few such designations included the terms
"minister," "pastor," and "priest," but no one mentioned a "rabbi"
or "nun." Although some mention was made of reading and sing-
ing in church, no one referred to the Bible, prayer book or hymnal.
The fact of differences among churches or religions was, apparently,
quite acceptable to children for not a single instance of bias, intoler-

ance, or disparagement was evident in their remarks. Instead, they showed very real appreciation of the opportunity to be selective as far as going to church was concerned.

> It tells of um, different families um, going to um, several different churches on um, Sunday morning.   (6RB)
>
> Well, that's a Sunday morning when everybody's going to church. They go to whatever church they want to, and there's two churches there. And I think some are leaving and some are going.   (6UB)
>
> On Sunday many people go to church. There are many churches in the city so the people can go to whatever church they want to; that is, usually families that go to church.   (6UG)

The highest level of interpretation based on a *synthesis* of structure and function was achieved by 25 per cent of the children. In spite of the fact that many did recognize the church, the limiting factor was the relatively small number of children who showed an awareness of religious functions. Such understanding was exhibited by an older rural girl who also added the idea of denominationalism:

> (Part I—What story does this picture tell?)
>
> It looks like Sunday. There's two different churches; maybe they're Catholic and a Lutheran. They're going to church or they're coming home from church; some are goin' and some are coming home.
>
> (Part II—Which boy or girl belongs in this picture?)
>
> The happy boy.
>
> (Why?)
>
> Because he's goin' to church. He should be happy that he's got a church to go to, and he's got parents, and that he can go and listen to God's word.
>
> (Part III—Which picture would you like to keep for your very own?)
>
> (Third choice) People going to church.
>
> (Why?)
>
> Just . . . the mother and father and boy and girl are going all to church together, and they had a good—they have a father to go with, and their parents are still living, and they can be glad they got a church to go to.   (6RG)

Nonrecognition. Only 5 per cent of the pupils were unaware of the religious meaning of this scene. This lack of recognition took the form of general comments about elements in the situation devoid of any particular religious significance rather than outright errors in putting various clues together. The data are insufficient for purposes of generalization, but are in keeping with responses of a similar nature to other life situations which have tended to focus upon people's activities in the main rather than upon the natural environment or upon cultural artifacts. The former included such ideas as "people crossing the street," "people standing near a big house," and "people going to that place." Although none of these is incorrect, they certainly exhibit no awareness of religion as such.

Children soon learn that going to church is one of the things that people do. As a consequence, they have little difficulty in recognizing a Church, but have considerably less awareness of its religious significance. Their consciousness of certain outward forms of religious practice is greater than an understanding of the moral and spiritual values involved. Whatever the concept of "worship" and "prayer" might be for those who are grasping at their meaning, religion is a very personal relationship with a very personal God or Jesus. That there are different churches and the freedom to express this relationship in different ways is a growing realization on the part of some pupils.

Children's Setting for the Church

Of all the pictures in the series, children were most familiar with the background for this life situation. The Church ranked first both in spatial settings and temporal settings assigned to it, but of the two, boys and girls were definitely more conscious of space than of time.

Almost every pupil, 94 per cent, designated a *spatial setting* for this scene. For children, the people in the picture were undoubtedly involved in activities having a church background. Consequently, its placement was associated in such terms rather than specified according to geographical or political units. As would be anticipated, all of the associational designations were institutional in character; no child related this life situation to places in Nature nor, quite obviously, to a home background. References of this type were necessarily linked with structural recognitions for the place which people were "going to," "at," "in," or "were leaving" was the church.

> People are going to church . . .
> I see some women and children getting out of Sunday school . . .
> A big family at church . . .
> There's a lotta people and they're coming outta church . . .
> I see a church and some people walking to the church . . .
> It tells of um, different families um, going to several different churches . . .
> The churches let out and people are walking away from the church while some people—they're coming . . .

Some boys and girls were mindful of the community setting for a Church. Those who were, seemed to be under no compulsion to mention a specific city, not even their own. As a result, not a single child placed this scene in any other political unit be it state, nation, or the world.

> That's all in a big city . . .
> All the families in the town are gittin' ready to go to church . . .
> That's in the town again . . .
> Um, looks like a nice friendly city . . .
> There are many churches in the city . . .
> That looks like a nice town . . .
> It's on a city street . . .

A *temporal setting* was provided for the Church by 41 per cent of the pupils. This was the only picture in the series for which the number of children conscious of temporal setting was almost as great as those who were not. In indicating time, systematic measures were used more than associational, this distinction being shared with only one other picture in the series, the Mansion. Associations in time were made with events occurring in the world of Nature there being no instance when human events were used. Time and religious activities, moreover, were much more a matter of daily events than seasonal or annual, both of which are illustrated in the following:

> Well, they woke up in the morning real early . . .
> One morning they went to church . . .
> It's on a Sunday morning . . .

About a family that goes to church and then they go on with what
they do with their afternoon . . .
Well, it looks like a sunny day . . .

Looks like a summer day . . .
How thankful they were after this dry season . . .
It looks like a nice summer morning . . .

Except for one child who referred to the Church scene in terms
of the present ("this is in the new days . . ."), all other time measures were chronometric rather than historical. Although religious
services often meet definite time schedules, the former did not include one reference to clock time. It was the calendar to which
children referred in establishing a time perspective for this scene
of religious activity. Except for an occasional reference to a religious holiday such as Easter, children saw this as a stereotype for
a "Sunday scene." An older urban boy put it simply and directly:
"Well, that looks like a church *on Sunday*, and the church is just
letting out."

That church going follows a highly prescribed pattern is soon
made apparent to boys and girls. It is for Sunday morning. No
other life situation was so definitely "set" as this. So strong was this
connection that children often appeared to regard religion as being
synonymous with attending church. Off-setting this were a few
children who regarded religion also as a code of ethics or way of
life. They were the ones who thought about "helping the poor"
and "praying at home." For them religion was a part of everyday
living, not just a Sunday event.

Children's Attitudes toward the Church

Children displayed "correct" attitudes toward this picture of
religion. Sixty-eight per cent of the boys and girls spoke with approval of what they saw (Rank = 2.5) and only 12.5 per cent
expressed negative feelings (Rank = 13). Neutral attitudes (9%)
and mixed responses (10%), moreover, were in the average range
for the series. The consistency of attitudes toward the Church,
however, was low for the series, ranking 11th. Only 22 per cent of
the pupils exhibited the same emotional "set" each time they viewed
this scene indicating that considerable shifting took place with repeated exposures to this life situation.

Positive attitudes toward this life situation were not only numerous, but they were also quite varied in nature. Children reacted to the practice of going to church and relationships with God as well as to religious values, including religious freedom, and human relationships involved in going to church. Church attendance was regarded as a happy experience by most children—or it was " 'sposed to be"—for going to God's House made it possible to "see God," "to worship God," and to "make Jesus happy." To some, His direct answer to their prayers was very real. Fewer children regarded this situation from the standpoint of moral or ethical conduct. Those who did, spoke approvingly of helping others—including God in His work, and unfortunate people in general—and showed a concern for meeting standards of goodness in their behavior. Attitudes regarding religious freedom were not expressed very often even when children recognized that there were two "different" churches. This was something that, apparently, was being taken for granted or approved for not once was a show of negativism based on such difference. As for social aspects, religion was regarded as a family affair and church as a friendly meeting place, both relationships being highly prized by boys and girls. The variety of ways in which these feelings were expressed is illustrated below:

Going to church

He's happy going to Sunday school. (1RB)
They're going to church, and he should be very happy. (1UB)
You're always kinda happy to go to church. (6RG)
They're going to church, and I think they're 'sposed to be happy. (6RB)
They're going to church. They should be happy, because that's a nice place to be going on Sunday. (6UB)
'Cause they're coming outta church. They're glad that they went to church. (1RG)
They just came from church and, well, they don't feel angry after they're there. (6RB)

Relationship with God

She's gonna see God. (1RG)
You should be happy when you go to God's House. (6UB)
They're going to church, and happy to learn to worship God. (6RG)

They're excited because they're going to church to worship God.
(6UG)

We all should be happy when we are going to church—that Jesus
is happy, too.   (6UG)

Moral conduct

They're going to church. They can help God and make Him live.
(1RG)

They're walking together, and they're showing their love to Jesus,
and helping the poor.   (1RG)

Maybe he's doin' something for another person, and so he's happy
about it.   (1RB)

The boys are all happy, because there isn't anything wrong with
them or anything.   (1RB)

Religious freedom

They could go to the church that they wanted to, and could be
happy 'cause they could worship God wherever they wanted to.
(6RG)

Human relationships

They'll be able to go with their mother and father to church.
(6RB)

Because he's nice. He's going to church with his father and mother.
(1RB)

Because they're meeting everybody.   (1UG)

Because they're going to church, and they're meeting their friends,
and they're going to church with their family.   (6RG)

Everybody's coming out of church, and it looks like they're talking
and having a reunion.   (6UB)

The few *negative* feelings displayed toward this life situation
were, more often than not, vague or indirect in their manner of
expression. A young city boy identified this scene with an angry
girl because "she just looks to me—she just feels like this." A
member of the same group claimed the girl was angry because, "she
just doesn't like going across the street." In a few instances, a
definite preference was indicated for other activities. In each of
these cases, it should be noted, the dissenter was a first grade child.

He wants to go to bed.   (1RB)

He doesn't wanna go to church. He wants to play home.   (1UB)

Those who were *neutrally* disposed toward the Church scene described church attendance as the thing to do; a part of the routines of living which is not necessarily "exciting."

> He's just walking along to church. (1RB)
> They're going to church. (6RB)
> (In-between boy and girl) He's just walking to a church. She's just walking to church like any girl would. (6RG)
> He's not surprised that he's going to church. (6UB)
> When you go to church you feel sorta in-between. (6UB)

The majority of mixed attitudes were the result of shifts from positive to negative or vice versa as children proceeded from one phase of the interview to the next. Some of the older girls, however, recognized that some people or under certain conditions there could be opposing attitudes regarding this church scene.

> (Which boy or girl belongs in this picture?)
> The happy girl and boy if they liked church. And if they don't, they would be sad, or else mad 'cause that they couldn't go—I mean, that they had to go. (6UG)

> (Which boy or girl belongs in this picture?)
> The in-between boy. Sometimes when you go to church you don't feel like you want to go or something and sometimes you're happy, but a lot of times when you go you don't feel like you want to go, it might be cold out or ... something like that. (6UG)

It is evident that most of the children have "caught" the importance with which religion is held in our culture. Even though some may not find church going very exciting or may have little understanding of what is taking place, they do know that it is "good." This may be the reason why those who are just beginning to differentiate among various forms of religion have not, as yet, acquired certain feelings about peoples of other faiths. As far as religion is concerned, no one could be more tolerant than a first grade child; even the sixth grader thinks it's a good idea to be able to go to "whatever church you want to." If religious prejudice develops, it is probably learned after the elementary school years.

Children's Preferences for the Church

Only 18 per cent of the pupils wanted this Church scene. It accounted for 7 per cent of their three choices for a rank of ninth in the series. Neither was the Church highly rejected, 2 per cent of such designations being centered on this particular life situation (Rank = 11). In short, children placed only low-average value on this picture but did not show great hostility toward it.

In general, children gave their approval to church attendance because they like to go, and because it was considered "good." They valued opportunities to worship and to express certain feelings that they had about God. Many also appreciated such human relations aspects as family attendance and meeting friends at church. Against all this, a little voice was raised by a first grade urban girl who was distressed because, "There's a lot of things I don't know about and everything." Those who desired a copy of this picture supported their decisions as follows:

Church attendance

'Cause I like to go to church.   (1RG)
It's a nice picture, and it just reminds yourself of going to church.
                                                                      (6UG)
It's good to go to church.   (1RG)
It's just a lotta good ideas, like you should go to church.   (6RB)

Religious expression

It shows your faith in God.   (6RB)
I think it's nice to go to church, and to thank the Lord for all the things we've got.   (6RB)
I liked it, because the children seemed excited, because they were going to church to worship God.   (6UG)

Human relations

The mother and father and boy and girl are all going to church together, and they had a good—they have a father to go with, and their parents are still living, and they can be glad they got a church to go to.   (6RG)
I like the people.   (1UG)
Well, you're always kinda happy to go to church, and seeing that I'm a Catholic, I always ride to church with someone.   (6RG)

Why is it that in spite of its high prestige the Church is only moderately valued by these children? One reason, probably, is because they find religion difficult to understand. Many of the concepts are abstract, the language often difficult, and much that happens is based on the far away and long ago. Compounding this problem for young active bodies is the generally restrictive nature and length of religious services planned more for adults than children. Yet, many young people like going to church because the whole family goes. For them, social values outweigh the moral and spiritual. If nothing else, going to church gives them an opportunity to "dress up" and "meet friends."

Group Comparisons

No life situation was perceived in more diverse fashion than the Church. It is one of the scenes on which all groups of children revealed some differences. The most pronounced were on the part of age groups. Boys and girls reacted quite differently, and to a lesser extent so did rural and urban children, but the variations between intelligence groups were minor. Differences in perception involved the emotions fully as much, or more, than ideational components. Regarding the latter, it is interesting to note that some difference in the recognition of this Church scene appeared in each of the group comparisons.

Age Differences. These were reflected both in the cognitive and feeling components of perception. Older pupils were not consistently superior in their recognition of this life situation, but excelled with respect to its functional aspects. More of them noted the expression of religious sentiments, and they were aware of a greater variety of such practices. With regard to such things as religious differences and religious freedom, they were markedly superior; in fact, not a single first grade pupil showed this kind of sensitivity. As a result of their limited consciousness of religious functions, relatively few of the younger pupils reached the level of synthesis (structure and function) in recognition, thereby falling far behind sixth graders in this respect. Too limited for purposes of generalization but interesting to speculate about, is the fact that only first graders saw a "Sunday school." As for the context in which this life situation was viewed, sixth grade pupils were definitely more temporally minded. They used more associational referents, more systematic time designations, and hence were generally more aware of the relationship of time to the observance of certain religious practices. Sixth graders, moreover, tended to express favorable attitudes toward the Church whereas more of the younger children were decidedly negative.

These differences can be accounted for in terms of acculturation *(early)* and learning processes. In our culture, children are introduced to religious experiences at an early age. By the time they are six and one-half years old they are on familiar terms with church buildings and church going. As would be anticipated, their understanding of these concrete manifestations of religion develops quicker than for their spiritual significance. Hence, some of the younger children are less likely to accept some of the conditions imposed by church attendance. After five more years of additional opportunities to develop the more abstract concepts of religion and for social sanctions to make their imprint, a decided growth in these respects is evident—although much still remains to be accomplished.

Sex Differences. Boys and girls differed principally in their emotional reactions to the Church. The one exception occurred in their consciousness of function, the difference being not in number of pupils but that girls visualized far more religious activities underway in this scene. Attitudinally, the contrasts were more marked. More boys had a tendency to be neutral and negative; girls tended to regard this scene with favor, and more of them expressed mixed reactions usually because they could see "both sides." Reflecting the former was the greater preference for this picture exhibited by girls.

It is quite clear that girls come closer to socially approved ways of regarding religion as symbolized in this Church scene. This is true in spite of the fact that the majority of children identified this life situation as being suitable for both boys and girls. The explanation may lie in the more rapid social development commonly attributed to girls. A greater sensitivity to social values and processes would, by definition, include a greater awareness of the importance of religion in society, and the social opportunities—other than religious—that it presents. Increased social maturity might also help to explain the greater number of mixed responses produced by girls, for with greater insight comes the awareness that people do regard church attendance differently. It may be, however, that these girls were merely reflecting the difficulty they were experiencing in accepting certain social mores in connection with religion.

Rural-Urban Differences. Rural children were more perceptive of this religious situation than urban in somewhat the same ways as girls when compared with boys. Their superiority regarding function was not in the number of pupils involved, but in the greater number of religious activities observed. Also, more rural children valued this picture than urban.

These reactions fit in with the popular conception of the church as one of the most important focal points of rural life. Although urban religious institutions may have more extensive programs and present a greater variety of experiences, they may have less impact upon children's consciousness than rural churches simply because they are in competition with more "attractions," and because of their generally larger and more impersonal characteristics. Rural children's heightened awareness of religion, therefore, is not so much a matter of more rapid socialization as in the case of girls, or greater ability to learn socially approved ways of living as for sixth grade pupils. Theirs comes from a kind of experience provided by the type of community in which they are reared, one in which the church is giving a more important role if for no other reason than the lack of other highly organized social institutions.

Intelligence Differences. Bright children differed from those with less intelligence in their perception of structure. Below-average children had a tendency to concentrate on the more limited type of structural recognition, the church, as compared with high-ability children who tended to take a more extended view encompassing the idea of different churches or a church and Sunday school. Greater intellectual endowment, apparently, enables its possessor to take more things into account, and thus offers greater possibilities for seeing relationships and integration. This intellectual power, however, does not necessarily mean outstanding performance in other aspects of perception. How one feels about the Church or religion in general is more than a matter of intelligence.

THE CAPITOL

There Are Many Men in Office to Help

This is an important building, the Capitol in Madison or Washington. It is a great big building with a statue on top of a dome, pillars, and many steps leading up to it. People are coming and going. There are important government men, Senators and Representatives, and other people who work in the Capitol. And there are lawyers and businessmen, for very business-like things go on there. They may be working on problems, bills, or on a case, and some may be going to a meeting. There's a policeman standing there to guard. Some people are visiting, and they are excited because not very many people get to see their Capitol.

CHILDREN's perception of this scene compared very unfavorably with others in the Life-Situation Picture Series. This symbol of our democratic values was, apparently, a difficult one for children to apprehend. They had very little to say about the Capitol, as was reflected in the length of time and number of words in their responses, and the limited number of meanings they attached to it, many of which were inappropriate. The one prevailing trend was the average success met by pupils in placing this scene, but in terms of temporal orientations this picture was lowest of all. Neither did the Capitol evoke strong attitudes for relatively few children came out definitely for or against what they saw. In spite of the fact that this life situation was regarded as being suitable for both boys and girls, it was not highly valued.

Children's Recognition of the Capitol

This picture symbolizing civic values was recognized by a bare majority of pupils (51% or a rank of 13). Those who did show some recognition of its governmental significance were far more likely to grasp it as a whole than to single out one or more of its relevant aspects. More often than not, this awareness was confined to external or physical features rather than inclusive of both its structure and function.

A consciousness of *structural* aspects was displayed by 43 per cent of the boys and girls. With very few exceptions, attention was focused upon the immediate scene, the government building, rather than upon an extended view of the situation including the idea of a capital city. The extent to which this picture was regarded as a stereotype is indicated by the fact that except for a young urban girl who called it a "state building," the only appropriate term used by children was "capitol." Pupils usually were satisfied with this general designation although some did specify that it was the Capitol of "our state" or "nation" or more specifically mentioned Wisconsin or the United States. The range in children's responses centered on structure is indicated by the following excerpts which include an identification of a capitol building based on experience and its placement in the capital city of Wisconsin.

> Well, two men with glasses on and mustaches on—they're going to work. And there's a big place where—there's the Capitol there. And women, and men, and little children go there to see the things —and nice things, and nice furniture. And in there, and way on top—you have to climb lots of stairs so you can get up there to the top of the Capitol. (1RG)

> Well, it looks . . . it's in a great big city, and there's a couple businessmen around. And they're a lot of people there. They're looking at the Capitol or some . . . looks something like the Capitol in Madison that everybody's looking at it. And there's a lot of people talking to each other. (6RG)

One young rural boy, while recognizing structure, misplaced another important symbol of our democracy and stated, "The United States Capitol is there. A big big statue's way up on top— the Statue of Liberty."

Relatively few pupils (14%) were sensitive to governmental *functions* and in each case this was accompanied by an awareness of structure. Those who were conscious of functions were more aware of processes involved in governing than they were of civic or democratic values. The former represented a wide variety of activities, none of which seemed to be of greater interest than another to children. Some pupils merely stated that the Capitol was the place where important people did their work; others mentioned certain specific activities such as "going to meetings," "talking over bills," "reading papers," "making rules." These ideas were expressed in the following ways:

> That's probably an important person that works in the Capitol . . .
> (6UB)
> Some of the Senators and Representatives are a . . . going in there, and some people, and are going in to hear the meeting . . .
> (6UB)
> It'd be a Capitol building where they make rules and everything . . .
> (6UB)
> They finished their papers they were reading, and after a while they went to the President to a little meeting . . . (6RB)
> There are many men in office to help their city with the problems they have . . . (6UG)

Children who showed any consciousness of certain characteristics of our form of government were the rare exception. A sixth grade rural boy recognized that Congressmen were elected (". . . they have just been elected . . . one of the House of Representatives . . ."), and one of his companions noted that "maybe something wrong at the Capitol; they had an argument with one of the Senators or something." Pupils, apparently, took elections, free speech, and law-making for granted or assumed that everybody knew that these existed. Regardless of which interpretation is correct, it is significant that not a single child was prompted to mention our democratic way of life either in terms of its freedoms or responsibilities.

This scene of government was recognized in *structural and functional* terms by only 14 per cent of the pupils, a figure which was set by their limited perception of social processes. An example of such synthesis are the remarks of a sixth grade urban girl, who identified this as a very specific Capitol and showed an awareness of what Congressmen do, but was not always sure how she felt about the whole business of government.

(Part I—What story does this picture tell?)

Well, that looks like our Capitol in Washington, D.C. And there are two men with briefcases, and they're walking past each other, and they look maybe like one of the Senators or in Congress or in the House of Representatives. And then there are some children, and mothers, and fathers, and they're um, looking at the Capitol. And then there's a policeman, and he's guarding the Capitol so he sees that nobody tries to wreck it or steal anything from it. And then there's some—three, there's three men in the background, and they're Congressmen, I think, and um, they're probably talking—discussing a new bill that came up or something.

(Part II—Which boy or girl belongs in this picture?)

The in-between girl.

(Why?)

And because a . . . she visits the Capitol, and um, it can be exciting, and it can be in-between, and I think the in-between girl.

(Part III—Which picture would you like to keep for your very own?)

(Second choice) The Capitol.

(Why?)

Because, um, it would be interesting to visit the Capitol, Capitol, and I don't have a picture of the Capitol.

Few pupils (8%) were *partially* successful in recognizing this governmental situation. Although no broad generalizations can be made from such limited responses, it is interesting to note that they were focused about equally upon people and things. In the former case, the policeman was selected as a symbol of authority controlling the movements of people. In the latter category, "Washington" was referred to most frequently, but without elaboration or implication of its governmental significance. Typical of this level of recognition is the following:

Um, it's Washington with the big—a thing there, and people are talk—talking. Those people are talking in the street, and people are walking across the street.   (1UG)

Nonrecognition. Almost half (49%) the boys and girls failed to recognize this as a governmental scene either in whole or part. The majority responded with general descriptive statements which greatly outnumbered inappropriate or indefinite reactions. *Inappropriate* or incorrect interpretations were made by 9 per cent of the pupils. All of these were errors at the structural level, the majority of pupils confusing this scene with other public buildings. The White House or "where the President lives" was mentioned most frequently, but a young city girl reported that it was a post office and an older city girl thought it was a museum. Other buildings were the "store," "bank," and a "factory" seen on a certain TV program:

> "...I think I've seen that factory somewhere around here, and um um, no, I guess not around here, but I know I've seen that on um um um, Mr. District Attorney..."   (1UB)

Almost a third of the pupils (31%) responded to this life situation in such a *general* way that they gave no indication of having been aware of its connection with government. In these cases the focus of attention was placed upon people far more often than upon things, and in no instance was Nature the object of attention. Children appeared to be most conscious of people's movements, noting in a general way that they were "walking," or "crossing the street," and to a lesser extent, that these people were "going to work" which in some cases meant "going to the office." Pupils who were not concerned with locomotion, the minority, observed that some people were "talking," that some men were "carrying a briefcase" (or "bookbag"), and that others were engaged in sightseeing. Children who gave all their attention to the things in this scene, concentrated on the building (which impressed them as being "big") about as much as on the fact that this was "downtown" or a "city." A young rural boy, for example, was attentive to both people and things, but failed to realize the governmental significance of this scene.

> There's a great big a, I don't know what you call them, but that's a great big thing. And a peop—men, and a little girl, and a policeman is standing there. And there's a lotta buildings. And they're crossing the street. And a, there's lines on the building, and there's a little um, top on the ... a those windows and oh! there's a bank.
> (1RB)

Almost as many responses were *indefinite* (8%) as were inappropriate. For the most part, these reflected indecision regarding the structural aspects of this situation rather than garbled reactions. As was true of inappropriate responses, a considerable number of children were uncertain as to whether this was a Capitol, the White House, a courthouse or a museum. One young girl recognized this as being "George Washington's thing."

It is clear that a consciousness of government is in process of developing during the elementary school years. Approximately half the pupils were able to recognize this stereotype for government, and those who confused the Capitol with the White House were thinking in essentially similar terms. At the same time, a considerable number of boys and girls had no way of dealing with this scene in terms of its citizenship meanings. Lacking basic concepts about government, they were unable to apprehend "this thing." As alternatives they could reduce the situation to one of urbanization and general sightseeing or, in fewer cases, "take a guess" as to what it was. Even those who did recognize this life situation, were far more conscious of its objective characteristics than the dynamic or abstract. All in all, the evidence indicates that children have very little conception of how government "works," and least of all about democratic processes. The reason for this may be that children are not concerned with the abstraction, "government," but are more interested in the activities of people in government services. As a sixth grade rural boy observed, "Looks like Mr. Smith, the Treasurer, or somebody."

Children's Setting for the Capitol

Children's consciousness of the "where" and "when" for this scene of government followed the common pattern for the series: a greater command of space than of time. Although the Capitol ranked sixth in the number of children who placed it in a spatial setting, it was second in the number of such responses given, indicating that many pupils used two or more types of space dimensions in referring to this scene. In terms of time, however, children had so little to say that this life situation ranked last in the series.

A *spatial setting* was designated for the Capitol more often than not, 70 per cent of the pupils having done so. Of the relatively greater number of specific designations provided by pupils, most were associational in nature rather than defined in more precise terms. As would be expected from the nature of the life situation, there was an overwhelming tendency to relate this scene to an institutional background. The interesting variety of such orientations is indicated in the following excerpts. Included are a number of institutional settings other than Capitol which were regarded as inappropriate for reasons noted in the preceding section.

> The Capitol's in the background, and there's all different sorts of men and women coming to see it . .
>
> It's in front of the President's house . . .
> Well, that's at the White House . . .
> Bobby's father always likes to go to the store, too . . .
> They're coming out from a . . . a . . . the post office . . .
> Visiting . . . a . . . looking at a museum . . .

Although outnumbered by associational referents, the use of geopolitical terms to designate location was greater for this picture than for any other in the series. These responses, moreover, were widely distributed among the various categories—community, state, and nation. In fact, this scene accounted for the majority of responses falling in the latter two areas. Interesting, too, is the Americanization of this symbol of government. Not a single child who identified this government building located it in any other country.

> Mens are walkin' downtown . . .
> She's going to town . . .
> Well, that's a city . . .
> I think these could be lawyers or even doctors coming home from work, from the downtown . . .
> It looks like a nice city . . .
>
> They're in Madison . .
> Some people visiting the Capitol in Madison . . .
> These men are walking near the Capitol of our state . . .
> That's the Capitol of Wisconsin . . .
> That looks like the nation's Capitol . . .
> They are near the Capitol of the United States . . .
> It's in Washington . . .
> That looks like our Capitol in Washington, D.C. . . .

Children definitely failed to see any relationship between government and time, only 5 per cent placing the Capitol in a *temporal setting.* What limited development there was in this connection is indicated in the following responses:

> One morning there was two men and ladies walking by . . .
> Well, there's some men going home from work . . . they go home and eat dinner and supper . . .
> This was in the long, long years ago . . .

Children are also learning that there is such a thing as a "seat" of government which is fixed. Madison, the state capital, and Washington, D.C. figured prominently in this connection but no other was mentioned. Was it the characteristic of the domed capitol that limited their associations? Are they aware that each state has a capital or have other government centers little interest or meaning for them? Although one could hope for greater familiarity with their own state capital on the part of children living only 50 to 100 miles distant, it is encouraging to note that no child misplaced it.

Children's Attitudes toward the Capitol

The Poor House was the only picture which drew forth fewer favorable attitudes than were expressed toward this scene (47%). At the same time, the Capitol was tied with the Church and Bedroom for last place in the series with negative feelings shown toward it (12.5%). Further setting this life situation apart was the greater total of neutral (22%) and mixed (19%) feelings which combined almost equalled the percentage of positive attitudes, and was the highest for the picture series. That children approached this governmental scene with a fair degree of consistency is evident in the fact that 31 per cent were unchanged in their attitudes at various points in the interview, this degree of "set" ranking fifth in the Life-Situation Picture Series.

Sightseeing is what children were most favorably disposed toward. In general, they liked the simple act of just walking, of going "someplace" or "somewhere." They were interested in visiting a big building which they had never seen before.

> She's going somewhere, and she should be happy.   (1UB)
> He's been someplace, and he's had a good time.   (6RG)
> 'Cause I think she likes to go there, and that's 'cause I think she likes to learn, too.   (1UG)

> She's seeing this building that she never saw before.   (6RG)
> She likes to see that big building, and she likes one like that one.
> (1UB)
> She is very happy, because she sees a pretty building with a few
> flowers around it.   (6RG)

With reference to government places and activities, the city, and human relations, there was less agreement. Some children were *attracted* and others *repelled* by what they saw. For a number, the opportunity to see their Capitol was greatly to be desired. It was important; they learned about it in school, and were very curious to see what went on in such a place. Others, however, associated governmental activities with wrong doing and unpleasant happenings, or felt that they would be out of place in such an environment.

Positive	*Negative*
Government	
Because she's going to the Capitol to look around. (6RB)	Maybe something wrong at the Capitol—they had an argument with one of the Senators. (6RB)
She's going to see her Capitol— in school she learned what it was. (6RB)	He's probably gotta go in the courthouse or in some building, 'cause maybe he's got some case that came up, and he has to be there or somethin' to figure out what's wrong. (6RG)
They're going to see the Capitol, an important building. (1RG)	
She's looking at the Capitol, and she's enjoying herself. (6RB)	
Maybe it's their first time; they just went to Washington, D.C. to see the Capitol. (6UB)	If you went to a big office (Capitol) or anything, you wouldn't know what to do. (6UB)
Because she likes to go to Washington. (1UB)	She's probably not too happy, because she has to go in the (Capitol) building with her mother, and her mother'll probably stay there talking. (6UG)
Not very many people get to see Washington or the big buildings. (6UB)	

Going to town was an attractive adventure to those children who saw it as a place for shopping, and for carrying on "important business." Yet, there were those who had more important things to do than to go downtown. A few just didn't like "crossing the street." All these activities seemed to be more enjoyable when shared with some member of the family: mother, father, and even sister—in that order. Mother, at the same time, was the person toward whom more negativism was directed than any other. In the city, too, many instances were noted by children where people didn't seem to "get along" very well.

Positive　　　　　　　　　　*Negative*

The city

She's with her mother and she can go downtown shopping.　(6RG)
It looks like a nice city, and it looks like she wouldn't have nothing to be sad about.　(6UG)
They're all businessmen, and looks like they're going somewhere important.　(6UB)
Because the men are out of work, and they get to go home to their families.　(6UG)

His mother sent him downtown, and he didn't want to go—see, him had to plow.　(1RB)
He doesn't like to go across the street.　(1UB)

Human relations

Her sister took her along. (1RG)
Because he's getting out of something, and his daddy might be waiting for him.　(1UB)
'Cause she likes to go with her mother.　(1UG)
That she can go to town with her mother.　(1RG)
She's able to go with her mother to the Capitol.　(6RB)
Some of the fathers and mothers are taking the children to the Capitol or White House. (6UG)

She's not happy with her momma, 'cause the momma wants to hold her hand.　(1RG)
The mother is pulling her, and she doesn't wanna go there . . . and she gets stubborn.　(1UG)
She doesn't want to help her mother.　(1RB)
Maybe she got a lickin'.　(1RB)
He don't like anybody because, he don't let him do anything. (1RB)
They look angry, 'cause they're walking away, and they don't speak to each other.　(6RG)
Because, maybe, somebody coulda hit him, and the policeman told him not to hit back.　(1UG)
That guy's got his hands out; he wants them to forgive him. (1RB)

The relatively large number of responses which indicated *neutral* feelings applied to all of the categories described above. An older rural girl, for example, justified the inclusion of neutral children in the Capitol scene with the simple statement that, "they're going someplace." Her counterpart in the city did likewise for the reason that, "nothing really exciting is happening." Going someplace and government, in and of themselves, had little emotional appeal to these girls. In much the same vein, children referred to working in the city, and to various relationships with mother, without revealing strong emotional overtones.

Working

They're going to work.	(6RB)
He's just going about his work.	(6RG)
He's not surprised that he has to go to work or something like that.	(6UB)

Human relationships

She's going with her mother.	(6RG)
She's walking along with her mother.	(1RB)
Because she's with her momma.	(1UG)
She minds her mother.	(1RB)

Mixed attitudes were usually the result of changes taking place in feeling tone as children viewed the situation at different times. Again, however, some of the older pupils were aware of the pros and cons which applied to it. A sixth grade rural girl, for example, was conscious of the price one pays for sightseeing when she noted, "She's sorta happy and sorta tired, too, because she's been walking so much." The dilemma in which children may find themselves when visiting strange places was expressed sympathetically by a sixth grade urban boy:

> There isn't too many pleasures just lookin' at a big building. And she'd be a little happy, and I imagine she'd be a little scared with those strange people.

Although some children were aware of the Capitol's importance in connection with government, they did not include democracy. Boys and girls seemed to accept the fact of government including its forms and functions. The word "democracy" seldom appeared, and no one compared our system of government with any other. There was some evidence of their knowledge about our country's past which might, presumably, include concepts about the "struggle for freedom," but it cannot be said that children associated this scene with democratic values. It may be that these attitudes require more time for their development or that children lack the facility to express such feelings. It might also mean that only a small beginning has been made in developing the civic consciousness of young people. They may appreciate democratic values in face to face relationships, such as in the classroom, but have not bridged the gap between this and governmental processes.

Children's Preferences for the Capitol

The Capitol enjoyed little popularity with children. It accounted for 5 per cent of their picture choices and 7 per cent of their rejections. These represent rankings of 10 and 3.5 respectively in the series. Only the Poor House was *both* less valued and more rejected.

The few boys and girls who placed a high value on this picture were influenced by its symbolization of government rather than extraneous factors. Their reasons for wanting a copy of the Capitol were centered on the site of government rather than the governing process itself. They reflected a sightseer's point of view rather than an appreciation of the importance of government for the general welfare, and a desire to learn more about democratic processes in government.

Acceptance	*Rejection*
Government	
I want a picture of the Capitol. (6RG)	'Cause I don't like Washington. (1UB)
I went there once, and I know how it looks. (1UG)	
Because I like the building there. (6UB)	
I think it would be interesting to visit the Capitol, and I don't have a picture of the Capitol. (6UG)	
Human relationships	
Because my father wants a copy of it—'cause he never went there before. (1RB)	It just don't look like they're happy—those men. (6RB)

Children's reactions indicate that they have not as yet identified themselves with government. Recognition of the Capitol generally carried with it a sense of its importance, but this was not translated into correspondingly favorable attitudes and value judgments. Hence, although few pupils spoke in derogatory terms about government, many rejected it as having little import for themselves except in connection with sightseeing. They regarded government as something "good" for grown-ups, but outside the domain of childhood, and voiced their misgivings about going to such offices with parents. As far as boys and girls are concerned, government is of the adults, by the adults, and for the adults.

Group Comparisons

Two of the four groups of children differed in their perception of the Capitol. Most pronounced were those between the first and sixth grade pupils, and of some consequence were variations between rural and urban dwellers. Although politics may be primarily a "man's game," no such affinity was discovered on the part of boys of elementary school age. Neither was intelligence related to the perception of this civic situation. That children do not become particularly involved in government may be gathered from the fact that the majority of differences between groups were matters of ideas rather than emotions.

Age Differences. First and sixth grade pupils differed in their ideas and feelings about the Capitol. The older ones demonstrated their superiority by reacting to the situation as a whole whereas many first graders concentrated upon a portion of the scene. The latter did recognize the Capitol in terms of its structure, but they were far exceeded by sixth graders with regard to the number of pupils showing this awareness and the total number of their responses. This superiority was especially evident in references to the immediate scene or governmental building. Older pupils referred to it more frequently as a capitol, state capitol, or "the United States Capitol." Not one of the younger pupils was aware of the functional aspects of this life situation. Sixth graders, therefore, excelled both numerically as well as in the total number of such responses, especially with reference to governmental processes. In view of this, no first grade child reached the highest level of recognition, synthesizing structure and function, whereas this was achieved by 27 per cent of the older pupils. Unable to grasp its significance, younger children could do no more than describe general features and so out-numbered sixth graders in failing to recognize the scene, and the total number of such general responses, especially those regarding people.

Sixth grade pupils were also far more likely to associate this scene with an institutional background and, on the whole, placed the Capitol in some kind of spatial background more often than was the case with lower grade pupils. The distribution of attitudes for these grade groups was likewise markedly different. Whereas more sixth grade pupils tended to be positive or neutral, more of the younger children tended to be mixed or decidedly negative in their feelings toward this scene of government.

The above represents one of the sharpest contrasts in the picture series, and is convincing testimony of the growth taking place in children's perception of civic values and activities during the elementary school years. Boys and girls enter school with little conception of government, only one-fourth managing to achieve a partial or structural recognition of this scene. By the time they are in sixth grade, the proportion of recognition has about trebled. The fact that only a little more than one-fourth of the older pupils have a grasp of governmental *processes,* however, indicates how much more need there is for continuing in this development. Ideas and attitudes about government are slow to appear and to mature.

Rural—Urban Differences. Children living on farms and in the city differed in some of their ideas about the Capitol, but not in their attitudes or value judgments. Discrepancies occurred in their recognition and spatial perception of this scene. Rural children were much more conscious of structural aspects although at the highest level of interpretation, which also included functional awareness, the groups did not differ appreciably. In referring to the Capitol, however, more rural boys and girls than urban were contented to identify it in a general way rather than label it specifically as the state or national capitol. At the other end of the scale was a greater number of urban children whose perceptions were inappropriate or indefinite. The greater proportion of nonrecognition responses was caused by confusing this scene with the White House, post office or museum, possibilities which were not voiced by rural children.

In designating a spatial setting for this situation, rural and urban pupils varied in their use of geopolitical referents. The former tended to place the Capitol in their own state, Wisconsin, or in Madison, the capital. Not a single urban child revealed such local orientation. All those who indicated a specific placement for the Capitol located it in Washington or regarded it as the United States Capitol.

It appears that rural children are more locally oriented than urban. The dome of the capitol building for Wisconsin is similar to that in Washington, and this clue was all that farm children needed to "see" their state capitol in Madison. It is probable that rural people have so many direct and personal contacts with representatives of state agencies that the state, including its government, is a focal point in their lives. There is a suggestion, too, of a differential in the experiences of farm and city children. The latter mentioned institutions other than the capitol in identifying (incorrectly) this scene. Few rural children regarded this as anything other than the Capitol. They did not confuse it with the post office or museum for the reason that their contacts with such buildings would probably be more limited.

THE SCHOOLROOM

Learning a Lot of Things They Didn't Know Before

Here is a schoolroom with probably the second grade class. It has a blackboard with arithmetic problems, a map, telephone, and a sign that shows the United Nations. There are lots of children in chairs around a table, and the teacher is sitting in the background watching. The pupils are learning a lot of things, and doing like their teacher told them. Now, they are showing their pictures to the class. The others are watching, and listening to what they say. These children are of different nationalities but they don't have to argue. They are working together and sharing everything—it shows democracy. This is a nice picture for Brotherhood Week.

THE Schoolroom was included in the Child-Adult Block to elicit ideas about education and human relations experienced by children in school. In terms of the latter, it was paired with the Dock which was considered to represent more adult relationships. On no picture were children as much divided. High as it was rated in preference by some pupils, this scene ranked even higher in its rejection by others. Positive attitudes, moreover, were in the low-average range for the series while negative feelings ranked in the high-average zone. The "sides" taken by children toward this life situation were not the result of uncertainty or confusion as to its nature. The Schoolroom was one of the few pictures which ranked high both from the standpoint of the ideas it stimulated and their appropriateness. There certainly was no question regarding children's recognition of the spatial backdrop for this scene, but very little thought was given to time. Children were in agreement, however, that this life situation was most suited to girls. These reactions were not the products of prolonged deliberation and much wordiness. Most children knew what they wished to say, and said it quickly with a minimum of words.

Children's Recognition of the Schoolroom

This was certainly a familiar scene to children. In spite of the fact that a deliberate attempt had been made to avoid picturing conventional classroom seating arrangements and a teacher-led class activity, 94 per cent of the children recognized this as a school situation (Rank = 4). Not only was the likelihood great that this scene would be recognized, but the chances were that children would respond to it as a whole rather than to only its parts. Regarding the former, there was equal certainty that children would recognize the Schoolroom from the standpoint of its structure and function rather than either one alone. In recognition, therefore, children's perception of the Schoolroom was of a very high order.

Attention was given to the *structural* aspects of this life situation by 83 per cent of the boys and girls. Unlike the majority of pictures, children were more inclined to view this scene in its extended dimensions, the school, than to limit their observations to the immediate representation of a schoolroom. Those who concentrated upon the latter, applied four concepts to the situation. They referred to the more inclusive ideas of "class" or "grade" not much more often than to the strictly physical "schoolroom" or "classroom." Such choice, however, did not seem to present itself to those who were going beyond the limits of one room to encompass the larger institutional structure. Except for a few scattered responses such as "Sunday school," "library," and "catechism," the only designation used to any great extent was "school." This very definite mind set is illustrated in the remarks of the following children who simply voiced their recognition of the School but went no further in describing what goes on in such an educational institution:

> They're in school.   (1RG)
> This tells about school, and Sunday school.   (1RG)
> It...it's a school. There's a boy with a...a nigger boy, and there's some girls, and there's a kid standing up, and there's a girl over there sittin', there's a telephone, telephone behind her, and there's some chairs, and there's some paper on the table, and there's another one, and that's all. And there's a table.   (1RB)

Almost as many children (78%) responded to the *functional* aspects of this life situation as to its structure. By far the greater number of pupils were sensitive to the teaching-learning processes being depicted than to the human relations being worked out in the situation. Of the great variety of processes identified by children, almost five times as many were centered on what pupils were doing as compared to the teacher's activities. The latter was described as "telling them what to do," "watching and listening to the children," "the teacher gives them work to do," or simply, "teaching." In noting what children were doing, there was a very real preference for stating specific activities rather than using general terms having an educational significance. It is not surprising that most of the efforts were concentrated on the girl holding the picture. Pupils were conscious of the drawing and painting aspect of this activity as well as the showing and telling. Markedly fewer were children's consciousness of other school activities such as arithmetic, reading, writing, storytelling, and for one first grade rural girl "seatwork." In contrast with such specificity were the few children who recognized "learning," "working," and in a few instances, "studying" as the processes underway in this scene. Illustrating this type of sensitivity to function are the remarks of a first grade rural girl who was engrossed in drawing and the teacher's role, but did not mention the school as the site for these activities—or else assumed this could be taken for granted.

> (Part I—What story does this picture tell?)
> A . . . they were drawing lots and lots of pictures, and that one little girl went and drew one, and she wouldn't leave them see it —that was a surprise—'cause she drew on the other side and showed it, and then, and then she showed the other one. And then she went back, and wrote somethin' on the board, and the teacher was watching 'em all the while. And then she drew another pic—two more pictures and then showed 'em, and and then they all drew pictures and showed 'em. And I see a telephone there, too.

> (Part II—Which boy or girl belongs in this picture?)
> The happy boy and girl.
> (Why?)
> 'Cause they're happy about what they're doing to help all the other people—they're teaching 'em to draw real good.

Although far fewer in number, children who were sensitive to the human relations aspect of this life situation exhibited some of the same tendencies as those who concentrated upon the teaching-learning functions. They identified themselves with the children rather than with the teacher, and were more concerned about peer relationships than with those existing between pupil and teacher. The latter were limited to expressions indicating a pupil's liking for his teacher or objecting to her being "too strict." A more involved interaction was sensed by an older rural girl who explained, "The teacher's mad because they don't learn their . . . the stuff they're supposed to learn; they're mad because she's scolding them." In talking about peer relationships, children gave about as much attention to interaction in general as to relationships among people who were "different." The former included a sensitivity to "sharing" and working together, being liked by classmates, and a general spirit of friendliness pervading the classroom. On the other hand, a young urban girl pointed out someone who "hits everybody," and a sixth grade rural boy indicated his fear of being ridiculed by the class when it came to drawing pictures. A first grade rural girl, however, was happy that "they let him play games with him."

As for differences recognized by children, race and nationality were mentioned, but not wealth or social position. Concepts used to express these differences were about equally divided among those based on race, nationality, and the idea of "differences." These are listed below for each of the groups in descending order of frequency:

Negro	Chinese	different races and color
colored	Japanese	different nationalities and countries
nigger	Italian	different creeds and religion
brown boy	German	foreign
		mixed group

Pupils representing these differences were invariably seen as sharing and working together under conditions of equality. The few abstractions regarding this type of human relationships were limited to democracy ("it shows all of democracy, of all the ways to live"), "Brotherhood Week," and the U. N. Without mentioning the school as an institution, a sixth grade urban boy revealed his sensitivity to both the teaching-learning and human relationship processes being depicted in this life situation as follows:

(Part I—What story does this picture tell?)

That looks like a . . . like . . . a well . . . it looks like the children, they look like they are sort of talking over Brotherhood Week, because there is all different races and creed there, and they have all different colors. And in the back there's a U.N. symbol, and it has U.N. on it, and it has all different children on there. And the teacher is in the back, and it looks like that teacher is listening to the conversation. And that one little girl next to that colored boy, looks like she's Chinese, and she's holding up some kind of a picture that she has drawn.

(Part II—Which boy or girl belongs in this picture?)

Mad boy.

(Why?)

Because he's just sittin' there, and his face is turned down, and he's looking real sharp at that girl.

As would be anticipated from the foregoing, the proportion of children who reached the highest level of recognition, *synthesizing* both structure and function, was achieved by 76 per cent of the pupils, this proportion being one of the highest for any of the pictures. The range of such responses is indicated by the remarks of a young rural girl who recognized that this was a class in school engaged in reading, and by an older city girl, who in connection with schoolroom activities, was conscious of or was justifying "a mixed group" by appealing to certain altruistic principles.

There's a teacher at school, and they're, they're having class, and they read their ta- ta- readers, and they are Americans. Then their teacher gives them work. And the little boy that's standing up, he does not have a chair, and he stands up part of the time. And a they all read, and he has to look on with somebody, and then the teacher gave him a chair and a book. (1RG)

That looks like a schoolroom with a . . . that are a, a younger group, that are coloring around the table like we were. And they are from all different races and creeds. And that shows that it's really not bad to be in with a mixed group at all; that there's nothing wrong about it. And that there's other things that white children can teach other children to give them an opportunity to have the freedom of America. (6UG)

It appears that once having identified clues, most children proceeded to synthesize in terms of the whole situation. Only 9 per cent failed to go on, and thus remained at the level of *partial* recognition. These pupils were more attentive to what people were doing than to the things depicted in the life situation. As was true of functional responses, activities involved in showing or telling about a picture were noticed most frequently, but in none of these cases was it implied that the activity was taking place in a school or for an educational purpose. A few children noticed the teacher sitting in a corner or telling a story, but again, the school or educational implications were lacking. The same could be said for such remarks as: "they're doing their arithmetic," and "they're having reading." The following is an example of a young rural boy who reacted to several significant clues, but did not state explicitly their school nature or educational purpose.

> There's there's children, and a telephone, and a picture up on the blackboard, up on the wall. And um, the—there's lots lots of children in chairs, and a the teacher is telling them a story. And there's one boy standing up, and one girl's got her pictures, and the other boy has got their pictures. And um, there's a, there's a pe—and there's a some cardboard up there with somethin' on it.
>
> (1RB)

Nonrecognition. Few pupils (6%) failed to achieve some kind of recognition of the Schoolroom scene. Failure to do so took on a number of different forms. A young rural boy said, inappropriately, "They're eating their supper." So convinced was he of this interpretation that on second contact with this life situation, he introduced the sad boy into the picture because, "He eats, but he don't wanna eat." A member of the same group of pupils merely listed a miscellany including "some boys, and some girls, and a table, and a floor, and a picture, and a wall." Also, there were general statements to the effect that children were "sitting on chairs," "working," and in one instance mention was made of someone who "can't do as good as the others." In short, failure to recognize this school situation was limited but varied.

We would expect school children to be on familiar terms with a school situation, and this anticipation was borne out in a number of ways. Their consciousness of this scene encompassed the school as a whole, they were as much aware of educational functions as they were of external appearances, and they described the former in specific rather than general terms. Yet, these children were largely dealing with surface manifestations rather than with the subtleties involved. They described what was going on, but gave little indication of a sensitivity to the purposes behind such activities, to the informality as portrayed, or to the prominent role being played by pupils. These are all related to the teacher's "methods." Children are either unconcerned about this phase of school work— taking for granted that this lies in the teacher's province—or they don't understand it. This raises an important question: how much should children know about the purposes and procedures involved in their learning experiences?

That elementary children may perceive the more obvious differences among people was shown in their greater awareness of race and nationality as compared with wealth and social position. To be sure, the former are generally more easily detected in a classroom situation than social status differentials. Hence, we cannot be certain that such differences have less import for children than race or nationality.

One cannot help but notice the great emphasis children placed on the children in this situation. Compared with teacher-oriented observations, they were much more aware of pupil activities and peer relationships. Quite understandably, children were better able to identify with the pupils in this scene than with the teacher. They could project when it came to the thoughts and feelings of the learners, but the teacher was viewed principally as the authority assigning and supervising school work, and only seldom as a guide or helper having thoughts and feelings of her own. This concentration upon children would seem to imply that pupil-pupil relationships are at least as crucial to the learner as the more traditionally emphasized relationships between teacher and pupils.

Children's Setting for the Schoolroom

Boys and girls had a definite notion as to the location of this educational situation, but gave very little thought to its orientation in time. This greater awareness of spatial setting as compared with temporal is evidenced in the rankings of the Schoolroom in the series, the figures being 2 and 11.5 respectively. No picture was significantly higher in its capacity to elicit designations of space; neither was any markedly lower with respect to time.

The very real inclination to offer a *spatial* dimension for this life situation was exhibited by 83 per cent of the pupils. The great majority of responses were associational in character, and in every case revolved around the school as an institutional setting. As the following excerpts indicate, there was little doubt in most children's minds as to where events were taking place:

> They're at school . .
> Well, there the children are in school, and they're in class . . .
> It shows a schoolroom . . .
> This is in a classroom . . .
> This looks like (Name) School . . .

Except for a few children who thought they recognized certain atypical elements in this educational situation, the Schoolroom was seldom located with any degree of preciseness. There seemed to be nothing in this scene which prompted boys and girls to think of their own state or a particular region of the United States. The few exceptions were mainly on the part of those who were rejecting this scene by denying its existence in this country. Expressions having a geographic or political basis such as the following appeared only infrequently:

> That looks like a schoolroom . . . to give them an opportunity to have the freedom of America . . .
>
> That looks like a foreign school . . .
> Looks like children in another land . . .

The children who viewed the Schoolroom in terms of *time,* only 8 per cent of the total, offer convincing evidence that a school scene such as this has no temporal significance as far as young people are concerned. Not only did most pupils fail to provide such a setting, but those who mentioned time did so with reference to their own activities instead of the situation pictured, and thereby were scored as being mixed or indefinite in their consciousness of time. Some notion of the use of personal associations, and the calendar as a more precise instrument, as well as mixed kinds of responses is indicated by the following:

> They had learned very much that day they went to school . . .

> This tells about school and Sunday school . . .
> They are sort of talking over Brotherhood Week . . .
>
> They're at school making pictures, just like we did today . . .
> These, I think, are little children doing what we just did . . .

Children's perception of a suitable field for this scene did not reach the high level of their recognition. Although most pupils placed it in a school setting, they did not attempt to define its spatial outlines more specifically and almost ignored its time dimensions. Is school so much a part of the child's world that for him it is a kind of universal: the school exists everywhere and is timeless? Has he developed a stereotype for the classroom which leaves no room for rural-urban, sectional, and even national differentiations? In such case, school would be school, and pupils would not be impelled to draw more exact boundaries for the background in which this scene would be most meaningful. Neither would the mixed group of classmates pictured in the Schoolroom offer any particular clue regarding time or place.

Children's Attitudes toward the Schoolroom

Few children (9%) were unmoved by this life situation. Although positive feelings (49%) constituted the largest single category, they ranked only 9th in the series. It is significant to note that the number of children showing an aversion to the Schoolroom in the form of negative (20% or rank of 5.5) and mixed attitudes (22%), was almost as large. In fact, the Poor House was the only scene which elicited a markedly greater number of negative responses. Furthermore, only 17 per cent of the group maintained the same attitude toward the Schoolroom throughout the interview. This was the lowest for any of the Life-Situation Pictures and is another indication of the mixed feelings or conflicting emotions which children had about school.

In spite of the relatively high degree of negativism and inconsistency of reactions to the Schoolroom, only favorable attitudes were expressed toward learning itself. There was no question but that it was "good!" One should appreciate having an opportunity to learn, learning new things is important and can be fun; in fact, one should like to learn.

> They should—they should like to learn their education.   (6RB)

They can be glad that they've got enough money for, their parents that they can send them to school.   (6RG)

They're happy about doin', to help all the other people. They're teaching 'em to draw real good.   (1RG)

Because they're at school. It looks like a low—a pretty low grade, and they're learning a lotta things they didn't know before, and having fun.   (6RB)

Opinions were divided about other aspects of the educational scene such as the school, classroom activities, school achievement, and relationships with both teacher and children. There were some who reacted to school in a general way indicating that they liked it or that it was fun to go. In contrast, others expressed a dislike for school which they felt made them "like most kids." Others were more specific finding fault with the building, the teacher, and overcrowding. Attitudes toward classroom activities were centered primarily on art which was looked upon as an enjoyable experience by most pupils although by no means by all. The importance of success in school was brought out in positive ways by some children, but more especially in remarks reflecting the lack of success or achievement. These applied not only to artistic endeavor but to achievement in general, and involved evaluations made privately by the learner as well as those by the class and teacher. The effect of failure upon the learner, the teacher, and the class as a whole was vividly depicted by a number of children.

Positive	*Negative*
School (In general)	

Positive	Negative
She likes school. (1RG)	She doesn't want to go to school.
He likes to go to school. (1UG)	She don't like her school. (1RB)
They can have fun at school, and do art and everything and draw. I think it's kinda fun. (6UB)	She probably doesn't like school, like most kids. (6RB)
	Because it doesn't look like a good school. The school doesn't look too big, and there's a lot of children in the class. (6UB)
	They didn't like school too well. The teacher was kinda strict. They didn't like the school—it was so poorly built. (6RB)

Classroom activities

He likes it at school, and he likes to color pitchers, and he likes to look at them.   (1UB)
Because they're having lotsa fun drawing, and the girl is showing pictures.   (6RB)
She's showing the pitcher to the classmates. It makes her feel happy that she's got somethin' to show them.   (6RB)
Because every, everybody's happy here, even the teacher, because they got um, work to do, work they like to do.   (1UG)

(Angry girl) Because she's doing this. (Drawing and showing her picture)   (1UB)
Most kids—sometimes they don't like showing pitchers and that.   (6UB)

School achievement

She draws good pictures. (1UB)
They're showing pictures, and some of them are happy of their pictures.   (1RB)
They're happy—they can read, and write, and draw.   (6RG)

Because she has to show her picture, and I think she doesn't like it.   (6UG)
He can't do as good as the others.   (1UB)
'Cause the girl right there don't, well, she don't look like she's quite —knows what she's doing. (6RB)
He looks like he's trying to answer the question, and he don't know the answer, and he might get a little mad.   (6RG)
Because it looks like the teacher's mad, because they don't learn the stuff they're suppose to learn. They're mad because she's scolding them.   (6RG)

Human relations in the classroom were given great emphasis by children. The significance of being chosen by the teacher and other rewards which can be bestowed on pupils for being "good" were balanced against the factor of disobedience and the punishment which could be meted out. One child, apparently, regarded school relationships as a haven compared to what must have been more severe disciplinary measures used at home. Relationships with peers were equally, if not more important to children, than those with the teacher. The importance of being with others, of being allowed to play with them, and sharing their experiences were highly regarded by pupils. Some were even appreciative of the differences in race and nationality among children in a classroom, and the significance of "Brotherhood Week." Yet, there was recognition that all children might not be friends, and that some would tolerate but not particularly welcome the presence of certain minority groups in the classroom.

Positive	*Negative*

Human relations (*Teacher*)

Because the teacher has chosen her to show her picture, and she will talk about it, and I think all the other children will like her. (6RG)	'Cause he doesn't wanna do what his teacher says. (1RG)
A, she's, she was good and she could draw a picture 'cause she wanted to. (1UG)	Maybe she has to sit in the dunce's chair, because she hits everybody. (1UG)
'Cause she likes to go to school, 'cause she doesn't get a bawling out from her mother and father. (1RG)	

Human relations (*Children*)

She likes everybody, and she's happy—she's having fun. (1RB)	He's just sitting there, and he's looking real sharp at that girl. (6UB)
Because they let him play games with them. (1RG)	Well, maybe she doesn't like to go to school with colored children. (6RG)
Because it looks like all the children are happy, because they're at school with other children. (6UG)	
They're all together, and playing, and in school. They are sharing all their papers and stuff. (6RG)	
They're doing their work together, and you can see that they are different nationalities. (6UG)	
It's a nice picture for Brotherhood Week. (6UB)	

Children were *neutral,* speaking with little or no feeling, about only one of the above factors. Although they could not be dispassionate about attending school, school achievement, or school relationships, pupils did regard certain classroom experiences as being "nothing to be happy about or nothing to be sad about either." In and of themselves, without any knowledge of their content or purpose, some children were indifferent to such activities as writing, looking at pictures, listening to stories, or doing school work in general.

They're just doing their work.	(6RB)
'Cause he has to write.	(1RG)
She's got that picture, and they're all trying to look at it.	(1UB)
She's listening to the girl.	(6RG)
She's just telling a story to some kids.	(6RG)

Of the relatively large number of *mixed* reactions to the Schoolroom, the majority were caused by shifts in the attention given to various aspects of the life situation. A young rural boy, for example, when first viewing this scene was favorably impressed by the boy who "likes to learn," but his second contact was concentrated on a girl who wasn't doing what she was supposed to. Some pupils were able to see favorable as well as less desirable aspects, and thus exhibited both positive and negative feelings. In some cases, furthermore, as children became more involved they changed from an outward show of neutrality and acceptance to one of negativism.

Mixed attitudes were expressed in connection with each of the major areas analyzed above. Regarding school attendance, an older city girl stated, "I think girls like to go to school better than boys." As for classroom activities, a sixth grade urban boy recognized that, "kids aren't too happy to go to school, and yet there is some pleasures like art and other things like that they're having in session now." Differences that can arise in the evaluation of school work were recognized by a young urban girl who remarked, "'Cause I think she likes her picture, and the other children don't." A rather interesting illustration is that of an older urban girl who was highly verbal on the subject of human relationships and yet was, apparently, finding it difficult to accept certain ideals:

(Part I—What story does this picture tell?)

This looks like a, ____(Name)____ School, because in __(Name)__ School there are different children of all different races and they get along well together. And a ... you can see in the background the U.N., and it a ... that means that everybody is united no matter which color or religion they are. And a pe- children, there's a Japanese girl or a Chinese girl; she is showing a picture that maybe she drew. And then there's a colored boy, and maybe there's Italian and German, and different people. And the teacher's sitting there, and she's listening. And on the board you can see arithmetic problems, and they have a phone in there, and um, may-maybe some of the other children are going to show their pictures that they drew.

(Part II—Which boy or girl belongs in this picture?)

The in-between boy and girl.

(Why?)

'Cause it's um, nice to um, be united with all the children from different countries, and um, maybe, sometimes you get ... you aren't happy but you do feel nice.

(Part III—Which picture wouldn't you like to keep for your very own?)

(Points to Schoolroom)

(Why?)

Well, a there isn't anything happy about it, and there isn't anything sad, and it doesn't look like anybody isn't really doing anything.

It appears that children are not as fond of school as adults would like them to be. The fault does not lie in their disregard for learning as such. Rather, it seems to be based on the kinds of things pupils do in school, the way they get along with others, and the evaluation made of their efforts. If we may judge from their comments, many children do not find school activities very interesting. Compared with a steadily increasing diet of movies, television, travel experiences, school is "work" and not very stimulating at that. Their activities include people, and here the child has the dual task of relating himself to his classmates as well as to his teacher. That this is not always an easy task is reflected in the number of children who do not feel "safe" in their group, who seem to miss the warmth and support of the people surrounding them. This factor, and others, are probably reflected in feelings about evaluation. For whether it is done by the teacher, the group, or by the individual himself, there is a great need to achieve at something, to be "as good as the others."

That elementary school children exhibit little prejudice is also quite apparent. Only one-fourth expressed any notion of "differences," and the few which might be considered biased were limited to the use of "nigger" by some of the younger children—which may reflect a limitation in vocabulary as much as prejudice —and a few reservations by older pupils about the presence of mixed races in the Schoolroom. Elementary children are either exceedingly clever at concealing their true feelings, and remarkably consistent in doing so under the varying conditions of this interview, or else they have not developed strong attitudes against people who are different in race or color. For six-year-old children, at least, the former hardly seems likely.

Children's Preferences for the Schoolroom

The Schoolroom was valued about as much as it was rejected. It appeared among the three selections made by 32 per cent of the pupils, accounting for 11 per cent of their choices. Two pictures, the Farm and the Bedroom, outranked the Schoolroom in popularity, but the difference was negligible. In terms of rejection, this scene accounted for 12.5 per cent of the choices only the Poor House being less preferred. For almost half the children, therefore, the Schoolroom was something about which they felt rather intensely, and at both extremes of the scale.

The values which prompted children to make their decisions encompass the school in general, and certain classroom activities as well as a broad range of human relationships. For many children, school had become a matter of "I like" or "I don't like." Art, too, was a subject which represented different values. Rarely, however, did a child justify his picture selection in terms of the importance of learning for meeting immediate or future needs, and never was his opinion based upon whether or not this scene suggested success or failure in school. Human relationships which seemed most important for children were those involving their classmates although broader relationships with the world outside the classroom were also mentioned. No one mentioned excellent teacher relationships as a reason for desiring this picture, but extreme disciplinary measures were cited as a cause for its rejection.

Acceptance	*Rejection*

School (*In general*)

Acceptance	*Rejection*
Because I go to school. (6RG)	'Cause I don't like to go to school. (6UB)
Because I like school. (1RG)	'Cause it's school. (6RB)
Everybody looks happy 'cause they like to go to school. (1RG)	Well, I don't especially care for the a school, and things like that.
Well, I like to, I like school. I learn so many things from it—I learn right from wrong. (6UG)	There's nothin' else special about it. (6UB)

Classroom activities

Acceptance	*Rejection*
Well, it's because I like to do that in school, too. (1UB)	Well, it doesn't have such exciting things. It just shows some of the boys and girls showing pictures. (6RB)
They're drawing pictures. (1RB)	
Because they're coloring, and they might be cutting and coloring. (1UB)	There isn't anything happy about it, and there isn't anything sad, and it doesn't look like anybody isn't really doing anything. (6UG)

Human relationships

Acceptance	*Rejection*
I think it shows friendliness. (6UG)	'Cause somebody could sit in the dunce chair. (1UG)
It's got so many children. (1UG)	
Because I think all the kids in my room I like, and I just hope they like me except, even though they are different nationalities. (6UG)	
It's a nice picture for Brotherhood Week. It looks like a picture of some children sitting down and discussing Brotherhood Week and the United Nations. (6UB)	
'Cause I think it's a democracy. (6UB)	

It seems that children generalize about the values of school at an early age, and that a considerable number take an extreme position "for" or "against" it. Most influential in shaping a child's judgment are the things he does in school, and how he gets along with other boys and girls. He values learning experiences on the basis of whether they are exciting or interesting rather than whether they prepare him for future "needs." There can be no question about his great concern for being liked by his classmates and having friends. It may be that the child takes for granted the kinds of relationships he will have with his teacher. He is less sure about himself in relation to the others in the class.

Group Comparisons

There was some variation in the responses of different groups of children to the Schoolroom. The greatest contrast was provided by age groups. Community background and sex were associated with minor differences, but none were discovered in relation to intelligence. With one exception, in connection with children's preferences, discrepancies between groups of children were matters of recognition. An awareness of the school setting for this scene, a lack of consciousness of its temporal orientation, and the great variety of attitudes expressed toward this life situation were demonstrated to about the same degree by all groups of children.

Age Differences. As was the case for all differences in recognition of the Schoolroom, those between first and sixth grade pupils were matters of kind or emphasis rather than the number of pupils involved. None of the recognition levels was characterized by a preponderance of either young or older pupils. Older pupils, however, were more responsive to the immediate scene (structure) to which they applied a greater number of concepts such as "class," "grade," "schoolroom," and "classroom." A greater divergence appeared between grade groups in their sensitivity to the functions being portrayed. The total number identified by older pupils exceeded that of younger pupils, and this was especially noticeable in the area of human relationships. Sixth grade children were far more conscious of the interaction of mixed groups, and the over-all problem of peer relationships in the classroom. They also identified more specific learning activities involving art, reading, writing, and arithmetic as well as referring more generally to "learning," "working," and "studying."

In contrast with the superiority of older pupils in recognizing this scene was the marked preference given it by younger children.

No other picture outranked the Schoolroom in the estimation of first grade children. Older pupils were far less attracted to it, and ranked it eighth or of average value.

A general notion about school seems to be acquired early in life, and for first graders the institution has undoubtedly a high place in their scale of values. As children grow older, they develop more extensive and refined concepts which enable them to discriminate in their perception of the objective features of school and, particularly, of educational processes. This development is marked by a greater sensitivity to the social aspects of school life, and by a devaluation of the worth of the institution as a whole.

Why does the school lose out in the value system of many sixth grade pupils? The answer may lie in the changes which accompany adolescence. Vacillating between child and adult roles, there is both a resistance to symbols of authority as represented in the school, and a negation of childish things associated with "grade" schools. Furthermore, their quest for new experiences and expanding interests may come in direct competition with school concerns which have lost much of their novelty by this time. This lessening of enthusiasm for school may also be an outcome of the kinds of experiences the child has had in school some of which, apparently, have not kept the original flame burning as brightly as before.

Community Differences. In no instance did the number of rural children differ markedly from urban with respect to the kinds of recognitions made of the Schoolroom. In their awareness of the teaching-learning functions being carried out, however, urban children had a tendency to concentrate on art activities involving the creation and sharing of pictures whereas rural children emphasized other activities such as arithmetic, reading, writing, storytelling, and even "seatwork." The attention given to different types of school activities may be a reflection of the emphases placed upon creative and academic learning experiences. It may be that in covering all the classes for all the grades there is less time for "art" in the weekly program of rural schools than is the case in urban systems having special teachers and facilities to promote an active interest in creative experiences.

Sex Differences. Although the number of girls and boys who perceived the functional aspect of this life situation was not significantly different, girls were more aware of human relationships in the classroom. Their sensitivity to the interaction of people was especially noted with regard to children of different color, nationality, and creed. The result was that the total number of peer relationships mentioned by girls was far greater than for boys. Both groups, however, were equally tolerant of such differences. This is another indication of the greater concern that girls have for the human element in life situations than is the case for boys. From this standpoint, at least, it bears testimony of the more rapid socialization of girls during the elementary school period.

THE DOCK

Getting Ready to Go Across the Ocean

At the dock of a seaport on the ocean, a ship is ready to go to sea. It might be the Queen Elizabeth! Another ship has come ashore and crowds of people are waiting for it. They are loading and unloading all kinds of cargo and luggage. There are thousands and thousands of people, some coming and some going, some meeting their relatives and friends, and some saying good-bye. The captain, stewardess, sailors, and passengers from the ship are standing around. Soldiers are coming from war, and newcomers in native costume have come from other countries. There are people that have to go overseas and all over the country for their jobs and pleasure.

THIS scene was designed to stimulate ideas about transportation and human relations. In the latter capacity, it was regarded as being more adult in character than its matching picture, the Schoolroom, because of increased possibilities for broadening human relationships to encompass world-wide dimensions. The Dock was not the most meaningful situation for children; neither did they dismiss it lightly. Boys and girls spent more than an average amount of time in responding to it, and on only one other picture (Mansion) were they more vocal. Their efforts, as far as interpretation was concerned, were in the average range for the series, the number of pupils achieving some form of recognition ranking higher than the number of meanings produced. This lack of ideas was most noticeable with respect to its background, for the Dock was close to last in the number of spatial and temporal settings in which it was placed. Feelings about it were not entirely consistent. The picture was the object of an average amount of favorable opinion, and was selected as one of three favorites an average number of times. It was exceeded, however, by only one (Poor House) in the number of negative attitudes which it aroused, but was seldom rejected out-right. The Dock, interestingly enough, was regarded as a fitting life-space for both boys and girls.

Children's Recognition of the Dock

The Dock ranked sixth in ease of recognition, 89 per cent of the children managing to see something appropriate in it. For the most part, recognition was based on a reaction to the picture in its entirety rather than consideration of one or more of its parts. Children seemed to be far more conscious of what was going on in this scene than of its physical characteristics; comparatively few grasped the significance of this situation in both structural and functional terms.

Not quite one-fourth of the children (23%) were conscious of the *structure* of this life situation. Such recognition was focused more upon the immediate environment (Dock) than upon an extension into more inclusive areas such as harbor or port. "Dock" was by far the most common concept brought to the immediate scene. So firmly was this stereotype fixed in the minds of children that only occasionally was another term used ("shipyard," "wharves," "boat station"). The few responses indicating that children were thinking in broader terms were based on such concepts as "harbor" and "seaport." Differences in awareness of structure are illustrated by a young city boy who recognized the harbor and then proceeded to enumerate all the things he saw there, and by an older rural boy who recognized people at a dock but did not indicate the significance of all this in terms of social processes.

> In the harbor, I see a airplane, a bo- is that a boat? A big thing way on this side, something real big, well, I'll call it a boat, a boat, people . . . boxes—are th- are those boxes food? Food, boat, airplane . . . a crowd, and more boxes of food, and that's all— and suitcases. (1UB)
>
> Some people standing on the dock waiting for the—waiting for some other people to get on the boat or get off. (6RB)

The *functions* being portrayed in this life situation were apparent to the majority of children (57%). Rather than being associated with a "dock," these processes were tied more directly to the vessels involved. Hence, sensitivity to the life activities underway was not likely to be linked with a consciousness of the over-all physical environment in which they were taking place. The movement implied by this scene was also more indicative of transportation activities in general than of their possible implications for world relationships.

For children, transportation was more a matter of people than of goods. The most common idea applied to the former was that of people taking a trip which, combined with the general notion of "travel," accounted for the majority of responses as compared with simply "leaving," "arriving," and "going some place." Goods being transported were described about equally as "cargo," "boxes," and a miscellaneous list including "things being loaded" as well as "baggage, food, and clothes." A young urban boy, apparently impressed by the magnitude of what he saw in this situation, demonstrated a rudimentary sense of the transportation of both people and goods as he proceeded with his identification of certain well-known ships.

> Well, it looks like they're going on that big boat. Mm, maybe that one there, I think is the Queen Elizabeth—one of them is—I think that one's the Queen Mary and that's the Queen Elizabeth. And there's some airplanes up in the air. And there's thousands, and thousands, and thousands, and thousands, and thousands of people there. And um, but, and they're all gettin' on the ship, and there's some boxes there that they're gonna carry.   (1UB)

Children were not unmindful that transportation made possible the interaction of people from different lands. They regarded this as a two-way process with people of this country going "across the ocean" and vice versa. World intercourse, for them, included such peacetime activities as travel, commerce, and immigration as well as wartime activities involving the embarkation or return of "the Navy," "Air Force," or simply "servicemen." None of these ideas about world relationships was more crystallized in the minds of children than another. Their variety is suggested by the following:

> Aeroplanes in the sky, and boats are sailing across the sea, and men are going on, get—getting on that ship.   (1RB)
> That tells about some people gettin' off a vessel from Europe.
>   (6RB)

There are people that have to go overseas and all over the country
for their jobs and for pleasure.   (6UG)
Some people are from other countries, and they want to become like
a—citizens of the United States . . .   (6UB)

Well, a they're . . . they're gettin' just home from Korea . . . They're
coming home from the war.   (6RB)
It looks like Navy or a Air Force men going on the—overseas.
                                                                    (6UB)

Relatively few interpretations of this scene (17%) were based
on a *synthesis* of both its structure and function. Unlike the majority of pictures, it was the lack of attention to the physical aspects
of this situation rather than to functions being performed which set
the limits. An illustration of a high level reaction is that of an older
urban girl who, in addition to recognizing the dock, was also aware
of its far-flung influences bearing on people from other lands including the factor of war.

(Part I—What story does this picture tell?)
    Well, this looks like a dock, and there's a big ship back there,
    and maybe that's the Queen Mary. And then they have planes
    going across. And they have a . . . a—it's another ship that's just
    getting home, and people are coming off of it. And it shows um,
    people are meeting each other, and maybe it's people they haven't
    seen for a long time. And then there's, and then there are a,
    there's a Army man back—there's a person who's in the Army,
    and he met his, maybe his brother or something. And then he—
    it shows a . . . a two men in native costumes, and I think they're
    from China, and they're getting off. And maybe that's in the
    United States.

(Part II—Which boy or girl belongs in this picture?)
    The happy boy.
(Why?)
    Because um, it shows Army people in there, Army men, and a,
    maybe she's happy to see her brother or father come home.

A *partial* grasp of the significance of this life situation was
exhibited by 22 per cent of the pupils. Responses of this kind were
centered on people more often than upon the objects portrayed in
the scene, and in no instance were they focused upon the body of
water or other natural features. The majority of ideas regarding

the human elements in this life situation implied participation
rather than the role of a spectator. Children preferred to think
about people "getting on," or "getting off" a boat or of "going for
a boat ride" rather than "waiting for" or "seeing" a ship coming in.
Among the miscellaneous ideas expressed were those having to do
with the reunion of family or friends, safety factors in water
transportation ("the drivers—they are careful so nobody will get
hurt . . .") and whether or not children cared to accompany their
parents. As would be anticipated, the few comments centered on
things were directed in the majority of cases to the vessels rather
than to the boxes or cargo piled on the dock. Such partial recognitions were usually limited to statements that there were "boats in
the water" or that "a boat was coming in." Illustrating such partial
interpretations involving people and things are the following
"stories":

> Well, um, a big boat is on the water, and people are standing there,
> and it seems that they're going to have a ride on it.   (1UG)

> A ship coming ashore with crowds of people waiting for it. (6RB)

Nonrecognition. The Dock was not recognized by 11 per cent of
the children. Failure to respond to any significant part of this scene
of transportation was primarily due to children's absorption with
general features of the situation. No child arrived at an inappropriate interpretation of this scene, no one merely listed a number of
items, and only one child's responses were so garbled as to result
in an indefinite conclusion regarding interpretation.

Children who described common elements were definitely more
conscious of people than of things. The former were about equally
distributed among three categories: (a) the holding of a baby,
(b) general activities such as talking, walking, looking, and
standing, and (c) miscellaneous ideas about "minding mother,"
someone who "had a licking," as well as another who "wouldn't
let him play with them." The occasional emphasis upon objects
was indication of the priority which airplanes had over ships in
the minds of some first grade children.

From the above account, we may conclude that children were
moderately successful in their interpretation of this transportation scene. Their consciousness of the functions of boats was
greater than that for the dock. Although children play with boats,

make models, and collect boats, they are quite limited in their concepts of the operations of real ships. Where and how do they dock? Where will they go? What do they carry? Who will travel aboard them and why? These and other ideas are still vaguely defined in the mind of a young child. Hence, the meaning of this scene held by the majority of children was the limited stereotype: people riding on a boat.

Children's Setting for the Dock

Children appear to have little conception of the "where" and "when" for this life situation. Their perception of space and time for the Dock was low, the rankings being 12 and 11.5 respectively. As was true of most scenes, however, spatial consciousness exceeded that for temporal.

An orientation in space was exhibited by 55 per cent of the pupils. Thus, the odds were about even that a child would perceive this transportation scene in some kind of *spatial setting*. Although this picture presented a very real opportunity for specifying geographical or political names, the use of such referents was very limited in comparison with those which were of an associational nature. Approximately the same number of responses were confused or mixed as far as spatial designations were concerned as in the associational and geopolitical categories combined. This was the largest number of such mixed responses, and may be an indication that for children the Dock scene was not as clear cut as others in the series.

Pupils associated this scene with institutions more often than with places identified with Nature. In the former, the referent which was used for locating events "by," "at," or "in" was the same as the name of the structure itself. In effect, children were limiting the field of action to their structural recognition of the scene. Such responses as well as associations with Nature took on the following forms:

> Well, this is by a harbor . . .
> They're all gathering at the boat station for a big ride . . .
> There's a boat coming in the dock . . .
> They were going to meet them at the dock . . .
> A boat that's just comin' in, just by the wharves . . .

> That's is on the ocean . . .
> By a seashore . . .
> It's on a oceanside . . .
> That looks like it's at the coast . . .

The few children who relied upon more systematic measures of space divided their attention between community and national referents. Although world relationships was one of the bases on which this life situation was designed, it is significant to note that not a single child placed this scene outside the United States. Some did sense that these ships and airplanes were either "going across the ocean" or "coming over from a different country." They saw the ship as having come from "Europe," "China," or from the Army "overseas," but the immediate scene was always in this country. One first grader felt that they were gathering "for a big ride going to Nebraska or some place." As far as communities were concerned, one sixth grade urban boy claimed "it's on a seaport," and a sixth grade urban girl saw the people as "newcomers coming into the new town," but not one child named any specific port or city where this could be taking place.

Only 8 per cent of the boys and girls designated a *temporal setting* for this life situation. The size and types of vessels as well as the suggestion of servicemen did not stimulate children to think of a time-field for the Dock—past, present, or future. The limited number of such designations was about equally divided between associational referents and those which were mixed indicating, as was true for spatial settings, the confusion which some children experienced in interpreting this scene. Associations were based on human events of a personal and social origin, but in no case was referral made to natural events such as tides or weather. In the examples which follow, the use of mealtime and war give some feeling of time for the events being discussed:

> The mother's just coming off the boat . . . and then they went home, and and then when it was suppertime, they ate their supper . . .
>
> Father's just come away from the war . . .
> Well, it was in the Army, and then when the Army was over, the men came back to marry the girls . . .

This scene seemed to have no particular time nor place in the perception of most of these children. While it is true that it was drawn as a stereotype of modern docks and harbors which would be representative of many different localities, pupils made no attempt to elaborate in their stories and other responses about where or when this scene might be taking place. The fact that children lived within a relatively short driving distance of such busy "ports" as Milwaukee and Chicago, has done little to sensitize them to such facilities. They, apparently, have not been introduced to the harbors of these communities; to them these are cities but not ports. The extent of travel envisioned by boys and girls was also limited indicating that they are only beginning to think in world-wide terms.

Children's Attitudes toward the Dock

Reactions to the Dock were more positive than negative. Exactly 50 per cent of the children were favorably impressed by this transportation scene, this figure ranking eighth in the series. Negative attitudes, the next largest group, were expressed by 27 per cent of the pupils. This degree of aversion was exceeded only by the Poor House, and was definitely greater than neutral (10%) and mixed (12.5%) attitudes which ranked in the average range for the series. Attitudes toward the Dock were not hard and fast predispositions, however, for only 23 per cent of the children were consistent in their feelings (Rank = 10).

Children's attitudes were directed toward transportation and accompanying human aspects. The former were mainly centered on the boat as a means of transportation and upon various aspects of travel. Human relationships involved the family, broader social contacts, and war. In each instance, children responded to what they considered to be desirable and less attractive features.

Positive and *negative* attitudes shown toward boats and travel reveal children's interests and fears. They liked to watch boats come in and out of a harbor (or thought they would); they wanted to take a "boat ride" (some were aware of the fact that a fare was charged). "Going somewhere," and taking a trip or a vacation were heralded with apparent enthusiam. Others were more specific in their desire to meet new people, see new things, and even "get new things." Attractive as these may have appeared, there were some children who objected to boats in general, and the hustle and bustle that accompanied their use. A number simply didn't want to leave home—even with father and mother, nor did they want a loved one to leave them at home.

Positive	*Negative*

Boats

They're meeting everybody, and it seems like they're gonna go on a boat for a ride and stuff. (1UG)	Because she isn't—she don't like that boat. (1UG)
Because she likes to go on the boat. (1RG)	'Cause I guess he doesn't like to ride on boats. (1UG)
She likes to ride in the boat, and she never saw a boat, and she likes to see all the people. (1UB)	'Cause she doesn't like to be in a, crowded places. (6RB)
The other kids forgot their money. The happy girl had her money, and she paid him and got on. (1UG)	

Travel

'Cause they can go somewhere. (1RG)	I think she's going someplace and she's not too happy about it. (1UB)
He is probably going on the trip on a big ship, and I know quite a few boys like ships and trains. (6RG)	The girl is crying, because she doesn't want to leave the house. (1UG)
They're going on a vacation. (6UB)	He has to go along with his mother and dad, and he didn't want to. (6RG)
They're happy to see their parents, and things that they never saw before. (6RG)	(Sad girl) These people are leaving to go across the ocean. (6RG)
Because this is the first time they'd been on a boat . . . and they thought the ocean was so pretty. And they went by the sailor that was steering, and they thought he (the happy boy) could learn lots of things that way. (6RB)	
Because they're going on a trip, and they're looking forward to it. And they can see many new people, and probably get a lot of new clothes and other things. (6UG)	

Positive and *negative* feelings expressed in connection with the family made quite clear the great need that children have for a sense of family unity, their sensitivity to family discord, and fear of separation. On the other hand, reunions were not always happy affairs for boys and girls if the baby in the family received the attention or if mother and dad had too much news to exchange. Children's need for friends and the sorrow occasioned by losing them was also evident in their reactions to the Dock scene. The immediate nature and limited social contacts children experience outside the home was illustrated by the scarcity of responses directed to people living in other "continents" or people coming here "from their home country"; they expressed neither curiosity about them nor prejudice. War, too, was viewed largely in personal terms usually revolving around the comings or goings of some member of the family.

Positive	*Negative*
Family relationships	

Positive	*Negative*
They're happy to see their father again. (1RG)	Their father or mother's going on the boat. (6UG)
She's glad to see her children and her husband. (1UB)	He can't go with his father or mother on the boat. (1UB)
He's home again and he's happy. (6RG)	Because they aren't too happy they're going away from their mother or father's home . . . Well, I 'spose it's probably gonna be about their first trip or something on a boat or something. (6UB)
Because they've got people coming home to them from off the ship, and they're probably glad that they're coming home. (6RG)	
'Cause he likes to go with his mommy and daddy. (1UG)	'Cause he's going away from his mother; his dad's taking him somewheres. (1UB)
	Because her mother is gonna go away for a long vacation, and she's gonna stay with her daddy, and her daddy hits her. (1UG)
	Because his mother and father pay more attention to the baby then they are to him. (6UB)
	Because his parents are talking and that, and he probably just doesn't like to stand and listen to them. (6UG)

Social relationships

He's gonna meet somebody (6RB) Because he met somebody, his old friends or somethin'. (6UB) 'Cause they can go on trips, and maybe they could have lots of fun. And they could hear about the other people when they are going on trips, and what they'd done. (6RB)

She might be goin' to a . . . going to different continents or something, and she might wanna see what it looks like. (6UG) Because they just got off the fishing vessel, it looks like, and they're away from their home country. (6RB)

They have seen some people leave that they like. (6RB) He didn't want to see all his friends—he want 'em to stay at home. And them won't; they want to go. (1RB) To see some people—gonna meet some relatives of his going away. (6UG) Probably he has to leave his best friend or somethin'. (6UB)

War

They're coming home from war. (6RB) Because father's just come away from the war, and he's happy to see him. (6RB)

Maybe her brother is going to the war or something. (6UB) She looks kinda sad, because her husband is going overseas. (6UG)

As was true for all of the life situations, some children were quite *neutral* about what they saw. For them, a waterfront would not be particularly exciting, because what could one do but look? The many things going on at such a place were meant for adults, and all that a child could do would be to wander around aimlessly. This lack of feeling is evident in the following reasons to support the choice of an "in-between" figure in the picture:

> Because he's down at the dock, and he's just normal. (6RB)
> He's just looking someplace. (1RB)
> Because there's so much going on there, and they probably would just be wandering around. (6RB)

The majority of children who exhibited *mixed* attitudes toward the Dock did so because they saw both attractive and undesirable elements in the life situation, and not because they shifted from one position to another on repeated contacts with it. With respect to travel, for example, an older rural girl voiced the conflict which arises when one leaves a familiar and well-liked place, and faces the hoped-for possibilities but uncertainties of moving. The hardships of travel were weighed against love for one's home country by another pupil. Regarding human relationships, some of the older children were aware of the fact that the people on the dock would be feeling differently depending upon whether their loved ones were returning or leaving. One older city boy contrasted the feelings of those who might be going on a trip with those of the children being left behind.

> They're leaving the place that they liked so well, and they're going to another. (6RG)

> They might be coming over from a different country and telling about the hardships they had, but they still might think it's nice to get back. (6UB)

> I think the sad one would be—if some people have to go off and leave their family, they'd feel awful sad. And other people can be very happy when someone that they love comes home. (6UG)

> (The happy boy and the sad boy or girl) Because some people git to go on the boat for the trip—and because their mother and father might be going away. (6UB)

That there are many facets to a Dock situation is strikingly revealed in children's attitudes. It is more than "having a boat ride" or "taking a trip" both of which are in keeping with children's desire for activity and new experiences. It also has to do with the separation of family and friends, a major problem to many children, and a hoped-for reunion. Relationships outside this immediate circle appear to be less crucial to children and less understood. They are only beginning to develop an appreciation of the interdependence of peoples, and realistic attitudes toward war. Neither have they learned to make distinctions among peoples of other lands for prejudicial ideas were not held by children—or, at least, were not expressed.

Children's Preferences for the Dock

The degree of acceptance for or rejection of the Dock was not so greatly different as to be considered significant. It was chosen by 24 per cent of the pupils, accounting for 8 per cent of their choices, and representing a rank of 6.5 in the series. On the other hand, this picture was rejected only 2 per cent of the time ranking 11th in the series. The latter was markedly lower than negative attitudes shown toward the scene, an indication that although children found much to be critical about, their feelings did not run strong.

Reasons given to support the selection of the Dock were centered on the same factors as those which prompted the identification of attitudinal figures. These included a general liking for boats, an enthusiasm for travel as well as the excitement associated with "war stuff" and crowds.

Boats

Oh, I just like the ships and boats.   (6UB)
Well, I like the boats . . . a, I've been on boats and I like them.
                                                                   (6UB)

Travel

I like to go somewhere.   (1RG)
It looks like they're traveling. I like to travel.   (6UG)
It looks like they're going on a trip, and they're going to have a good time.   (6RG)
'Cause I never rode on a boat, and I wanted to. And that would remind momma and daddy that I wanted to ride on a boat.   (1RG)

War

Because I like to go to the Navy.   (1UB)
I like the war stuff.   (6RB)

As was true of their expressions of attitudes, however, some children did not take kindly to having too many people around or to be separated from loved ones.

Acceptance	*Rejection*
Human relationships	
It looks like a whole crowd of people around. (6UB)	There are so many people to color. (1RG)
	If I had to leave somebody—or even my father, going away on the boat—it would hurt like anything, and I wouldn't like that. (6UG)

It appears that transportation and travel have moderate attractions for elementary children when weighed against other values found in the Life-Situation Picture Series. This may not be in keeping with the importance attached to the factor of mobility by our culture, but for children a number of needs seem to have greater priority. Adults may yearn to travel to far-away lands of their choosing, but to a young child a trip "somewhere" seems quite satisfactory. What is important is to be on the move, and to see new things. Although representing a small minority of responses, it is significant that this picture was selected because of "war stuff." To some elementary school boys, war is synonymous with travel, excitement, adventure, and they like it without having much comprehension of what is involved—other than ACTION.

Group Comparisons

Perception of the Dock by various groups of elementary children were not uniform. Reactions of first grade and sixth grade children represented the greatest differences; rural and urban children varied in minor ways. In spite of the popular notion of the affinity that boys have for ships, their reactions were not very different from that of girls. The same was true of bright children as compared with those having less intelligence. Differences were greatest with respect to the cognitive aspect of perception. Some attitudinal variations did occur, but none of the groups of elementary children differed greatly in their preference for or rejection of the Dock.

Age Differences. Sixth grade children were markedly superior in their recognition of this scene, and displayed greater maturity regarding setting and certain of their attitudes. In their *recognition* more of the older pupils were conscious of this life situation structurally. This was evident in attention given to the immediate scene, and especially in their use of the concept "dock" to label it. The difference between grade groups was even more marked in sensitivity to functional aspects. Older pupils excelled in their awareness of both transportation and world relations. They brought a greater number of concepts to bear on the transportation of goods, and although there was little difference in the number of ideas regarding the transportation of people, sixth graders were definitely more conscious of the notion of a "trip." As for concepts dealing with world relationships, older pupils referred to a greater number of peacetime activities involving travel, commerce, and immigration as well as more wartime activities. In all, therefore, they applied a greater total of concepts in each of the functional categories. As would be expected from the above, many more sixth grade pupils recognized both structure and function the proportions being 32 per cent and 2 per cent for the respective groups.

In contrast with the ability of older pupils to view this life situation as a whole, was the greater tendency for younger children to seize upon one or more elements. Accordingly, more first grade pupils achieved only partial recognition; their responses included more types of such awareness, and were primarily centered on people. With respect to the latter, more lower grade children were satisfied with the simple explanation of a "boat ride." Regarding statements of a general nature (nonrecognition), the above pattern was almost duplicated with respect to: first grade pupils outnumbering older pupils, responding with a greater total of general concepts, and concentrating on human activities.

Grade comparisons were the only ones which revealed differences in a consciousness of the background for the Dock scene. These involved space but not time. Sixth grade pupils were more productive in their thinking about spatial setting than were younger children, and this was especially noticeable in the number of times they associated this scene with an institutional background or the natural environment.

Attitudes toward the Dock also varied with age. The difference was not that one group was more favorably or adversely oriented toward this life situation than another, but in the number of times that mixed feelings were expressed. These were not the result of changes in attitudes with repeated contacts, but the ability to regard it from a number of points of view. As would be expected, this flexibility in perception was greater on the part of older pupils than first graders.

It is clear that a very real gain takes place with age in the cognitive aspects of perceiving the Dock. Whereas practically all sixth grade pupils managed to synthesize various clues and arrive at some form of whole interpretation, the majority of younger pupils were dealing with parts—about as many being relevant to transportation as not. The broader range of concepts brought to bear on the Dock scene, the increased sensibility to processes involving goods as well as people, and the extension of mental horizons to include the world were part of this maturation in perception. Development with respect to perceptual field seems to be less marked, for the superiority of older pupils in dealing with space was not carried over into time. In fact, it appears that a sense of orientation for this scene is only in its beginning stages by sixth grade for pupils were not inclined to use geographical or political terms. Emotional reactions to this scene appear to be less influenced by age. The change which takes place is not one of direction, but of flexibility. Young children have more limited possibilities for interpreting a life situation. Once having adopted a point of view toward a particular scene, they appear to be more "set" in their attitudes. With age comes a consciousness of the different feelings which may be attached to the same situation by different people, a development which may reflect the shift from the egocentrism of the young child to the more socialized orientation of older boys and girls.

Rural-Urban Differences. Children living in rural and urban communities differed in their recognition of the Dock and in their attitudes. More rural pupils failed to achieve some measure of recognition of this scene than was the case for city boys and girls. Nonrecognition took the form of general statements about the universals in this life situation. Farm children produced a greater number of such responses, especially with reference to people, in which case the total number of concepts describing various activities was much greater.

In comparison with rural children, the attitudes of urban pupils was similar to that of sixth graders when compared with younger pupils. City boys and girls surpassed the rural in the expression of mixed attitudes toward the Dock. The reason was the same as for the sixth grade group, namely: a greater capacity to perceive this life situation from a number of points of view.

The above differences are evidences of the keener perception of this Dock scene by urban children. Theirs is not a widespread superiority, but one which manifests itself at both ends of the scale. At the lowest level of recognition were found more rural cases; the most mature level of attitudes was reached by more urban children. Between these extremes, and hence, for the most part, rural and urban childrn fared equally well in their reactions.

The superiority of urban children comes as no surprise when one recalls that they live in an industrial center located on the Great Lakes. One would expect them to be on more familiar terms with docks and shipping than would be the case for children living on farms some distance inland. Yet, transportation by water, despite the automobile and airplane, is so much a part of our culture that the majority of country children are on an equal footing with those living in the city as far as a generalized awareness is concerned. Whether through visitation, the influence of mass communications, or schooling, rural children's perceptions were similar to those of urban boys and girls except at the most insightful level of attitudes.

SUMMARY

A NUMBER of interesting trends appear among children's responses to the pictures in the Child-Adult Block. For five of the ten aspects being studied, all three paired comparisons based on rank (*See* Table 2) varied in the same direction. For example, Word Productivity for the Bedroom ranked lower than that for the Dam, the Church was below the Capitol, and the Schoolroom was lower than the Dock. In two cases (Attention Time and Appropriate Recognition) the rankings for all three pictures in one set exceeded those in the other. Hence, as was true for the other life-situation blocks, it cannot be said that children are more perceptive of one group than of the other. On the whole, however, greater perception was shown to the child-situation pictures in the following ways:

Children react with greater facility to child-situations than to adult-situations. For each pair of pictures, boys and girls took less time and required fewer words in responding to the child-situation. Yet, they produced a greater number of ideas for each of these scenes.

Children are better able to recognize child-situations than adult-situations. In each of the three sets of comparisons, a larger proportion of the ideas associated with child-background scenes were appropriate. Not only were children more accurate in their recognition, but they reached a higher level of perception. On the child set, more pupils recognized both structure and function or structure alone whereas for the adult scenes there were more nonrecognition responses in all three categories (general description, inappropriate, and indefinite).

Children have a better orientation for child-situations than for the adult. The Church and Schoolroom were the highest ranking pictures in spatial setting although the Bedroom did not follow this pattern. In temporal settings, however, the child scenes equalled or exceeded their adult counterparts, the total number of such settings being significantly greater.

There is a tendency for children to prefer child-situations rather than adult. Although no discernible trends appeared in the attitudes of boys and girls toward either set of life situations, there was a definite trend in their preferences and rejections of these pictures. In every case, more children selected the child scene, and in all but one the adult picture was more rejected. The only exception to this general trend was the Schoolroom toward which pupils exhibited strong reactions for and against. The reversal in direction noted for the Schoolroom scene complicates the interpretation of the value placed by children on each set of pictures. The preference of children for the child-situations must be considered a tendency rather than characteristic of the entire set.

The easy familiarity of children with life situations which they experience as opposed to adult situations is what we would expect from the standpoint of recognition and setting or background. That young people would have a preference, however slight, for familiar situations rather than those regarded as adult also fits into this pattern. Familiarity in itself, however, is no guarantee of the development of favorable attitudes as was evident in the reactions of some children to the Schoolroom.

Age Differences

Differences in the perception of the life situations in this Age Block by first grade and sixth grade pupils were the greatest for any of the groups being compared. These were more evident in responses to the adult-situations than to the child. They suggest the following generalizations about developmental differences in perception:

As children grow older they gain in the ability to recognize adult-situations. Sixth grade pupils reached a higher level of recognition (synthesis, structure, function) on each of the adult scenes whereas many first grade children did no more than describe them in general (nonrecognition) terms. On the child-situations, however, no sweeping generalization is warranted. First and sixth grade pupils either did not differ in their recognition (Bedroom) or these differences were qualitative in nature (Schoolroom) except for the Church where older pupils again excelled.

Older children have a better sense of orientation for adult-situations than do young children. In every instance, sixth grade pupils designated a greater number of spatial settings for the adult scenes than did first graders. A similar trend was noted in the awareness of temporal settings for child-situations, but it was less consistent in not including the Schoolroom scene.

Young children tend to express more negativism toward adult situations whereas older children have a tendency to regard them more favorably. These tendencies were statistically significant with respect to the attitudes revealed toward the Dam and Capitol but less marked for the Dock. A similar trend appeared in attitudes expressed toward the Church, but no grade differences occurred in feelings about the Bedroom or Schoolroom. Also, in keeping with these tendencies is the fact that more first graders valued the Schoolroom whereas more of the sixth grade pupils indicated a preference for the Dam.

The above observations are convincing testimony of the superiority of sixth grade pupils in dealing with what has been termed adult-situations. This has been most evident in the recognition aspect of perception followed by setting, and then feelings or emotions. The young child, inexperienced in the world of grown-ups, has so few concepts to bring to these situations that he does not even recognize them for what they are; neither does he see these situations in a larger context. So little meaning do they hold for him that he is less than attracted to them, and sees little of value for him in these situations. Given five more years of experience, some of which has brought him into closer contact with these situations, either directly or vicariously, the child has acquired a considerable stock of concepts and orientation to these scenes. With these ideas comes a tendency for his former negativism to change in the direction of more neutral or favorable attitudes.

Differences Associated with Intelligence

Bright children differed from those having less intelligence in the recognition of and attitudes toward adult-situations. For no single picture was the difference between these groups statistically significant. So consistent were their perceptions, however, that there resulted a marked variation between the two groups in the sum total of their responses to the adult-situations. The following conclusions, therefore, are warranted:

Bright children tend to surpass less intelligent children in the recognition of adult scenes. In each case, more of the former achieved the highest level of recognition (synthesis) in contrast with lower I.Q. pupils, more of whom failed to recognize the scene (general description). Although higher I.Q. children were more aware of the Church structurally in generalized form (religious center) no similar over-all superiority characterized their perception of child-situations.

Bright children tend to have more favorable attitudes toward adult-situations than do children with less intelligence. In every instance, high I.Q. was associated with positive attitudes; low I.Q. with greater negativism. No such consistency of attitudes characterized the responses of intelligence groups to the child-situations.

Differences between intelligence groups parallel those of the grade groups. High I.Q. pupils displayed some of the same superiorities over less capable children that were exhibited by sixth graders as compared to younger pupils. The advantage that goes with higher intellectual ability, however, is not as extensive or as great as that which marks a difference of five years in mental age and experience. There can be little doubt, however, that intelligence is an important factor in the perception of adult-situations.

Sex Differences

Boys and girls differed most strikingly in their *feelings* about the child-situation pictures constituting this block. The only instance of variability in recognition was qualitative rather than quantitative (more girls were aware of human relationships in the Schoolroom scene). The only difference of any kind on the adult-situations was the greater preference shown by boys for the Dam picture, but this was not consistent for all adult scenes. The one generalization which pertains to the responses of these groups, therefore, is as follows:

Girls have a higher regard than boys for situations which are more directly experienced by children. They displayed more positive attitudes and a greater preference for the Bedroom and Church scenes whereas more boys were neutral or negative. Similar trends were evident to a lesser degree in responses to the Schoolroom.

It is quite clear that as far as this block of pictures is concerned the differences between boys and girls are not matters of degree but of kind. The two groups are equally adept in the cognitive aspects of perception, but girls have acquired a much higher appreciation for one set of life situations. This is not the equivalent of saying that girls are more perceptive for it could be argued that superiority would be evidenced in more positive feeling tones for the adult-situations as was the case for sixth grade and high-ability pupils compared with younger and less capable children. The more plausible explanation is that elementary children are already cognizant of the feminine role played in the home, church, and school. This is borne out by the fact that two of these situations were regarded as better suited to girls (Bedroom and Schoolroom) whereas none of the adult scenes enjoyed such distinction. This role is, apparently, quite acceptable to elementary girls. In way of contrast, however, the masculine role in the adult-situations was less clearly defined by children and less acceptable to boys. It might well be that sex roles are not as sharply differentiated in these instances or that it takes children longer to apprehend what these roles are either because of a lack of experience with such situations or because of their complexity.

Rural-Urban Differences

There is no pattern or trend distinguishing the perception of Child-Adult situations by rural children or urban. In recognition, for example, rural boys and girls were more aware of the Capitol structurally whereas more inappropriate or indefinite responses were given by urban children. Yet, the former failed to recognize the Dock (general description) more so than urban pupils. In the functional awareness of the Schoolroom scene, qualitative differences appeared. As for feelings, rural children showed a greater preference for the Church scene; urban boys and girls displayed more mature (mixed) attitudes toward the Dock. In short, differences between these two groups were centered on isolated pictures and not on any one set of life situations. Hence, there is reason for maintaining that:

Rural and urban children do not differ systematically in their perception of child- and adult-situations. The one possible exception to this generalization lies in the greater total of temporal settings provided by rural pupils in responding to adult scenes. Although there is consistency in this set of pictures, so much of the weighting is produced by the Dam that without it no real tendency could be established.

What this means is that, generally speaking, neither of these groups is more mature nor socially perceptive than the other. Furthermore, rural children are not necessarily more closely oriented to the home and urban children more "worldly" minded. It is the type of life situation rather than the mere factor of immediacy or remoteness which accounts for differences in the perception of farm and city children.

Part V

WHAT HAVE WE LEARNED ABOUT CHILDREN'S SOCIAL PERCEPTION?

Then said a teacher, Speak to us of Teaching.

And he said:

No man can reveal to you aught but that which already lies half asleep in the dawning of your knowledge.

The teacher who walks in the shadow of the temple, among his followers, gives not of his wisdom but rather of his faith and his lovingness.

If he is indeed wise he does not bid you enter the house of his wisdom, but rather leads you to the threshold of your own mind.

The astronomer may speak to you of his understanding of space, but he cannot give you his understanding.

The musician may sing to you of the rhythm which is in all space, but he cannot give you the ear which arrests the rhythm nor the voice that echoes it.

And he who is versed in the science of numbers can tell of the regions of weight and measure, but he cannot conduct you thither.

For the vision of one man lends not its wings to another man.

And even as each one of you stands alone in God's knowledge, so must each one of you be alone in his knowledge of God and in his understanding of the earth.[7]

[7] Reprinted from *The Prophet* by Kahlil Gibran with permission of the publisher, Alfred A. Knopf, Inc. Copyright 1951 by Administrators C.T.A. of Kahlil Gibran Estate and Mary G. Gibran.

Chapter	TOWARD A THEORY
XXIII.	OF SOCIAL PERCEPTION

THE foregoing analysis of children's reactions to the Life-Situation Picture Series leads to a number of important conclusions about their social perception. These have a bearing on the nature of social perception, its development during the elementary school years, and factors influencing the perception of social situations.

Nature of Social Perception

There is substantial evidence to the effect that *children try to apprehend the world with which they have contact.* Of the 4400 specific directives given to the children in this study no reply was elicited by only 1.8 per cent.[8] For only two of the 1232 picture summaries were no data available in all three parts of the social interview. As might be expected, 92% of the failures to respond were on the part of first grade pupils. Another indication of children's tendency to give meaning to their world is the fact that if the social significance of the situation eluded their grasp they centered on the common activities of people rather than "giving up" as it were. Thus, the Capitol, which proved to be one of the most difficult for children to interpret, was often regarded as an instance of "people walking downtown" or "people meeting each other and talking." It seems as though children want to be on speaking terms with their world. Few, apparently, dismiss a new or unfamiliar experience with the thought that it is too "hard" to understand or consciously table the experience for interpretation at some future date when they are older.

It is interesting to note also, that regardless of whether or not

[8] *See* Frank J. Estvan, *Studies in Social Perception: Methodology, op. cit.,* p. 237.

children recognized a life situation, they dealt with it in realistic terms. Although the instructions, "what story does this picture tell?" left much room for the play of imagination and fantasy, few exotic stories were produced, and these were generally of the "who-done-it" type on the part of children who volunteered a liking for detective stories.

Children's social perception is related to type of life situation. As has been demonstrated, elementary children are not consistently superior in dealing with any block or set of pictures depicting a particular type of social background. Perception seems to be related more to the social functions depicted than to rural-urban, social status, or age differentials. The great variability in the picture series for each of the perceptual aspects being evaluated as well as differences in the average performance level among these aspects would indicate that social perception is not a generalized or unitary trait. (*See* Table 3 in Appendix.) This would argue against a theory based upon innate or *à priori* determinants for in such case there would be more uniformity of response to various life situations, and greater relationship among the various components of perception. In lessening the force of nativistic explanations for perception, greater credence may be given to environmental (experiential) influences.

Children's social perception is highly individualized. The wide range in children's perception of a life situation has been demonstrated in every chapter of the preceding sections. Differences have occurred in connection with the recognition of a life situation, the perceptual field in which the situation has been viewed, and in feelings expressed toward it. These differences are strikingly illustrated in responses to the Poor House. Those of a sixth grade rural boy represent the highest level of recognition:

> (Part I—What story does this picture tell?)
> Well, it looks like a poor family and haven't . . . they haven't got too much food or clothing or anything . . . they haven't got a very good house, and it looks like there's one of them sick . . . they probably haven't enough food, and the father probably hasn't got a good job, and there's holes in their clothes and everything.
>
> (Part II—Which boy or girl belongs in this picture?)
> The sad girl.
> (Why?)

Well, because the room and everything, and they haven't got a very good place to live.

In comparison are the responses of a first grade urban boy which are nothing more than a simple enumeration of clues having no particular significance for poverty:

> (Part I—What story does this picture tell?)
> A man, and a girl, and a mother, and a boy.

> (Part II—Which boy or girl belongs in this picture?)
> The happy girl.
> (Why?)
> 'Cause there's another girl.

Both of which stand in contrast to the sense of time exhibited by a sixth grade urban boy, inappropriate though it may be:

> (Part I—What story does this picture tell?)
> Um ... it's probably in the pioneer days, um, let's see ... maybe it tells about the pioneers or something.

> (Part II—Which boy or girl belongs in this picture?)
> The in-between girl.
> (Why?)
> Well, they don't look happy or sad. She might be crying, I don't know, could be. Well, maybe she couldn't play with her friends or somethin'.

Individualism is also apparent in the degree of involvement which children exhibit in connection with the situation being perceived. This is, indeed, a subtle dimension of human behavior. Just how much empathy is represented in the three above statements is difficult to determine. In mode of expression, they appear to be more impersonal or objective than the comments of a young city boy who said:

> (Part I—What story does this picture tell?)
> Um, a lady with her baby, and a little girl, and a little boy in bed and ... and a husband ... that looks like my daddy and ... no, it looks like my Uncle Ben ... and ... and ... and ... my Aunt with her little baby ... and ... and my sister over there and my ... other children in the bed.

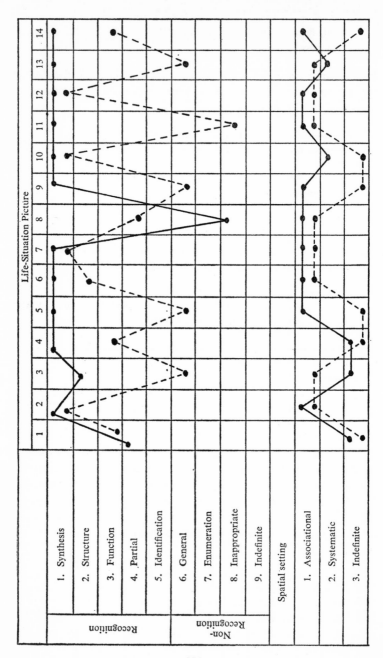

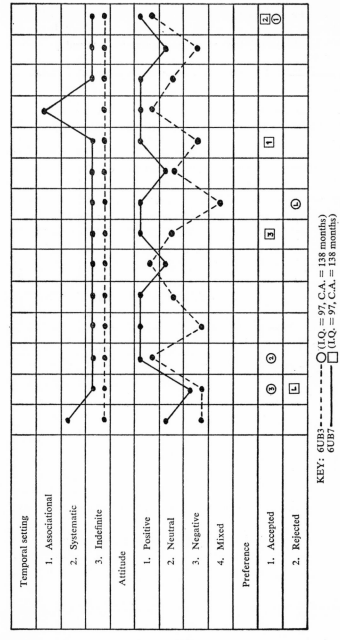

KEY: 6UB3 ----○---- (I.Q. = 97, C.A. = 138 months)
6UB7 ———□——— (I.Q. = 97, C.A. = 138 months)

Fig. 5. Social Perception Profile of Two Sixth Grade Urban Boys.

(Part II—Which boy or girl belongs in this picture?)
    The in-between girl.
(Why?)
    'Cause she doesn't look mad and she doesn't look sad.

Or the sixth grade girl who felt that a sad boy belonged in the picture because:

> Well, he doesn't look very happy in a home like that and . . . um, I don't think I'd be very happy in a home like that neither.

Individuality in perception may also be regarded from the standpoint of differences among children belonging to the same group. For within each group there are wide variations. This is rather convincingly demonstrated in the profiles for two sixth grade urban boys attending different schools but who were identical in chronological age and intelligence quotient. (*See* Fig. 5.) For the 14 pictures in the series, they disagreed on 10 in their recognition, six times on spatial setting, twice regarding temporal setting, and nine times in attitude. As for picture preference, they disagreed in five out of six selections, and on their rejections. This does not constitute a negation of group differences or cast doubt upon the reliability of differences noted in the preceding sections. It means that within the general trend established by a group of children individuals may vary considerably; that differences among the members of a group are likely to be as great as or greater than those found in comparing groups of children.

Development of Social Perception

The responses of first grade and sixth grade children offer a number of clues regarding the development of social perception. The performance of these two groups was markedly different with respect to every perceptual component: recognition, perceptual field, and attitude. No other group comparisons provide such great contrasts.

Recognition.[9] An impressive gain takes place during the elementary school period in children's ability to recognize life situations. Sixty-seven per cent of the first graders achieved some

---

[9] The data on which this presentation is based are summarized in Table 4 in the Appendix.

measure of recognition of the Life-Situation Picture Series in comparison with 90 per cent of the sixth grade pupils. Quite obviously,
a great deal of development has taken place before children even
enter elementary school and, as shall be evident when the nature
of children's recognition is examined in greater detail, much remains to be done after they leave elementary school. The differences between younger and older pupils suggests a number of
trends in the development of children's ability to recognize life
situations.

*Development in recognition proceeds from enumeration of
clues to a description of parts to an interpretation of the whole.*
For the most part, children have gone beyond the point of simply
enumerating what they see in a life situation by the time they enter
elementary school. Fewer than 2 per cent gave such responses (correct or inappropriate) in comparison to 38 per cent who described
parts of the scene (relevant or inappropriate), and 58 per cent
who interpreted various clues in terms of some kind of whole (appropriate or inappropriate). The developmental sequence of enumeration—description—interpretation is given further support in
a comparison of recognition levels reached by young and older
pupils. No sixth grader, for example, stopped short at the point
of simple enumeration. The few such responses were made exclusively by younger pupils. At the other end of the scale, sixth
grade pupils were superior in recognitions classified as synthesis,
structure, or function the proportions being 74 per cent as compared to 32 per cent. On the other hand, first grade children exceeded older pupils in each of the partial recognition categories
except the one dealing with the natural environment.[10]

*Children are more sensitive to the human element in a life situa-
tion than to Nature or things.* This tendency was revealed whenever pupils reacted to parts of a life situation. Whether they concentrated on a relevant aspect of the scene (recognition) or described something in general (nonrecognition), the focus on people
and their activities was greater than the combined attention given

[10] Intellectual levels of three, seven, and twelve years assigned to comparable stages in picture interpretation are reported in:

Alfred Binet and Th. Simon, *The Development of Intelligence in Children,*
pp. 188-194. Baltimore: Williams and Wilkins Company, 1916. (Translated
by Elizabeth S. Kite.)

to the physical world and the things which constitute our culture. This was just as true for partial recognitions as for general statements about life situations, for first grade children as for sixth. This emphasis upon people is clearly characteristic of the elementary school child.

Generally speaking, recognition of structure precedes recognition of function. This was especially noticeable in the reactions of first grade children. In every comparison of the number of pupils reaching these levels of recognition or the number of types (immediate or extended) of such recognition made by pupils, structural responses significantly out-numbered the functional. However, the rapid progress made by children in their awareness of function is indicated by the fact that by sixth grade structure was greater than function only with respect to recognition level. In comparisons involving types of responses, function had caught up with structure.

Structural and functional recognitions tend to be immediate rather than extended throughout the elementary school period. In the case of each life situation structural recognitions were centered upon the objective characteristics of the immediate scene rather than looked upon more broadly or at a higher level of abstraction. Similarly, functional recognitions were more likely to be descriptive of ongoing processes than attempts to abstract their essential characteristics or reflect qualitative judgments. These findings hold true for both groups. The evidence is conclusive, therefore, that no real trend in generalizing about types of life situations develops during the elementary school years.

As children grow older some of the causes for nonrecognition tend to disappear but others remain constant. General statements made with reference to people and things, and the enumeration of general (miscellaneous) items in a life situation are much more often the cause of nonrecognition for the first grade children than for sixth. Moreover, the proportion of general types of nonrecognition as compared with those which are inappropriate, indefinite, or due to failure to respond combined is decidedly greater for young children than for older pupils. On the other hand, there is very little difference in the number of inappropriate responses which occur at either end of the elementary school period. It appears, therefore, that with age there is a very sharp decrease in general type reactions which fail to single out significant or relevant aspects of a life situation, but no appreciable difference in the number of errors made. This would seem to indicate that young children are not in the habit of "taking a wild guess" if they do not recognize a life situation. Instead, they seize upon something familiar—usually a person—and this they do in an egocentric way regardless of the nature of a particular life situation. The fact that there is no corresponding decrease in errors can be explained by the greater number of choice-options open to the more mature child. His more extensive background increases the possibility of making finer distinctions among social stimuli, but failure to discriminate carefully enough can result in a greater number of faulty associations.

Perceptual Field.[11] A very real development in children's awareness of the orientation for life situations takes place during the elementary school years. This is evident in the sheer number of such designations, their preciseness, and certain characteristics peculiar to the growth of spatial or temporal consciousness.

One of the more obvious trends is *the great increase in the use of perceptual settings which takes place as children grow older.* In about half the cases (53%) first grade children did not specify a spatial setting for the life situation under consideration. By sixth grade this proportion was significantly less, occurring in only 15 per cent of the scenes. Although children were much less aware of time, the same trend prevailed, the 89 per cent of unspecified reactions of younger pupils dropping to 78 per cent at the sixth grade level. Not only do older pupils fare better in these gross evaluations based on a lack of field consciousness, their superiority is evident in a more positive sense. For every one of the categories where a significant difference was established between first and sixth grade pupils (5 spatial and 4 temporal) the advantage was always on the side of the older pupils. Hence, although gains taking place during the elementary school period do not show up with respect to every specific type of spatial and temporal setting they are widespread and of considerable magnitude.

Development of spatial consciousness precedes that of time. This may be gathered from the figures quoted above pertaining to the number of life situations for which no setting was specified. For each grade group, the number of failures to denote time was

[11] The data on which this section is based are summarized in Tables 5 and 6 in the Appendix.

markedly greater than the omission of spatial orientations. Further evidence that space and time do not develop together is gained by noting the combination of *spatial and temporal* settings given for each life situation.[12] For more than half the scenes (55%), first grade children gave neither spatial nor temporal setting, and in no case was a systematic spatial referent used in combination with a systematic temporal setting. The largest group of sixth grade pupils, on the other hand, had moved from no awareness to a combination of an associational spatial setting and an indefinite temporal designation (45%). Only 2 per cent, however, used a systematic referent for both space and time. For neither grade group, can it be said that development proceeded from indefinite space and time to associational space and time to systematic space and time. In each case, gains were made in spatial consciousness before temporal.

Development proceeds from associational to systematic referents. First grade children placed only 9.61 per cent of the life situations in a temporal setting, and these were almost equally divided between associational and systematic referents. By sixth grade, this proportion had been increased two and one-half times (24.04% of the scenes), and a significantly greater proportion were associational as compared to systematic. This trend for growth to take place in associational type referents before the systematic is even more evident in the case of spatial settings where it was markedly greater at both grade levels.

Development in the use of systematic spatial settings proceeds from near to far but not in regular progression. First, it should be noted that both first grade and sixth grade children are strongly community centered, and that only a negligible number of life situations have been placed in a world setting. That older children have begun to expand their horizon beyond the immediate community is indicated by the fact that more of them used the state as their referent as well as regional, national, and world settings combined. It is interesting to note, however, that both first grade and sixth grade pupils were more conscious of the nation as the setting for life situations than the state or region in which they lived. The former, it would appear, is "psychologically" nearer than areas or

[12] See Appendix, Table 7 showing relationship of spatial and temporal settings.

divisions which are actually closer geographically speaking. In other words, children tend to skip such intermediate areas as the state or region in their expanding awareness of space rather than moving outward systematically in terms of size of unit.

Development in spatial orientation is characterized by greater use of specific referents. Although the number of specific place names used by sixth grade children was not large, they did outnumber those used by first graders to a significant degree. This was especially true with regard to institutional referents in which case older pupils would refer to "Boulder Dam" rather than simply "a dam" as in the case of younger pupils. Quite obviously, the added years of experience have increased the stock of place names which older children can use in their apprehension and orientation to life situations.

Development in temporal orientation proceeds on an irregular front. Unlike the pattern noted in the development of a sense of space, no one generalization describes what takes place regarding temporal awareness. With respect to associational time, a significant increment occurs regarding natural referents, both diurnal and annual. Of the human associations used to indicate time, growth takes place regarding social events but not the personal. As for systematic measures of time keeping, the chronometric is characterized by a great gain in the use of the calendar but none with respect to clock time; the historical shows no really significant gain, although there is some tendency on the part of older pupils to use the present and past in their thinking. In the latter connection, it is significant to note the absence of orientation to "the future." This may be a reflection of the type of life situations to which children were responding or an indication of the lack of "forward" thinking by young people. On the whole, therefore, there is no single explanation accounting for what happens in the development of temporal consciousness. This may indicate that time is a far more complicated abstraction than space for children to comprehend. It may also imply that children have fewer opportunities to develop a sense of temporal orientation—or less training.

Perceptual Attitudes.[13] As was true of recognition and perceptual field, the elementary school years do not constitute a period of relative stability in the attitudes which children display toward life

[13] See Appendix, Table 8 for the data on which this section is based.

situations. The change which takes place during these years is not quantitative: from no attitude to the formation of either positive or negative feelings. It is primarily directional: a shifting from one kind of attitude to another. Furthermore, the element of consistency is also involved.

It cannot be emphasized too strongly that *attitudinal changes which take place during the elementary school years are far reaching*. The kinds of attitudes expressed by first and sixth grade children were significantly different in each phase of the interview except the last where greater uniformity would be expected in reasons given for selecting or rejecting pictures. Even in the performance of this task, younger children gave a greater number of indefinite reasons (attitudes) for their choices. In all other phases of the interview (Parts I and II) there was a marked difference between young and older pupils in their expression of each type of attitude with the exception of negative feelings expressed in picture-story responses. The fact of attitudinal change is given additional support when analysis is made in terms of individual life situation pictures. In six cases out of fourteen, the distribution of the four types of attitudes for a particular scene was markedly discrepant between the two age groups, and for ten of the fourteen situations there was at least one attitude for which the difference was significant. The changes described above are the greatest of any of the group comparisons being made.

Generally speaking, children's attitudes toward life situations change from negative to positive. A summary of all the attitudes expressed toward the life situations in the series shows little difference in the number of neutral or mixed responses, but a decidedly greater number of negative responses on the part of young children, and a far greater proportion of positive attitudes expressed by sixth graders. This greater aversion of first grade children was found to be statistically reliable for exactly half of the fourteen pictures. The greater positivism of older pupils was evident on nine life situations being markedly so for the Resort scene. Hence, there is no denying the existence of very strong negative feelings on the part of first grade children. One explanation for this strong "set" is that young children and those who are older are reacting to different things in the life situation. As has been demonstrated, the former are not as capable of synthesizing various clues, but are more likely to deal with segments or parts of the scene. These parts, furthermore, primarily involve human beings—their activities, relationships, and feelings. It may be that a "natural" egocentrism of the six-year-old accounts for his greater tendency to fixate on child-adult or child-parent relationships as compared to the more socialized thinking of older children.[14] Without denying the validity of a theory of egocentrism, it is also possible to explain this strong negative current in terms of familiarity. The four scenes toward which no appreciable difference in attitudes were exhibited by first and sixth grade children are less complex and within the experiencing of young children: Bedroom, Schoolroom, Old Beach, Village. The first two rank very high in recognition and the latter are at least in the average range. It appears that in these cases young children were reacting to the social significance of the life situations and in so doing their attitudes were much like those of older pupils.

Changes in children's attitudes are in the direction of socially accepted attitudes. This fact is most apparent in the Social Status Block of pictures in which younger children expressed more positive reactions to the picture of Poverty and more negative attitudes toward the Resort—in contrast to sixth graders none of whom had anything favorable to say about the former and who showed a positive tendency toward the latter. The direction of change represented by these contrasts is in keeping with the aversion-value status generally held by these situations in our culture. This would seem to indicate, therefore, that attitudinal changes taking place during the elementary school years are more than a gain of positivism resulting from greater knowledge and familiarity with the life situation in question. Children also learn which things are to be avoided and which are to be sought for in this culture.

Children's attitudes become more consistent as they grow older.[15] A far greater number of sixth grade pupils exhibited the same attitude toward a life situation throughout the various phases of the interview than was the case for younger children. The latter responded with a greater variety of attitudes to the same situation than was true for older pupils. These combinations included attitude + neutral + indefinite and to a less degree attitude + indefinite.

---

[14] For the distinction between egocentric or syncretic thinking and that which is objective or socialized *see:* Jean Piaget, *The Language and Thought of the Child.* London: Routledge & Kegan Paul Limited, 1926.

[15] *See* Table 9 in the Appendix.

There was no difference, however, in the number of times an attitude was combined with a neutral response, this being a reflection of the increasing involvement which took place in all children as they began with a task requiring little personal involvement and proceeded to those calling for more definite expressions of attitude and decision making. Altogether this is the greatest difference in consistency to be found in any of the group comparisons. It constitutes convincing evidence that as children grow older they develop the ability to adopt a certain point of view with respect to a situation and to stick with it. To put it another way, with age there is a tendency for attitudes to crystallize.

Valuation.[16] Judging by their picture selections, *there is no systematic change in the valuations placed on various life situations as children grow older.* The distribution of picture preferences and rejections made by young and older pupils are not markedly divergent. In only two cases were they significant, the Schoolroom being selected by more first graders and the Dam being chosen more frequently by the sixth. Except for the suggestion of movement from immediate to more remote kinds of experience, this offers little in way of a pattern of development in valuing life situations. Extremes in likes or dislikes appear to be highly individual, and the resultant of many forces few of which operate in the same fashion for all the members of a group. Some children, for example, selected a picture because of its novelty. Some were guided in their choice by the content of the picture, whereas others thought of it in terms of its aesthetic qualities or possibilities for "coloring." Because life situations may be viewed in light of a multiplicity of values, it is quite probable that changes in valuation have to do with the value-elements perceived rather than the life situation taken as a whole. In short, a life situation may be highly regarded by both young and older pupils, but for different reasons.

Factors Associated with Perception

Perception is not unitary behavior. The variations noted in preceding sections imply that perception is influenced by a number of factors which interact in different ways to produce a wide range of individual differences. Evidence has been accumulated regarding

[16] Picture preferences and rejections are given in Tables 10 and 11 in the Appendix.

the relationship of experiential background, sex, and intelligence to perceptual behavior. In this connection, certain observations about the physical basis of perception, language, and personality will also be of interest.

Physical Basis of Perception. The parable of "The Blind Man's Idea of the Sun" recognizes the primary function of the sense organs in providing data to the perceiver. The chemico-electrical processes by which these impulses are integrated, interpreted, and acted upon as well as remembered for later recall are still largely matters of speculation and theorizing as was seen in tracing the philosophical and psychological backgrounds for perception study. That differences exist in the efficiency of individuals' sensory apparatus is well known. Since no two people receive exactly the same primary data of the world about them, each lives in his "own world." Yet, within a range of normality, however broadly it may be defined, a man is seen as a man, and a tree as a tree. It is at this level of sensory discrimination that social perception normally takes place.

Language and Perception. In addition to the physical basis for perception there must be language. For language is a means of dealing with experience. Experience is organized under certain categories depending upon the purpose behind such organizing, and the systems of classification available. In turn, verbal symbols are the basis for naming, describing, or responding to the things or events being perceived. Distinctions in conceptualization and perception must be contained in the language, and be mastered by the individual using this language. Otherwise magenta, burgundy, Chinese red, dusty rose, pink, etc., simply exist as lighter or darker shades of red. The concept precedes the percept, and must take linguistic form for utility in thinking and communication.

As important as language is in the process of perception, it is not sheer bulk alone that counts.[17] The fact that an individual has much to say about a life situation is not necessarily a sign of greater perceptiveness on his part. In fact, no relation was discovered between the verbal output elicited by a life situation and the number of ideas produced, the degree of recognition achieved, or its value-

[17] For a detailed analysis of children's Word Productivity *see* Frank J. Estvan, "Studies in Social Perception: Word Productivity," *Journal of Experimental Education* (June, 1959).

aversion status. Bright children, however, generally outproduced pupils of lesser intelligence, and the same was true of sixth grade pupils as compared to first. These trends are in keeping with the superiority exhibited by high I.Q. and older pupils regarding the ideational aspects of perception, thus, indicating a group relationship if not one for the individuals constituting these groups.

The part that language plays in children's perception is more apparent in the kinds of verbal symbols used than in the amount. Lacking the "right" terminology, the young child makes many substitutions and invents his own peculiar phraseology. The surveyor for him is a "veyor," the house is described as "rickety-rackety," and the farmer is in the process of "grabbing up some wheat." In time he can be depended upon to learn more acceptable or conventional ways of expressing himself. This will require a greater stock of concepts or vocabulary so that what was formerly a "town" will now become a "village" or a "city." His greater store of linguistic schemas will make possible greater precision in classifying or describing life situations. A "factory" may now be identified as a "coal yard," "refinery" or "power plant." In this developmental process intelligence plays a very important part as has been reflected in the prolific and specific character of the terms used by bright children. The influence of social environment is also apparent. The "semi" (truck) and "sheriff" of the farm child, for example, represent something more than linguistic equivalents of the city child's "truck" and "scout car." In much the same way the significance of "street corner" for boys probably has implications which differ from the use of "downtown" by girls.

Hence, we see that language development and perception go together. As the child acquires a greater stock of concepts, he is able to make finer discriminations in his perception of the world around him. As Piaget [18] has pointed out, such development is essentially a process of socialization in which the egocentrism of the young child gives way to a frame of reference outside the individual, and he begins to see the world more like other people constituting his social group.

Experience and Perception. Many evidences of the part played by experience in the act of perception have been revealed. When a young city boy says in response to the Resort scene, "It looks

[18] Jean Piaget, *op. cit.*

like, to me, the Y.M.C.A. . . . that's where I'm going to go swimming," the basis for his perception is quite obvious. The part played by experience and that due to mental age in accounting for the considerable difference found between first grade and older pupils, however, is less clear. A better measure of the relationship of experience to perception is found in comparing rural and urban children when intelligence, sex, and grade are kept constant.

Differences between farm and city children were spread over various ideational and feeling categories involved in perception. Although there was no difference in their over-all recognition of the series, there were significant variations in five of the fourteen life situations. Much greater disparities were shown with respect to the field or background orientations displayed by these groups of children. Regarding spatial setting, rural boys and girls were more state conscious and urban children more oriented to the nation both with respect to general terms and specific place names used to make these designations. Differences in the kinds of temporal referents used by rural and urban children were even more marked, the former showing a preference for associational settings and the latter for systematic. City children were also more conscious of the present ("modern") time setting for the series, but they also displayed more confusions in trying to identify time periods. The same general pattern was true of the feelings expressed by rural and urban children. There was no significant difference in the distribution of attitudes expressed toward the series as a whole. What was noticeable was that city children began the interview with a greater proportion of negative reactions and ended the interview with more neutral responses than was true of children attending one-room schools. Within this over-all picture there was a difference in attitude toward one life situation (the Dock) which urban children had more mixed feelings about, and a greater preference shown by farm children for the Church scene.

Another way to examine the relationship of experience to perception is to study social class differentials. This was the focus of an earlier study on social-problem awareness.[19] Quantitatively speaking, there was no difference in the perception of social prob-

[19] Frank J. Estvan, "The Relationship of Social Status, Intelligence, and Sex of Ten- and Eleven-Year-Old Children to an Awareness of Poverty," *Genetic Psychology Monograph,* XLVI (June, 1952), pp. 3-60.

lems by upper-status or lower-status children. There was, however, a very real difference in their sensitivity to 10 of 42 problem areas identified. Upper-status children were more aware of *qualitative* problems (kind of employment, kind of education, location of residence, and possession of recreational facilities). They also showed a greater awareness of the discomforts and hardships attending poverty. Lower-status children, on the other hand, were more aware of *quantitative* problems (having clothing, having employment, health factors including medical care), as well as personal or social disorganization involving family relationships and intoxication. As for setting, the upper-status child tended to think of poverty in national terms whereas the lower-status child noted its prevalence in his immediate surroundings. Also, he seemed to be more aware of its presence in other countries probably as a result of his closer contacts with ethnic groups.

Experience, then, does not mean that children will be more or less perceptive of life situations as a whole, but that they will show greater sensitivity to the areas with which they have more contact or which are more meaningful in their way of life. The difference is one of kind rather than degree, and is one which affects all phases of perceptual behavior.

Sex and Perception. The roles of the sexes are the outcomes of biological fact and social invention. Among others, Margaret Mead [20] has provided a wealth of material illustrating how patterns of behavior for the sexes are culturally defined. Whatever these factors may be in our culture, sex has been found to be associated with the way in which life situations are perceived. Some of the differences have to do with ideas. Far more striking are the different attitudes and overtones which color the boy's and girl's view of the world.

Boys are slightly more aware of the cognitive side of perception. There were more girls than boys, for example, who attained only a partial recognition of certain life situations. Regarding perceptual field, it was the boys who made greater use of social or historical events to orient scenes in time. Girls, in contrast, were more confused or mixed in their placement of life situations in

[20] Margaret Mead, *Sex and Temperament in Three Primitive Societies.* New York: New American Library of World Literature, Inc., 1950 (Mentor Edition).

a spatial context. These findings are in substantial agreement with the different ways in which boys and girls looked upon poverty. The former were slightly ahead of girls in their ideas about poverty. They were more sensitive to its health implications, they placed poverty in a world-wide setting, and were more realistic in their estimate of its prevalence.

The great difference in feelings between boys and girls was exhibited in every stage of the interview except for picture preferences. Girls were more definite in their expression of attitudes. They exhibited more favorable attitudes in their picture stories, and identified more angry figures with the life situations, whereas boys gave more neutral reasons for their figure selections. As a result, for the series as a whole, girls exhibited more mixed pro and con tendencies than did boys who were more neutral. Differences in feeling tone, as evidenced in picture valuations, were markedly variant for five of the fourteen life situations. Boys had a high regard for the Dam and Farm whereas girls preferred the Bedroom, Mansion, and Church.

That boys acquire a somewhat greater familiarity with the world, but that girls react to it more emotionally is quite clear. Areas of concern present the contrast between the girl's concentration upon primary institutions, and the boy's preference for the "outside" world. In making such a distinction, much greater emphasis is given to the symbols of "higher" social status by girls than by boys. The conclusion is inescapable that, already in elementary school, boys and girls are in the process of identifying themselves with their respective roles in society, and that this fact colors their view of the world.

Intelligence and Perception. Intellectual level as determined by the Stanford-Binet test has also been found to be related to perceptual behavior. Differences associated with intelligence apply to ideas, the intellectual components of perception, but have little if any bearing on emotional reactions.

Greater recognition power was displayed by high I.Q. pupils in almost every respect including synthesis, generalized structure, and both dimensions of function (immediate and extended). In way of contrast, more low-ability pupils went no further than to describe these scenes in general terms (nonrecognition). This represents the difference between generalization which is based on knowledge and generalization which is due to "ignorance." The former is perception based on specific and meaningful concepts, the latter a mode of approach reflecting the perceiver's inability to differentiate.

The superiority of bright children was equally pronounced regarding a consciousness of background or field. In connection with both spatial and temporal settings, they designated a greater number of associational and systematic referents whereas lower I.Q. pupils produced a greater number of indefinite responses. With respect to space, high I.Q. pupils made more use of specific place names than was the case for less able pupils. In their time designations, bright children were also much more likely to use diurnal references—time associated with natural events. This superiority of highly intelligent children in the ideational components of perception was also borne out in their awareness of poverty in which case they demonstrated both quantitative and qualitative superiority in terms of recognition, and the larger physical setting in which they placed the problem.

Attitudinally, there was no difference in the feelings or valuations bright and low-average children placed upon life situations. There was, however, a difference in their approach. More bright children began on a vigorous note which was expressed as positive or negative attitudes. As the interview progressed, more low-ability pupils identified "sad" figures with the life situations, and a greater number gave no definite reason to support their figure selections. At the end of the interview, however, the two intelligence groups were practically alike in their expression of attitudes.

Thus, it appears that with high intellectual capacity there is a corresponding high level of cognition which is revealed in greater powers of recognition, and a heightened sense of orientation. In spite of differences in the ideas brought to bear on a life situation by children of varying intellectual levels, they do not feel differently about them. Bright children may have more assurance in expressing their attitudes, but given time to react to a situation those of lower ability exhibit similar emotions. Quite obviously, there is a difference between *knowing* about and *feeling*. By definition, intelligence is the capacity to think rationally (comprehend, reason, judge), to act purposefully (adjust to, deal with the environment), and to learn from experience. These are mental endowments which function in providing the conceptual basis for perception, recalling related experience, and integrating all these into some meaningful pattern. These processes are not necessarily translated into affective or feeling states in the sense that the more ideas the perceiver has about a life situation the stronger or "better" he will feel about it.

Personality and Perception

The term, personality, is generally used with reference to kind of person or so-called "adjustment." Those who study personality are concerned with the dynamics involved in the organization of the individual's needs-response system. Looking at the totality of individual behavior, they seek to identify the unifying factors or integrating principles resulting in characteristic modes of behavior (syndromes). It is the unique combination of these various factors, and their relative strength as they interact in various situations which distinguish *the* individual from other people, and which are said to constitute his "personality."

Like all other forms of behavior, perception is part of the individual's response system and, therefore, of his personality. The past decade has witnessed an increasing interest in the distortions which can be brought about in perception through the influence of motivation and fear, need for conformity and achievement, bodily states, and personal-social values.[21] Not only does personality influence perception, but the reverse is being posited with equal vigor. In such cases, perception is regarded as a means of personality assessment.

Characteristic modes of response to the Life-Situation Picture Series are strikingly evident among children. These highly individualistic ways of responding to life situations took two forms. In the main, they were matters of feeling tone although cognitive aspects of perception were also involved. As far as typical school children are concerned, "personality differences" are not reflected in distortions of what the scene represents or bizarre explanations

[21] The extent of such studies may be gathered from: Jerome S. Bruner and David Krech (Eds.), *Perception and Personality: A Symposium.* Durham: Duke University Press, 1950; and

Robert R. Blake and Glenn V. Ramsey, *Perception: An Approach to Personality.* New York: Ronald Press, 1951.

•

of what is going on. A distinctive pattern of reaction is most often discernible in the feeling tones expressed or in the recurrence of the same theme regardless of the nature of the particular life situation. An illustration of an affective "set" are the responses of a first grade rural boy whose selection of figures and reasons for their selection in Part II of the interview gave evidence of conflict in nine situations out of fourteen.

Picture 1. A happy girl. 'Cause her mommy doesn't shame her.
2. The mad boy. 'Cause his mother doesn't like him.
3. He's happy. 'Cause hims mother didn't give him a licking nor nothing.
4. The sad boy. 'Cause he was crying going downtown. See him get . . . his mother told him to go downtown and him didn't want to.
5. The happy girl. 'Cause see, her mother didn't scold her.
7. The sad boy. Yes, see, his father told him to plow and he didn't want to.
9. The mad boy. 'Cause see, his mother sent him downtown and he didn't want to go, see him had to plow.
12. The mad girl. 'Cause she doesn't want to go to the school. She don't like her school.
14. The sad boy. He didn't want to go to see all his friends. He don't like them. 'Cause see, them didn't stay home. He want 'em to stay home and they won't, they want to go.

It is interesting to note, further, that he described the picture which he drew just prior to the interview in the following manner: "This is a dog, and this is me, and this is a tiger." Placed in the total context there might be reason for interpreting the tiger as a symbol of aggression, and concluding that this youngster is exhibiting mixed feelings about his world. This may represent a serious deviation from so-called normal development or be within the range of expected behavior for a six-year-old who is pulling away from his parents.[22] Whether or not this child was attempting to establish some measure of independence or whether his be-

[22] Arnold Gesell and Frances L. Ilg, *Child Development,* Part II, p. 110. New York: Harper and Brothers, 1949.

havior manifests something more serious we do not know, but conflict is characteristic of his behavior *at this time*.

In contrast to the above are the remarks of a sixth grade rural boy who, in his picture stories to all fourteen life situations, expressed friendly, optimistic, and appreciative feelings denoting good equilibrium and an adjusting outlook. The extent of the latter may be inferred from the picture he drew prior to the interview which was entitled, "A Trip to Space."

Picture 3. He's so glad to get this pretty scene . . .

4. The family told the little boy to thank the man very much . . .

5. He likes his home very much—he likes his parents very well.

6. 'Cause I think it's nice to go to church and thank the Lord for all the things we've got.

7. He was glad that he had moved to this part of the country and the neighbors were very kind to him, too.

8. They were glad, too, and they thanked their neighbors . . .

9. . . . They greet them with a friendly grin and a "hello."

The anxiety and fear of a young urban girl who had been seriously ill, and whose relative had met with a tragic accident was revealed in each of her picture stories, a sampling of which follows:

Picture 1 (Bedroom)

They're going to bed. And when you go to bed you should go to the toilet and say a prayer. And before you go to bed if your bed is wet, you should make sure it is dry.

Picture 11 (Resort)

If there's a swimming pond by your house, you should watch out because somebody might get a long stick or thing and stick it in the water and then they would hurt theirselves. And people that are sick should mind their mother.

Picture 12 (Schoolroom)

And when they're at school and show pictures they should be real careful because naughty kids could put their sticky hands all over it. And when their teacher tells them to do things, they should do it. And they have to go to gym and somebody ain't got their work done—they should mind their teacher. And the hard work they have to do—if they don't know they should ask their teacher.

Picture 14 (Dock)
And if you're going on a boat somewheres you should watch out so you don't get on the edge and try to stand on it, 'cause you could fall right in the water and git bit by a whale. And if you had a baby you should watch out so you don't slip and fall in the water, 'cause a baby would die that way. And if you had a package and you picked up the wrong one, you should watch the name and you should ask the people that got theirs right by you, and you should ask them if you got the wrong one and then they'll give it back. And if you're in the Marines you should be careful. And planes are having war where they shoot them down, you should watch out because one plane might be the dangerous one, and if they shot a bullet why it might go right out the plane. The stuff that you buy you should keep, 'cause if you go back and say you don't want it, they wouldn't give you any of your money back, and you go to a store, they shouldn't cheat.

The extreme degree of apprehension mirrored in the above "stories" coupled with a corresponding high regard for what "should" be done was also revealed in the picture drawn by this child before the interview took place which she explained in part by saying, "I like a fence so that the kids don't go out in the street."

In reacting to the Life-Situation Picture Series, some children exhibited a very strong preoccupation with a certain interest or value which would appear as a common theme in greatly differentiated scenes. The desire "to ride on a pony" was a repeated theme for a young rural boy. Another six-year-old had apparently just "discovered" father, and had centered his attention on the father symbols (man or men) in nine of the situations. All three of his picture choices were influenced likewise: "Because there's airplanes, and a boat, and lotsa people, and my dad likes lotsa people, an' airplanes." A sixth grader didn't like "lotsa people." He preferred the "open country," and expressed his dislike of crowds in four of the situations. On the picture he had drawn earlier, he showed himself walking alone with his dog and stated, "I like to go for walks in the forest."

In children, such interests may be short lived. Then, again, they may mark the beginnings of persistent personality "traits." Some appear to be "normal"; others seem to be grossly deviant. One such example might be a young urban girl whose obsession with monetary considerations appeared in 9 out of 14 pictures:

Picture 2. (Her mother) told her that she would give her some money if she got the baby some milk.

3. His daddy said if he worked with him, he'll get some money.

4. They're gonna go by—to the downtown, and buy something.

5. She's looking at some beautiful things and she's thinking if she could be one of them.

7. (Man) Wants to see if he could help and then he said he would give him five dollars.

9. They think you have to spend some money to go up there.

10. Nobody would go by this store where they sell clothes, because they don't have good clothes there, they cost too much.

11. The wife doesn't want him to build a new farm 'cause then he wastes too much money, and he wants to, and and the kids, they still think their mother is right.

13. If he (the little boy) would go to school his daddy would a . . . give him a dog house, and he would buy him a dog that wouldn't cost so much money.

In explanation of the picture which she drew beforehand, she said, "I dressed up in my mother's clothes and came outside. I like to, but I can't—my mother won't let me." Although a number of interpretations of these data are possible, including the idea of poverty and family differences of opinion over money matters, this girl's responses are so strongly fixated that one wonders if there isn't need for some kind of guidance. At any rate, there can be little question regarding the intensity of her present concern over money.

The above illustrations are convincing testimony of the relationship between perception and certain characteristic ways of behaving on the part of individuals or their "personality." Perception is more than a disinterested or dispassionate view of objective reality. By the time they enter school, many children have developed strong emotional or value "sets" which are brought into play as they view the world. The nature of these "view finders" and strength of their directional powers vary greatly among individuals, and is the reason why some writers refer to "objective" and "subjective" perception. It is more useful to think of these two as being the end points of a continuum, and to regard differences as being a matter of degree. Even so-called "normal" individuals perceive the world through a lens fashioned by the totality of their wants, experiences, and behavior patterns. Only because this image of the world falls within the band of normality as defined by the culture is it classified as "objective." The farther the image departs from this range of acceptability the more "subjective" it is held to be. Given a different culture or a change in the mores or values of the same culture, the classifications of these perceptions might be reversed—just as would the concept of personality adjustment.

Chapter	DEVELOPING CHILDREN'S

XXIV. SOCIAL PERCEPTION

THE variety of influences bearing on perception and its many ramifications are testimony of the inseparable relationship.between perceiving and living. In fact, were an individual rendered incapable of perceiving either because of a loss of his sensory equipment or experiential background, his survival would depend upon outside assistance. Less dramatic but, perhaps, more important because it can be easily overlooked is the relationship between perceiving and the quality of living. For it is a different thing in driving a car to be mindful only of one's desire to reach a destination quickly and to be perceptive of road conditions, road signs, speed regulations, and traffic both front and rear. The difference may mean life or death for the driver and for others, and in the long run will influence automobile design, road construction, driving regulations, accident insurance, and other institutional practices bearing on this form of transportation.

Perception may continue to develop for as long as an individual lives. The foundation for continued growth is laid from the first moments of consciousness. The infant's perceptions grow along with his physical growth. Through the functioning of his senses and intelligence, he defines and refines his concepts of the persons and objects surrounding him. His curiosity, explorations, frustrations, puzzled facial expressions are signs of such attempts. Later, his efforts take the form of a continuous string of "whys" asked of parents, brothers and sisters, playmates—anyone who will listen to and answer him. Right or wrong beginnings are made at this stage. The child with "problems" usually comes from a "deprived background" which does not necessarily imply slum conditions or the lack of basic physical requirements. It can be true of any child from any stratum of society who is deprived of the necessary guidance in growing mentally. Some may develop in spite of this, but it cannot be taken for granted. "Correct" perceptions cannot be left solely to incidental or accidental, trial-and-error learning. In this confusing world the child looks to others for "help."

Knowing about Children's Social Perception

Children seldom, if ever, regard a life situation with a blank mind and unvarying pulse. Is going to a summer camp a wonderful opportunity to learn to swim, row a boat, and "make a lotta new friends" or are his mother and dad just "getting rid" of him so that they can go on their vacation? From the very outset, camping takes on certain meanings which shape and color the child's experiences and influence his judgment afterwards as to how "good" summer camp really was.

Without doubt, beginnings are extremely important phases in any activity, and adults must make definite provisions for finding out what is in the minds and hearts of young people as they approach a situation. This is where guidance must begin: by taking the child's limited perceptions and correcting whatever erroneous ideas he may have, by relating his values to whatever possibilities are inherent in the situation and, if nothing more, by helping him to see that there are many ways of perceiving the same situation.

Knowing about a child's perceptions also enables adults to evaluate his development. The child who traces vein structure and uses shadings of color for his autumn leaves has moved beyond the point where he colored them a solid red. When he introduces other signs of autumn in his portrayal, we have evidence of his increasing perceptiveness of changes taking place in Nature at this time of year. If a child shows an awareness of things which he previously ignored or sees relationships among things which formerly stood in isolation, do we not have a most significant measure of his developing knowledges and insights?

The role of perception in evaluation is also important from the child's point of view. Crucial as adult judgment may be to the child, equally important is his own perception of achievement and that of his peers. The two are not necessarily the same, and the difference is not always in the direction of higher "standards" held by adults. For the grown-up who has some understanding of developmental stages in art, the product of eight- to twelve-year-old children may give evidence of "normal" growth whereas a child may be grossly dissatisfied with his efforts. In drawing a picture of "anything you are interested in or think about," a sixth grade girl drew a picture of herself as a secretary in a business office. Not satisfied with the figure drawn, she redrew the picture on the other side of the paper. It was a duplicate except that instead of a secretary sitting at a desk, there now was a sign "Out to Lunch." To find out how children perceive their accomplishments, and to help them understand the nature of growth and development would seem to be important ways in which adults can help children to appraise their progress realistically.

Providing a Basis for Perception

An individual perceives only what he can bring to a situation directly or through analogy. The development of perception, therefore, goes hand in hand with the development of a rich background of concepts. This is essentially a question of the kind and nature of children's experiences. As many pupils indicated, their ideas came from direct experiences with the situation in question, through television, and the school. They interpreted certain life situations by making analogies with everyday events in their lives ("I live on a farm, and I like to drive a tractor."), to some of their more special activities ("that looks like the Y.M.C.A.—that's where I'm going next week"), and to travel experiences ("that's Washington, D.C. where we went once"). References to school activities included such notions as "we're studying China and that would be a good picture to show how they live," and recall of field trips taken by the class. Certain TV programs or televiewing, in general, were also cited as sources of ideas.

These observations are not unique to this particular group. In an interview of first grade suburban children dealing with their social concepts and sources of information, it was discovered that in 19.4% of the cases knowledge was the outcome of direct contact or experience with the concept, and that television was given about equal importance contributing to approximately 19% of the responses. This latter source of information was cited nearly twice as often as parents. As might be expected for first grade children, the school supplied less than 5% of their information, and books (including comic books) provided even less.[23] It should be noted that the same source of information can result in valid concepts or in misconceptions. Experiences, in and of themselves, are no guarantee that correct interpretations will be made by children regardless of how realistic they may be. Moreover, there is no certainty that the experience will eventuate in the formation of concepts. As responses to the Dam scene suggest, there can be a vast gulf between the planting of a tree and the development of conservation concepts. Hence, the importance of providing children with concrete experiences as well as opportunities to verbalize about these experiences.

The availability of past experiences (concepts) for recall depends upon the "trace" left by the original experience. The impress which any event makes upon a young mind depends upon a number of factors. Included is an awareness of the significance of the experience for the achievement of *his* goals, the reality of experiencing governed by the avenues of sensory approach open to the experience, and the emotional quality of the experience giving it force and vitality. All these would imply that for children, at least, conceptual development should be focused upon fewer but more intensive experiences as compared with attempts to "cover everything." Instead of moving superficially over broad areas of human endeavor, children should stop long enough at key points to uncover the interplay of forces and concepts at work. Taking a little thing and "blowing it up," as it were, produces a network of ideas so that this "thing" no longer exists in isolation, but is integrated with a number of related concepts. Rather than only one stimulus having the power to evoke this concept, as in a simple stimulus-response connection, the experience is then available for association with all ideas included in the conceptual pattern of which it has become a part.

Guiding Children's Perception

Perception needs to be guided. Its highly selective nature, and susceptibility to the influence of habitual "sets" and temporary physical or mental states may result in an infinite variety of in-

[23] Charlotte Huck, *The Nature and Derivation of Young Children's Social Concepts.* Evanston: Northwestern University, Unpublished Ph.D. Dissertation, 1955.

terpretations for any life situation. The more complex the situation the more help children need in knowing what to pay attention to. This screening out of relevant stimuli from among those equally provocative but significant-for-other-reasons is achieved through the agency of purposes. Hence, one of the most important functions of the adult is to help children establish purposes or, if they have already been set up, make sure that they have been understood and accepted. For example, it is one thing to visit a large airport with nothing particular in mind, and another to note the important facilities and services provided by such a center. The former may result in a random series of impressions including the parking lot, the fascinating staccato of take-off and landing, the bustling terminal building, the "candy counter," drinking fountain, and eventually the restrooms. The trip back home will undoubtedly ring loud with the zooming and gyrations of budding pilots. A good time will be had by all, and if the purpose is to bring out the notion that an airport is a very busy place, this objective would probably be achieved. On the other hand, if the purpose is to find out how one travels by air, visiting the airport becomes less a matter of looking at anything that happens to come along and more a seeking out of the processes involved: finding out about schedules, how to buy a ticket, insurance, weighing in, what to do about luggage, meals, getting on a plane, what to do when on a plane, etc. Planes, the new "Jet" bubble-gum machine, and the restroom may still be parts of this experience, but they are seen in their proper perspective and do not constitute *the* trip.

Because perception involves an association of ideas, it would help the child if past experiences with airplanes are recalled as well as pertinent information about bus and railroad stations. In this way, concepts about transport terminals would be brought to the surface level of consciousness, and be available for the child's interpretation of his new experiences with airport terminals. Because perception involves discrimination, the child should be encouraged to make distinctions among the physical aspects and the processes involved in airplane transportation. All "counters" are not alike. Can the young child tell which are for information, purchasing tickets, weighing in—and which for refreshment? Does it matter which airplane one chooses or do they all go to the same places? What is the difference between first class and tourist travel?

The child's awareness would also be furthered by having certain relationships brought to his attention or by organizing experiences so that he may more readily perceive these relationships. In this case, guiding the child through the steps involved in plane travel would help him to integrate these various phases into an orderly pattern so that he would "see" not only what is involved, but the way in which these processes go together to constitute air travel. To carry this synthesis further, the child should be made conscious of the recency of plane travel, and come to regard it as one phase in the gradual evolution of transportation; he should appreciate the significance of the far-flung network of air routes, and their great impact on personal and social living. Naturally, all of this will not come from one visit to the airport, but this demonstrates the growth and expansion of concepts necessary for understanding and perception.

Focusing on the Human Element

In developing children's social perception the focus should be kept on the human element. We have already noted how the child directs his attention to people and is concerned about the personal-social relationships implied in various life situations. This means that instead of talking about "offices" and "work" we would emphasize the information clerk, the ticket agent, the baggage man, and what each does to make plane travel more convenient and dependable. Instead of talking about the handling of countless pieces of baggage in the abstract, we would trace through the weighing, tagging, and various ways in which a particular piece of luggage (preferably a child's) is handled in the course of traveling from one place to another. Instead of planes being "fueled" in the abstract, perception would be aided if children could observe Mr. Kelly driving the gasoline truck to the plane, and follow the operations involved from the standpoint of what maintenance men actually do.

In focusing on the human element, we cannot overlook the possibility that to a large extent meaning for the individual is largely in terms of himself. While it may be true that there is a change from egocentrism to socialized thinking as a child grows older, it is also probable that the self is always the center for the individual's life space.[24] In a sense, therefore, what is self becomes a matter of identification. How close the various segments of the *there* or elsewhere may be to the observer is essentially a matter of perception. By developing the notion that anything that happens ultimately affects everyone else, the dichotomy between self-interest and social welfare, and that between children's concerns and adult problems tends to disappear. Increasing sensitivity to how "all things affect me" would not necessarily mean that everything would be regarded as of equal importance for reasons which have been made explicit in this volume. Such an awareness, however, should increase the scope of one's preoccupations, and result in more socialized if not more effective thinking and acting.

The human element in any life situation, therefore, includes both the perceiver and "others." Yet, as we have seen, boys and girls did not make a practice of identifying themselves with life situations in constructive roles. They perceived themselves (children) usually as consumers rather than contributors or producers. Their desire for participation was in terms of the activity, and not because of a sense of responsibility or respect for the outcome of the total enterprise. Although they often showed sympathy for the people in a scene, it seemed to be disassociated with their own lives. They were conscious of the farmer in the field and the man in the factory being "all tired out," but did not consider their own father's connection with work or what a child's contribution could be.

The child's perception must, therefore, "get under the skin"— his own and others. The development of self-insight and empathy with others should be one of the major concerns of those helping children "grow up." Through role playing and other techniques, boys and girls should be given opportunities to examine their roles and that of adults. In this way they will gain a realistic awareness of functions, and acquire attitudes or feelings about them based on human values rather than personal considerations alone.

Thus we see the intimate relationship between perception and learning. Every experience, whether in school or out, requires dealing with something. One of the important outcomes of any

[24] For an elaboration of this idea and the concept of visual distance *see:* Andrew Paul Ushenko, *The Field Theory of Meaning.* Ann Arbor: The University of Michigan Press, 1958.

activity, therefore, is to be able to perceive things in a new fashion or to be conscious of things that previously did not exist in the mind of the perceiver. These are more likely to develop with guidance.

The Role of the School

The factors involved in developing children's perceptions are clearly things about which the school can do something. The dependence of perception upon conception defines one of the school's primary purposes: to develop systems of ideas which may be used as frames of reference for viewing the world. Such a viewer would include a number of overlays each consisting of a pattern of reference points. One would represent organizations of ideas or concepts, another would involve space, the third a scale of time. On them would be fixed the bench marks or key points giving form and structure to the ideas being dealt with. By using these in conjunction with each other, the child would learn that ideas are not free-floating but that they belong to systems or "fields." A horse, for example, is a form of transportation, a source of income, a means of carrying on work, recreation, a quadruped. The school can develop the broad outlines of these frames of reference, and fill in enough of the more important details to insure their usefulness. It could not hope to complete their development for there is no terminal point in learning. There will always be new concepts and more insightful cross references which can be made from one overlay to the others.

There is disagreement about the most effective method of developing patterns of ideas. The confusion often arises because of a failure to recognize the fact of multiple organization or to insist upon one system of thought as having priority over others. Proponents of the latter position are quite prone to look upon their organization as being "systematic" and to regard other forms as being of lesser degree and even "incidental" in structuring. A system of ideas does not exist in the form of a linear arrangement of concepts like beads on a string, one idea touching upon the next which, in turn, comes in contact with the following idea. Rather, a concept must be seen as coming in contact with or being related to many ideas constituting a pattern or integration of ideas. In such a complex, entry may be made at a number of points instead of only at the "beginning" as would be the case if ideas were confined in pipelines. The test of organization is whether movement from idea to idea answers the purposes of the learner (problem) rather than whether concepts are laid out end to end in some fashion determined by the nature of the content itself. Many of the same ideas would be accounted for in both plans of organization but, quite obviously, they would be perceived in quite different contexts.

Any plan for developing frames of reference for looking at the world must have continuity. As we have seen, perception is usually a matter of degree. A percept is not developed at one point in time, but is a growing thing ever broadening and more insightful. Much happens before the child enters school, a great deal develops during his school years, and one would hope for continued growth after "commencement." For school people, this means that elementary and secondary programs be viewed as a whole, and that the development of social perception, as for other areas, be regarded as a twelve year sequence or more. In such a scheme, every stage of conceptual development would be regarded as equally important. There would be no place for a "one-shot-treatment" based on the allocation of a specific topic to one grade or school level only. The community, for example, would not be studied once in the second or third grade, but would be perceived in more meaningful relationships as the learner's horizon was extended into "new" areas of knowledge, space, and time.

The nature and development of social perception suggest the need for both differentiation and synthesis in school programs. This has certain implications for organizing learning experiences and for teaching procedures. The former would have to take into account the limited perceptual field of the young child, and his difficulty in integrating or synthesizing clues to create meaningful wholes. Relatively speaking, his learning experiences should be organized in units which are not too broad in scope, which stress the relationship between structure and function, and are short in duration. Growth would take the form of increasing ability to make a more detailed and analytical examination of closely related ideas, to place them in a space-and-time setting, and to tie these ideas in with other bodies of knowledge. The first can be achieved within content areas through the conventional school subjects, but the second usually requires going "outside" the subject area—often to history. The broadening of perceptions achieved through the inter-relating of concepts from many content areas would seem to call for "integrated courses" at the end points of an educational pro-gram. The general design for a curriculum, then, would be to begin with rather general considerations of structure and function in areas of limited scope followed by a gradual extension into space and time which is accompanied by more analytical discrimi-nations, and ending with the broadest kind of experiences inte-grating the ideas and experiences of many related areas for the development of even greater insights—and perceptions.

In addition to what has already been said about developing children's social perception, teaching techniques must also give consideration to the semantics involved in perception, and the formation of the habit of perceiving. Any teacher soon acquires her own stock of misverbalisms: the youngster who salutes the flag "for witches stand," the young child from a city slum area who was proud to report that milk came from the "gutter," the boy who identified the fat little man in his Christmas drawing as "Round John Virgin." They illustrate the problem of communica-tion and its effect on perception. Except that the referent has a clear-cut meaning and is understood by children, perception is bound to be faulty, to say the least. The avoidance of such bizarre interpretations rests upon teaching skills and pupils' habits of awareness. The latter is more than "paying attention." It is an active seeking for clues going beyond the immediate and obvious to come out with something which makes more sense. To nurture an awareness of one's environment and the desire to respond to it more fully is one of teaching's greatest challenges.

In Conclusion

The perceptive person really "lives." He sees more in life and, as a consequence, he lives more richly. For him nothing is with-out significance. Everything is part of the mosaic of life, and he delights in discovering the pattern. Attuned to the world, he can adapt to changes. Whether they be personal or social, he per-ceives problems realistically, and because he does his solutions are more likely to be adequate. Never before have these qualities been more important for the individual or society. Development of the child's social perception, therefore, cannot be emphasized too much or begin too early. It is the responsibility of all—family, relatives, friends, school, church, social agencies, yours, ours . . . But in the words of "The Prophet":

> If (the adult) is indeed wise he does not bid (the child) enter the house of his wisdom, but rather leads (him) to the threshold of (the child's) own mind.

APPENDIX

TABLE 1

CHRONOLOGICAL AGE AND INTELLIGENCE
QUOTIENT OF COMPARATIVE GROUPS

	Group	C.A. (months)		I.Q. (months)	
		Mean	S.D.	Mean	S.D.
Grade	First (N = 44)	78.44	2.02	107.59	14.99
	Sixth (N = 44)	138.64‡	2.15	109.61	14.71
Community	Rural (N = 44)	108.73	30.06	105.45	15.18
	Urban (N = 44)	108.34	30.29	111.75	13.61
Sex	Boy (N = 44)	108.96	30.29	108.25	15.70
	Girl (N = 44)	108.11	30.06	108.95	13.93
Intelligence	High (N = 16)	108.88	27.54	128.94‡‡	7.72
	Low (N = 16)	108.56	30.89	90.25	7.37

‡ F (analysis of variance) = 19031.25 or P<.01

‡‡ t (difference between two means) = 14.04 or P<.01

TABLE 2

RANKINGS FOR LIFE-SITUATION PICTURES

Perceptual Aspects	Community Block				Social Status Block					Child-Adult Block				
	Rural		Urban		Upper		Lower			Child		Adult		
	Village	Farm	City	Factory	Mansion	Resort	Poor House	Old Beach	Bedroom	Church	School-room	Dam	Capitol	Dock
1. Productivity														
a. Attention Time	11	6	8	4	2	7	3	10	12	14	13	1	9	5
b. Word Productivity	5	7	8	10	1	6	4	9	14	13	11	3	12	2
2. Recognition														
a. Meanings	10	3	1	6	14	8	5	4	7	11	2	12	13	9
b. Appropriateness	8.5	1.5	5	7	14	11	12	8.5	1.5	3	4	10	13	6
3. Setting														
a. Spatial	7	3	4	9.5	9.5	8	13	5	14	1	2	11	6	12
b. Temporal	4	3	7	11.5	5	6	8.5	8.5	2	1	11.5	11.5	14	11.5
4. Attitude														
a. Positive	4	5	7	12	12	1	14	6	10	2.5	9	2.5	12	8
b. Negative	5.5	10	4	3	7.5	11	1	7.5	13	13	5.5	9	13	2
5. Preference														
a. Selected	13.5	1	11	13.5	4.5	4.5	12	8	2	9	3	6.5	10	6.5
b. Rejected	13	8.5	6	6	6	14	1	3.5	11	11	2	8.5	3.5	11
6. Sex Association	Boy	Boy	Boy & Girl	Boy	Girl	Boy & Girl	Boy & Girl	Boy	Girl	Boy & Girl	Girl	Boy	Boy & Girl	Boy & Girl

TABLE 3

COMPONENTS IN CHILDREN'S PERCEPTION OF LIFE SITUATIONS

Perceptual Components	Life-Situation Pictures														Mean %
	1	2	3	4	5	6	7	8	9	10	11	12	13	14	
1. Recognition	100	59	73	78	49	95	100	75	51	91	70	94	75	89	78.5
2. Field															
a. Spatial	20	50	57	65	65	94	80	73	70	75	66	83	68	55	65.8
b. Temporal	33	11	8	8	18	41	23	11	5	14	16	8	19	8	15.9
3. Attitudes															
a. Positive	48	7	68	47	47	68	55	53	47	53	74	49	60	50	51.9
b. Negative	13	69	17	26	19	13	16	19	13	25	15	20	20	27	22.3
4. Preference															
a. Selected‡	12	4	8	3	8	7	12	8	5	5	8	11	3	8	7.1
b. Rejected	2	44	3	5	5	2	3	7	7	5	0	13	1	2	7.1

‡ Per cent of choices instead of pupils as for other components.

TABLE 4

LEVEL AND TYPE OF RECOGNITION BY COMPARATIVE GROUPS

	Level and Type	Grade		Community		Sex		I.Q.		Total	
		1st	6th	Rural	Urban	Boy	Girl	Low‡	High‡	N	%
Recognition	1. Synthesis	86	273³	169	190	187	172	44	86³	359	29.14
	2. Structure	82	111¹	100	93	98	95	39	35	193	15.67
	a. Immediate	(109)	(304)³	(196)	(217)	(215)	(198)	(64)	(88)	(413)	
	b. Extended	(64)	(114)³	(93)	(85)	(95)	(83)	(24)	(43)¹	(178)	
	3. Function	31	71³	46	56	51	51	21	20	102	8.28
	a. Immediate	(104)	(293)³	(182)	(215)	(202)	(195)	(60)	(88)¹	(397)	
	b. Extended	(29)	(140)³	(80)	(89)	(86)	(83)	(23)	(41)¹	(169)	
	4. Partial	198³	101	163	136	131	168¹	53	48	299	24.27
	a. Human	(176)³	(96)	(146)	(126)	(115)	(157)¹	(48)	(40)	(272)	
	b. Natural	(12)	(18)	(16)	(14)	(16)	(14)	(6)	(3)	(30)	
	c. Cultural	(51)³	(20)	(41)	(30)	(39)	(32)	(11)	(16)	(71)	
	5. Identification	13³	0	5	8	8	5	4	0	13	1.06
Non-Recognition	6. General	156³	19	88	87	91	84	45²	21	175	14.20
	a. Human	(150)³	(19)	(86)	(83)	(88)	(81)	(44)²	(20)	(169)	
	b. Natural	(4)	(0)	(4)	(0)	(2)	(2)	(0)	(0)	(4)	
	c. Cultural	(28)³	(4)	(21)	(11)	(18)	(14)	(2)	(5)	(32)	
	7. Miscellaneous listing	6¹	0	4	2	3	3	5	0	6	0.49
	8. Inappropriate	31	32	32	31	34	29	11	11	63	5.11
	9. Indefinite	8	9	9	8	8	9	2	3	17	1.38
	10. No response	5	0	5	5	5	0	0	0	5	0.41
	Total (levels)	616	616	616	616	616	616	224	224	1232	100.01

Note: Figures in ( ) are types of recognition at the levels indicated.
¹P (X² > 3.841) = .05; ²P (X² > 6.635) = .01; ³P (X² > 10.827) = .001; ‡N =16 instead of 44 as for other groups.

TABLE 5

SPATIAL SETTING OF COMPARATIVE GROUPS

Type	Setting / Referent	Grade 1st	Grade 6th	Community Rural	Community Urban	Sex Boy	Sex Girl	I.Q. Low‡	I.Q. High‡	Total N	Total %
Associational	1. Nature	30	73[3]	52	51	50	53	14	14	103	7.91
Associational	2. Home	46	82[2]	65	63	60	68	22	27	128	9.83
Associational	3. Institution	115	244[3]	171	188	194	165	54	80	359	27.57
Associational	Total	191	399[3]	288	302	304	286	90	121[1]	590	45.31
Systematic	4. Community	39	115[3]	84	70	66	88	24	28	154	11.83
Systematic	5. State	0	8[1]	8[1]	0	5	3	1	0	8	0.61
Systematic	6. Region	0	2	0	2	1	1	0	2	2	0.15
Systematic	7. Nation	6	14	5	15[1]	8	12	3	6	20	1.54
Systematic	8. World	0	4	1	3	3	1	1	1	4	0.31
Systematic	Total	45	143[3]	98	90	83	105	29	37	188	14.44
Indefinite	9. Mixed	53	49	60	42	32	70[3]	17	25	102	7.83
Indefinite	10. Unspecified	328[3]	90	206	212	226	192	94[2]	55	418	32.10
Indefinite	11. No response	4	0	1	3	4	0	1	0	4	0.31
Indefinite	Total	385[3]	139	267	257	262	262	112[1]	80	524	40.25
	TOTAL	621	681	653	649	649	653	231	238	1302	99.99

‡ N = 16 instead of 44 as for other groups

[1]P (X² > 3.841) = .05
[2]P (X² > 6.635) = .01
[3]P (X² > 10.827) = .001

TABLE 6

TEMPORAL SETTING OF COMPARATIVE GROUPS

Type	Setting / Referent	Grade 1st	Grade 6th	Community Rural	Community Urban	Sex Boy	Sex Girl	I.Q. Low‡	I.Q. High‡	Total N	Total %
Associational	**Natural**										
	1. Diurnal	23	56³	46	33	40	39	8	21¹	79	6.22
	2. Annual	1	18³	12	7	8	11	4	5	19	1.50
	Human										
	3. Personal	6	7	9	4	3	10	5	6	13	1.02
	4. Social	1	8¹	4	5	9²	0	2	1	9	0.71
	Total	31	89³	71¹	49	60	60	19	33	120	9.45
Systematic	**Chronometric**										
	5. Clock	2	3	4	1	2	3	0	2	5	0.39
	6. Calendar	16	36²	22	30	23	29	8	14	52	4.09
	Historical										
	7. Past	4	9	5	8	6	7	1	0	13	1.02
	8. Present	7	13	4	16²	11	9	1	2	20	1.57
	9. Future	0	0	0	0	0	0	0	0	0	0.00
	Total	29	61³	35	55¹	42	48	10	18	90	7.07
Indefinite	**Indefinite**										
	10. Mixed	11	13	7	17¹	14	10	4	6	24	1.89
	11. Unspecified	549¹	483	525	507	516	516	195	178	1032	81.26
	12. No response	4	0	1	3	4	0	1	0	4	0.31
	Total	564	496	533	527	534	526	200	184	1060	83.46
	Total	624	646	639	631	636	634	229	235	1270	99.98

¹P (X^2 > 3.841) = .05; ²P (X^2 > 6.635) = .01; ³P (X^1 > 10.827) = .001; ‡N =16 instead of 44 as for other groups

TABLE 7

RELATIONSHIP OF SPATIAL AND TEMPORAL SETTINGS OF FIRST AND SIXTH GRADE CHILDREN

Spatial Setting \ Setting	Temporal Setting			
	Systematic	Associational	Indefinite	Total
Systematic	1st - 0.00% 6th - 1.96% (P<.01)	1st - 0.48% 6th - 2.38% (P<.01)	1st - 6.68% 6th -16.27% (P<.001)	1st - 7.15% 6th -20.62% (P<.001)
Associational	1st - 1.43% 6th - 6.17% (P<.001)	1st - 0.64% 6th - 7.43% (P<.001)	1st -28.46% 6th -45.30% (P<.001)	1st -30.52% 6th -58.91% (P<.001)
Indefinite	1st - 3.18% 6th - 1.40% (P<.05)	1st - 3.82% 6th - 3.79% (P = n.s.)	1st -55.32% 6th -15.29% (P<.001)	1st -62.32% 6th -20.48% (P<.001)
Total	1st - 4.61% 6th - 9.54% (P<.001)	1st - 4.93% 6th -13.60% (P<.001)	1st -90.46% 6th -76.86% (P<.001)	1st -99.99% 6th -100.01%

N (1st) = 629
N (6th) = 713

296

TABLE 8

PERCEPTUAL ATTITUDES OF COMPARATIVE GROUPS

Response			Attitude	Grade 1st	Grade 6th	Community Rural	Community Urban	Sex Boy	Sex Girl	Intelligence Low‡	Intelligence High‡	Total (N =88)
PART I	Picture Story	Figure	1. Positive	40	111[3]	76	75	60	91[1]	24	46[2]	151
			2. Neutral	520[1]	450	505	465	501	469	186	157	970
			3. Negative	47	55	32	70[2]	43	59	8	26[2]	102
			4. Indefinite	14[2]	3	6	11	12	5	6	1	17
PART II	Figure Selection	Figure	1. Happy	236	314[3]	274	276	261	289	102	101	550
			2. Neutral	180	232[1]	188	224	216	196	60	77	412
			3. Sad	113[3]	64	98	79	98	79	48[1]	30	177
			4. Angry	88[3]	19	59	48	43	64[1]	18	19	107
		Reason	1. Positive	265	362[3]	317	310	301	326	106	122	627
			2. Neutral	112	153[1]	108	157[2]	149[1]	116	39	48	265
			3. Negative	202[3]	128	172	158	148	182	56	64	330
			4. Indefinite	48[3]	8	30	26	34	22	28[2]	7	56
PART III	Picture Preference		1. Positive	123	127	123	127	123	127	44	46	250
			2. Neutral	1	0	1	0	1	0	0	0	1
			3. Negative	40	46	45	41	45	41	16	16	86
			4. Indefinite	11[1]	3	6	8	8	6	3	2	14
SUMMARY			1. Positive	273	362[3]	321	314	314	321	107	116	635
			2. Neutral	72	88	75	85	98[2]	62	27	23	160
			3. Negative	181[3]	94	144	131	137	138	60	42	275
			4. Mixed	88	72	76	84	65	95[2]	30	43	160
			5. No response	2	0	0	2	2	0	0	0	2

[1] $P (X^2 > 3.841) = .05$
[2] $P (X^2 > 6.635) = .01$
[3] $P (X^2 > 10.827) = .001$

‡N =16 instead of 44 as for other groups

297

TABLE 9

CONSISTENCY OF PERCEPTUAL ATTITUDES OF COMPARATIVE GROUPS

	Group	Attitude toward Life Situation				Total	P (Distribution)
		Consistent	Combined with:				
			Neutral	Indefinite	Neut. & Ind.		
Grade	1. First	134	419	15	48	616	$X^2 = 48.049$ d.f. = 3 P<.001
	2. Sixth	204	399	4	9	616	
	P	<.001	n.s.	<.05	<.001		
Community	1. Rural	151	426	10	29	616	n.s.
	2. Urban	187	392	9	28	616	
	P	<.05	<.05	n.s.	n.s.		
Sex	1. Boy	174	398	12	32	616	n.s.
	2. Girl	164	420	7	25	616	
	P	n.s.	n.s.	n.s.	n.s.		
Intelligence	1. High‡	66	149	1	8	224	$X^2 = 15.801$ d.f. = 3 P<.01
	2. Low‡	48	141	6	29	224	
	P	n.s.	n.s.	n.s.	<.001		

‡N = 16 instead of 44 as for other groups

298

TABLE 10

PICTURE PREFERENCES OF COMPARATIVE GROUPS

Picture	Grade		Community		Sex		I.Q.		Total	
	1st	6th	Rural	Urban	Boy	Girl	Low	High	f	Rank
1. Bedroom	18	13	15	16	8	23[2]	2	4	31	2
2. Poor House	4	7	5	6	6	5	3	2	11	12
3. Dam	5	16[1]	11	10	17[2]	4	3	3	21	6.5
4. Factory	3	4	5	2	6	1	0	3	7	13.5
5. Mansion	15	7	10	12	6	16[1]	4	3	22	4.5
6. Church	6	10	12[1]	4	4	12[1]	5	2	16	9
7. Farm	19	13	16	16	24[2]	8	4	7	32	1
8. Old Beach	8	12	10	10	13	7	3	6	20	8
9. Capitol	6	7	8	5	6	7	5	1	13	10
10. City	6	6	5	7	7	5	3	2	12	11
11. Resort	8	14	10	12	8	14	3	3	22	4.5
12. Schoolroom	20[1]	8	10	18	11	17	6	8	28	3
13. Village	2	5	4	3	3	4	0	1	7	13.5
14. Dock	11	10	10	11	13	8	7	3	21	6.5
Total	131	132	131	132	132	131	48	48	263	
X^2 (Dist.)	15.694‡		5.868‡		33.364‡		(Not		46.111	
d.f.	13		13		13		tested)		13	
P	n.s.		n.s.		>.01				≫.001	

[1]P $(X^2 > 3.841)$ = .05   ‡Yates' correction applied
[2]P $(X^2 > 6.635)$ = .01   Rho (Total) =+.054

TABLE II

PICTURES LEAST PREFERRED BY COMPARATIVE GROUPS

Picture	Grade		Community		Sex		I.Q.		Total	
	1st	6th	Rural	Urban	Boy	Girl	Low	High	f	Rank
1. Bedroom	1	1	0	2	1	1	1	1	2	11
2. Poor House	18	21	22	17	18	21	6	8	39	1
3. Dam	2	1	0	3	1	2	0	0	3	8.5
4. Factory	1	3	2	2	0	4	1	1	4	6
5. Mansion	3	1	2	2	3	1	0	0	4	6
6. Church	2	0	0	2	1	1	0	0	2	11
7. Farm	2	1	2	1	0	3	2	1	3	8.5
8. Old Beach	2	4	4	2	2	4	2	1	6	3.5
9. Capitol	5	1	4	2	5	1	1	1	6	3.5
10. City	2	2	2	2	4	0	1	0	4	6
11. Resort	0	0	0	0	0	0	0	0	0	14
12. Schoolroom	3	8	4	7	8	3	0	3	11	2
13. Village	1	0	1	0	1	0	0	0	1	13
14. Dock	1	1	1	1	0	2	1	0	2	11
Total	43	44	44	43	44	43	15	16	87	

For all comparisons: P $=$ n.s.

Rho (Total) $= +.235$

BIBLIOGRAPHY

Allport, Floyd H. *Theories of Perception and the Concept of Structure.* New York: John Wiley and Sons, 1955.

Blake, Robert R. and Glenn V. Ramsey (Eds.). *Perception: An Approach to Personality.* New York: Ronald Press, 1951.

Boring, Edwin G. *Sensation and Perception in the History of Experimental Psychology.* New York: Appleton-Century-Crofts Company, 1942.

Brandt, Herman F. *The Psychology of Seeing.* New York: Philosophical Library, 1945.

Bruner, Jerome S. and David Krech (Eds.). *Perception and Personality: A Symposium.* Durham: Duke University Press, 1950.

Dennis, Wayne (Ed.). *Current Trends in Psychological Theory.* Pittsburgh: University of Pittsburgh Press, 1951.

Estvan, Frank J. "The Relationship of Social Status, Intelligence, and Sex of Ten- and Eleven-Year-Old Children to an Awareness of Poverty," *Genetic Psychology Monograph,* XLVI (June, 1952), 3-60.

———— "Studies in Social Perception: Methodology," *Journal of Genetic Psychology,* XCII (June, 1958), 215-46.

———— "Studies in Social Perception: Word Productivity," *Journal of Experimental Education* (June, 1959).

Gesell, Arnold and Frances L. Ilg. *Child Development.* New York: Harper and Brothers, 1949.

Gibson, J. J. *The Perception of the Visual World.* Boston: Houghton Mifflin, 1950.

Kenworthy, Leonard S. *Introducing Children to the World.* New York: Harper and Brothers, 1956.

Parkhurst, Helen. *Exploring the Child's World.* New York: Appleton-Century-Crofts Company, 1951.

Remmers, Herman H. and D. H. Radler. *The American Teenager.* Indianapolis: Bobbs-Merrill, 1957.

Russell, David H. *Children's Thinking.* Boston: Ginn and Company, 1956.

Sherif, Muzafer. *The Psychology of Social Norms.* New York: Harper and Brothers, 1936.

Vernon, Magdalen D. *A Further Study of Visual Perception.* New York: Cambridge University Press, 1952.